Canada Among Nations 2004

Canada Among Nations 2004

Setting Priorities Straight

EDITED BY
DAVID CARMENT
FEN OSLER HAMPSON AND
NORMAN HILLMER

McGill-Queen's University Press
Montreal & Kingston · London · Ithaca

ISBN 0-7735-2836-9 (cloth)
ISBN 0-7735-2837-7 (paper)

Legal deposit first quarter 2005
Bibliothèque nationale du Québec

Printed in Canada on acid-free paper

McGill-Queen's University Press acknowledges the support of the Canada Council for the Arts for our publishing program. We also acknowledge the financial support of the Government of Canada through the Book Publishing Industry Development Program (BPIDP) for our publishing activities.

Canadian Cataloguing in Publication Data

Canada among nations.

Annual.
1984–
Produced by the Norman Paterson School of International Affairs at Carleton University.
Publisher varies.
Each vol. also has a distinctive title.
Includes bibliographical references.
ISSN 0832-0683
ISBN 0-7735-2836-9 (2004 edition ; bound).—
ISBN 0-7735-2837-7 (2004 edition ; pbk.)

1. Canada—Foreign relations—1945– —Periodicals. 2. Canada—Politics and government—1984– —Periodicals. 3. Canada—Politics and government—1980–1984—Periodicals. I. Norman Paterson School of International Affairs.

FC242.C345 327.71 C86-031285-2
REV F1034.2.C36

Typeset in 10/12 Sabon by True to Type

Contents

Abbreviations

3 PPCLI 3rd Battalion Princess Patricia's Light Infantry
187 BCT 187th Brigade Combat Team
ACPP Africa Conflict Prevention Pool (UK)
AIDS Acquired Immune Deficiency Syndrome
APEC Asia Pacific Economic Cooperation
ATA Afghan Transitional Authority
BBC British Broadcasting Corporation
BMD ballistic missile defence
BMGF Bill and Melinda Gates Foundation
BPG bi-national planning group
CCG Canadian Coast Guard
CF Canadian Forces
CFB Canadian forces base
CFI Canada Foundation for Innovation
CIDA Canadian International Development Agency
CIHR Canadian Institutes of Health Research
CJTL Combined Joint Task List
CPGGH Canadian Program on Genomics and Global Health
CPP Conflict Prevention Pools (UK)
CSI Canada Science International
CUSFTA Canada-U.S. Free Trade Agreement
CUSO Canadian University Services Overseas
DART Disaster Assistance Response Team
DDR Disarmament, Demobilization and Reintegration
DFAIT Department of Foreign Affairs and International Trade

DFID Department for International Development
DND Department of National Defence
DPSEP Department of Public Safety and Emergency Preparedness
EDC Export Development Canada
EEZ exclusive economic zone
ETAN East Timor Alert Network
FAC Foreign Affairs Canada
FELEX frigate equipment life extension project
FDI Foreign Direct Investment
GATT General Agreement on Tariffs and Trade
GCPP Global Conflict Prevention Pool (UK)
GDP gross domestic product
GHRI Global Health Research Initiative
GIS projections Geographic Information Systems projections
IAEA International Atomic Energy Agency
ICAO International Civil Aviation Organisation
ICARDA International Center for Agriculture in Dryland Areas
ICRC International Committee of the Red Cross
IDRC International Development Research Centre
IFI international financial institution
IFPRI International Food Policy Research Institute
IHA international humanitarian assistance
IMF International Monetary Fund
IPR International Policy Review
IPU Inter-Parliamentary Union
IRF Immediate Reaction Force
ISAF International Security Assistance Force
ISTAR intelligence, surveillance, target acquisition and reconnaissance
IT Information Technology
ITU International Telecommunication Union
ITWAA Integrated Tactical Warning and Attack Assessment
IWMI International Water Management Institute
IWRM integrated water resources management
JNBCD Joint Nuclear, Biological, Chemical Defence Company
JSSS Joint Support Ships
JTF2 Joint Task Force Two
LAV III Light Armoured Vehicle III
MAI Multilateral Agreement on Investment
MarCom maritime command
MCDV maritime coastal defence vehicles
MGS Mobile Gun System
MIF Multinational Interim Force (Haiti)

MINUSTAH United Nations Stabilization Mission in Haiti
MOCS marine security operations centers
MOD Ministry of Defence (UK)
MOOTW Missions Other Than War
MP Member of Parliament
MSF Médecins Sans Frontières
NAM Non-Aligned Movement
NATO North Atlantic Treaty Organization
NBC nuclear, biological or chemical (weapons)
NCE Networks of Centres of Excellence
NIH National Institutes of Health
NORTHCOM Northern Command
NAFTA North American Free Trade Agreement
NEPAD New Economic Partnership for Africa's Development
NGO non-governmental organization
NMD National Missile Defense
NORAD North American Aerospace Defence Command
NRC National Research Council Canada
NSERC National Sciences and Engineering Research Council of Canada
NSP National Security Policy
O&M operations and maintenance
ODA official development assistance
PCO Privy Council Office
PJBD Permanent Joint Board on Defence
PMO Prime Minister's Office
POGG peace, order and good government
PRT provincial reconstruction teams (Afghanistan)
PSO Peace Support Operations
R&D Research & Development
RCMP Royal Canadian Mounted Police
S&T Science & Technology
SARS Severe Acute Respiratory Syndrome
SMES small and medium enterprises
SOUTHCOM Southern Command
SSHRC Social Sciences and Humanities Research Council
SSR Security Sector Reform
U of T University of Toronto
UNAMA United Nations Assistance Mission in Afghanistan
UNDP United Nations Development Program
UNICEF United Nations International Children's Emergency Fund / United Nations Children's Fund
UNHCR United Nations High Commissioner for Refugees
USCG United States Coast Guard

WIPO	World Intellectual Property Organization
WMD	weapons of mass destruction
WMO	World Meteorological Organization
WHO	World Health Organization
WSSD	World Summit on Sustainable Development
WTO	World Trade Organization
YES	Youth Engagement Strategy

Preface

When the planning began for *Canada Among Nations 2004*, we fastened on the suggestion of Denis Stairs that we should devote attention to the notion that the Canadian government needs to choose some serious priorities in its foreign policy. Canada, as the prime minister admits, must "work smarter" in the world, and concentrate "what we do best and on what the world needs most." It is that theme which lies at the heart of our inquiry, and we thank Professor Stairs for agreeing to write the book's keynote chapter.

We have benefited enormously from the support of Philip Cercone, Joan McGilvray, and their colleagues at McGill-Queen's University Press. Trista Grant, Hector Mackenzie, and David Perdue provided invaluable research assistance, and Brenda Sutherland prepared the manuscript, asking all the right questions with characteristic forthrightness. Megan Sproule-Jones efficiently created the index. We also express our gratitude to Katherine Graham, the dean of Carleton University's School of Public Affairs and Management, and to the university's Centre for Security and Defence Studies.

This is the twentieth edition in the *Canada Among Nations* series. For each of the twenty volumes, Janet Doherty has organized the workshops, communicated with authors, and ensured that tight publication deadlines are met. We wish to recognize her quiet, tireless professionalism by dedicating this book to her.

D. C.
F. O. H.
N. H.
Ottawa, 22 August 2004

Canada Among Nations 2004

1 Smart Power in Canadian Foreign Policy

NORMAN HILLMER, FEN OSLER HAMPSON, and DAVID CARMENT

When Paul Martin became prime minister of Canada on 12 December 2003, he carried with him massive expectations: his own, and those of a foreign policy community which had become convinced that the country had lost its international lustre. Martin's internationalist credentials were impeccable. He was the son of another Paul Martin, Lester B. Pearson's foreign minister in the 1960s, and the protégé of Maurice Strong, one of the grand practitioners of Canadian globalism in the post-Second World War era. He had built a worldwide business giant, Canada Steamship Lines, in the 1980s. Entering Parliament in 1988, he was Jean Chrétien's formidable finance minister from 1993 to 2002; from that perch he won a reputation as a committed reformer of the international financial system. Now, the new prime minister confidently predicted, he was on the threshold of a decade in power, a decade to make Canada count once more in the world.

Shortly after taking office, Martin let his activist imagination roam in major addresses on foreign policy in Washington and Montreal, and on defence at Canadian Forces Base Gagetown, in New Brunswick.[1] Taken together, the speeches called for a forceful and focused multilateralism, with Canada assuming a "catalytic" leadership role, "concentrating on what we do best and on what the world needs most." Threats were everywhere and "unprecedented in our times," ranging from failed, failing, and rogue states to international criminal syndicates, weapons proliferation and terrorism. The first duty of government was to protect its citizens, and the best protection for them was a stable and cooperative international system. Canada thus intended to concentrate, much more than in the past and as "a major foreign policy thrust," upon institution building as the essential foundation of secure, modern states. To that end, Martin was binding together the traditional instruments of foreign policy – diplomacy, defence, and development, fashionably known as the 3 Ds – to respond, concretely and for the long haul, to the need of vulnerable states to build up their capacity for governing themselves in an effective and publicly accountable manner. The prime minister announced the establishment of the Canada Corps, an organization that would make available Canadian expertise in institution and capacity-building.

There was a fine line between assistance and interference, admittedly, and local customs and traditions had to be respected when fresh methodologies were being introduced. There were also times when the responsibility to protect the downtrodden became paramount. If a state violated the norms of acceptable behaviour in abusing its own citizens, its sovereignty would not confer immunity for crimes against humanity.

The imperative for better governance within countries was paralleled by the necessity for more efficient international regimes and multilateral institutions. Martin innovated in championing the establishment of a G-20 at the head of government level, modeled on the G-20 Group of Finance Ministers, which he had helped invent in the middle 1990s. Well-entrenched powerhouses like the US and Germany were members of the original combination, but so too were the emerging economies of China, Indonesia, India, Brazil, Mexico and South Africa. Where the G-8 was inevitably narrow, a leaders' G-20 would be broad, able to confront big global challenges like SARS, AIDS, greenhouse gases and terrorism which knew no borders. Only through the direct involvement of the top leadership, politicians like Martin were apt to think, could the world's intellectual, emotional and historical impasses be broken. The Doha round of multilateral trade negotiations was one example of a suitable case for treatment by a new G-20. At the same time, the prime minister underlined the importance of reforming existing multilateral institutions generally, while attacking, specifically, such urgent and transcendent issues as clean water, infectious diseases, market access for agricultural products and global terrorism.

The prime minister had pledged during his Liberal Party leadership run that the restoration of Canada's standing in the world would be a preoccupation. But foreign policy did not take centre stage in the early Martin era, nor did pressing domestic issues. They could not. Revelations about abuses in a Chrétien sponsorship program of the late 1990s rocked the government of his successor, putting Martin on the defensive. His eager team, which had pushed Chrétien from power, seemed unready to govern. Public support for the prime minister fell away. Even so, insisting that as a new leader he must have a mandate from the voters, Martin called an election for 28 June 2004, no longer assured of the huge victory that seemed his for the asking only months before.

THE 2004 ELECTION

In the May-June campaign, headlines were dominated by concerns such as health care, social policy, the Charter of Rights, and the stewardship of the economy – even as global pressures continued to be felt more keenly and acutely by Canadians. The SARS crisis of the previous year exacted a harsh toll on the country's biggest city, threatening the lives of Toronto's citizens, and damaging a lucrative tourist industry. A single case of "mad cow" disease was enough to send the Alberta beef industry into crisis when the US closed its borders to cattle exports from Canada. As the political and security situation in the Middle East and Persian Gulf worsened, moreover, fears about a terrorist attack on Canadian soil continued to mount. Canada's life does not stop at Canada's borders, but none of that came to the fore in the campaign.

Some disquiet about Canada's foreign policy priorities did lurk on the margins of the campaign. In the policy platforms of the major political parties, there were clear differences in stance and orientation. The Liberals publicly committed themselves to a thoroughgoing review of Canada's international strategies. They also pointed to the February 2004 budget, which earmarked an "extra" $600 million in defence spending, to demonstrate that they were serious about Canada's defence capabilities. The Conservatives, a newly-hatched partnership of the Progressive Conservatives and the Alliance parties, made Canada-U.S. relations the centrepiece of their foreign policy promises, stressing their desire for the improvement of relations after many years of Liberal "mismanagement" and "neglect." Leader Stephen Harper pledged to spend an additional $1.2 billion a year on defence over and above what the Liberals had promised, an amount which would rise to $1.6 billion over the next five years. The New Democratic Party warned of the evils of getting too cozy with the United States, especially in defence relations. For the Bloc Québécois, Canada's international commitments, capabilities, and credentials were obviously less important than the foreign policy opportunities that a sovereign and independent Quebec might someday bring.

There were times in the campaign when it seemed likely that Martin would lose not just seats in Parliament but the government itself. In the end, a bruised prime minister barely survived, with 135 Liberal seats to the Conservatives' 99, the Bloc's 54 and the NDP's 19. With substantially more seats than any other party, and no immediate predisposition on the part of the Opposition parties to bring him down, Martin formed what he euphemistically called a stable minority government. He named Pierre Pettigrew to the foreign affairs portfolio, switched Bill Graham from Foreign Affairs to the Department of National Defence, and kept Jim Peterson at International Trade and Aileen Carroll at International Cooperation. Of these the multilingual Quebecer, Pettigrew, a former trade minister, was the most interesting selection because of his personal flair and taste for ideas. But he made it clear on the day he was appointed that he expected to lead the country to where it had been before in the world. "I think as a foreign policy, we've got it right in Canada," Pettigrew declared.[2]

Caution and compromise usually prevail when governments cannot rely on a majority of House of Commons seats. Leaders of minority governments look to the next election and to those issues, largely domestic, where they can gain traction with voters. In the current case, a weakened prime minister will have to be careful to balance and build support when there is contention, rather than have backing supplied ready made. Martin will also be vulnerable to his own members, all of whom he needs and some of whom will regard closer defence relations with the US, for example, as anathema. As one pundit predicted, "[I]n foreign capitals there will be a nagging suspicion that, for a while, Canada might not mean what it says or be able to deliver on whatever position it takes."[3]

Yet there might be an opportunity. That is the suggestion of journalist-academic Andrew Cohen, who, in noting the Martinite ambition to arrest Canada's decline in the world, argues that international affairs offers the prime minister "the best chance to make a difference in a minority government – if he seizes the moment." He might not have a grand plan to address the central problems of Canada's place in the world, but "the elements of a new, smart foreign policy are emerging. It is a foreign policy of niches."[4]

HARD CHOICES ...

Niche thinking, as defined by the former Australian foreign minister, Gareth Evans, concentrates resources "in specific areas best able to generate returns worth having, rather than trying to cover the field."[5] The concept is now in lively play, and not simply in prime ministerial speeches, because it addresses a perception of drift in recent Canadian foreign policy and raises the attractive possibility of marrying specific problems to specific Canadian skills so that impacts will be real and measurable. Niche policies recognize, in addition, that there are more claims on the public purse than there were in the fondly remembered Golden Age of the 1950s, when defence and diplomacy were kings.

Scholars, commentators and think-groups like the Canadian Defence and Foreign Affairs Institute and the Public Policy Forum regularly demand significant new monies for Canada's foreign policy, defence, and development assistance establishments. But what if, as seems only too likely, an infusion of cash does not materialize under the Martin government? Does that not reinforce the argument for the identification and development of serious priorities to maximise the resources available? And if there are to be specializations, how are the choices to be made, employing what criteria?

Denis Stairs' keynote chapter to this volume confronts precisely these issues. When there are not enough bucks to go around, he muses, "perhaps they should not 'go around' at all, but be spent instead where they can do the most good." That prompts an examination of how to make what Stairs justifiably calls "hard choices." Hard in the sense of precise and concrete, but hard too because the forces, institutional and international, which will be arrayed against fundamental change are powerful and perhaps inexorable.

The point of the exercise is to magnify results by concentrating effort. The strategy is simple enough, on the surface. Start with Canada's needs, interests and preferences, and derive from the resulting analysis that which matters most, and that which matters least. Something more exact is required, however, particularly since the forces favouring inertia are so strong. Stairs suggests that geographical criteria be set aside, and functional ones adopted: how to engage, that is, rather than where. In development, for example, Canada could concentrate on treatable diseases and engineering for clean water, eschewing other activities and creating a specialization much as peacekeeping has been one in the military arena. In defence, Canada might make savings in the procurement of certain weapons systems, clearing the way for heavy investment in areas that fit the Martin strategy of assistance to nation-building endeavours.

The bulk of Stairs' discussion centres on the manner in which Canada's diplomatic, defence and development efforts have become over-extended in relation to the capabilities government has been willing to deploy. We are trying to do more with less, Stairs explains, and in more places. But we are where we are for good reason, and we have got there over many decades. Escape will not be easy, and it will be impossible without clear, coherent and insistent leadership from the highest reaches of government – from, indeed, the prime minister.

Beginning with Stairs, the first section of the book is devoted to the question of priorities. Gordon Smith, his chapter informed by long experience in the Ottawa bureaucracy, argues (in contrast to Graham Fraser) that the Martin way will be very different from the Chrétien era. Martin, Smith says, has already set his priorities straight. He is more cognisant of North American realities, and hence the need for strategic accommodations, and more conscious of the challenges of global governance, and hence the need to target investments and coordinate policy "so that Canada can make a difference."

Rob McRae of the Department of Foreign Affairs, a key figure in the government's international policy review, takes a tough look at interests in the making of choices about Canada's stance in the world, and implicitly weighs them up against values. Do Canadians, he asks, wish only interests, narrowly considered, to dictate policy? Philippe Lagassé carries out a calculus of defence needs measured against the budgets available to the Canadian Forces (CF). He concludes that the military's operational tempo must be reduced in order to replenish the CF's depleted equipment funds and adequately train and rest soldiers, and argues for a greater domestic focus for operations and platform acquisitions. Lagassé also sets criteria for the acquisition of new platforms that require that all new equipment have a domestic or dual domestic/expeditionary use. To complete the discussion, CARE Canada's Nancy Gordon stipulates that official development assistance (ODA) can be expected to follow foreign policy priorities, some noble and some less so.

... AND A FALSE CHOICE

Much of the current discussion about foreign policy priorities revolves around the importance and implications of Canada's intimate economic and continental ties with the United States. This is the preoccupation of Canadian foreign policy, a fact amplified by the increasing intensity of indiscriminate threats emanating from a wide variety of largely non-state sources. Terrorism, weapons proliferation, global warming, biodiversity loss, and pandemic and emerging infectious diseases all threaten the whole continent, not just one part of it.

No one would suggest that the United States is anything but the most significant of Canada's external relationships. The disagreement comes in the discussion of what that entails. There are those who argue that Canada's international relations should play second string to preserving the health of the Canadian economy and our trade and investment relations with the United States. With almost two billion dollars worth of goods and services crossing the border each day, Canada cannot afford to take any aspect of its economic and security relationships with the United States for granted. This view, which is shared by groups like the Canadian Council of Chief Executives and diplomat-academics like Allan Gotlieb, Bill Dymond, and Michael Hart, contends that Canada cannot risk alienating or antagonizing Washington with foreign policy flights of fancy. There is simply too much at stake for the country's economic survival and well being. What is needed, write Dymond and Hart, is a foreign policy grounded in "a conception of a national interest that accepts the primacy of the United States in securing both our national security and our prosperity."[6]

According to advocates of a more integrated North Americanism, the inescapable reality of Canada's close economic ties with the United States ought to bring a clearer focus to the government's international agenda and political alignments, not the other way round. Canada's economic and commercial interests must define its strategic priorities with a correspondingly greater commitment and share of resources going into continental security and defence, including coastal maritime surveillance and control, intelligence, public safety, and general border management with the United States. The North Americanists maintain that Canada cannot risk the closure of or disruption along the border if there are future terrorist or military attacks against the North American continent.

On another side are those who take exception to the view that Canada should be hamstrung, or hidebound, by its relations with the United States, even in a post September 11 world. Led by Lloyd Axworthy, the Canadian foreign minister from 1996 to 2000, internationalists emphasize global citizenship and resist allowing the market and Uncle Sam to decide the Canadian future.[7] They think Canada uniquely qualified, by tradition and talent, to assist those parts of the world that are wracked by civil strife and struggling to find democracy. They take pride that Canada's military, police, judiciary, and NGO communities have been actively involved in the great state building and democratic reconstruction enterprises of the past fifteen years – Namibia, Mozambique, Cambodia, El Salvador, Guatemala, Bosnia, Kosovo, and East Timor. They see the internationalist vocation demonstrated in what Canada is trying to do today, with uncertain effect, in Haiti and Afghanistan.

That vocation took eloquent flight in the O.D. Skelton Memorial Lecture, delivered by Michael Ignatieff in March of 2004 at the Lester B. Pearson Building in Ottawa in front of the minister and a large crowd of practitioners. Ignatieff argued passionately for a muscular multilateralism that would establish the Canadian principles of peace, order, and good government "as the *sine qua non* for stable states, enduring democracy, and equitable development."[8] Some of the same language found its way into the prime minister's major speech on foreign policy in Washington the next month.

The choice between North Americanism and internationalism is a false one, more of a rhetorical point of reference than a realistic basis for action. Paul Martin, Lloyd Axworthy, and Michael Ignatieff, each in his own way, make the case for both international activism and North American partnership. Canadians, indeed, have been delicately searching for a balance between the two for a long time, believing that a global foreign policy is an antidote to the tight clinch of bilateralism. But whether Canadians like it or not, and particularly so since September 11, the country is caught in the slipstream of American national security policy and action. There is no evading Canada's alignment to the United States, which paradoxically allows Canada to do many of its vaunted good works in the international arena.[9]

MANAGING THE PRIORITY RELATIONSHIP

How, then to manage Canada's priority relationship? The second section of this volume highlights Canadian-American relations, placing chapters by John Higginbotham and Jeff Heynen, Robert Bothwell, and Elinor Sloan alongside essays by Jean Daudelin and Graham Fraser, whose broader analyses of foreign policy are set firmly in the context of what Daudelin terms Canada's growing "North Americanization" over recent years.

Daudelin asserts that Canada has its priorities in order. The country has not sleepwalked into insignificance; its foreign policy is a success story. The continent is Canada's relevant international environment, and that file has been managed extraordinarily well, in spite of the astonishing external vulnerabilities that accompany North Americanization. The country's international footprint is shrinking, and activism on the global scene is largely inconsequential.

Higginbotham and Heynen see continental politics in a state of some confusion, and they find their optimism in incrementalism. Because there is no consensus in Canada about the future of the continental relationship, and because the United States is "highly distracted," they recommend that Canada work with what is already there, the multiple networks of personal and institutional linkages which have built up over decades. They call for a smarter use of existing transgovernmental channels as a means to advance issues one-by-one and sector-by-sector, and to prepare for the broader possibilities and bigger deals of the future, should they come into view.

This view of Canada-US relations as amenable to rational discourse accords with a long line of analysis emphasizing the striking similarities between the United States and Canada, and their sheer interdependence. Historian Bothwell is in that tradition. He details the many bumps along the road, but through it all he discerns shared geography, interests, values, and cultural heritage, which link Americans and Canadians inevitably, if not perfectly.

Although Liberal governments have moved in the right direction by establishing new domestic institutions and instruments of national security, that needs to be accompanied by a clear articulation of Canada's continental policies and priorities. An initial effort in that direction has been made with the National Security Policy, and while many are quick to dismiss the document, it does contain some important commitments and policy shifts. The Canadian public, certainly, appears to be ready to back a more substantial effort to deal with the threats that confront Canada and the United States. A Pollara poll in April 2004 showed that a majority of Canadians want the federal government to increase spending on fighting terrorism in Canada and on Canada's national defence.[10]

On the security front, three dimensions in particular require early and sustained attention. They are Canada-United States defence cooperation in the new security environment; a possible Canadian role in the American missile defence system; and border management, including issues of security controls and systems to address the problems of "cross-border terrorism," law enforcement, intelligence, and infrastructure protection. The challenges that have emerged in each aspect of the Canada-US security relationship suggest that traditional policy frameworks and assumptions will have to be carefully re-examined.

In the aftermath of the Cold War, Canada and the US strengthened bilateral defence ties. The Department of National Defence (DND) devoted greater attention towards 'interoperability' between the Canadian and American armed forces. Close defence ties ensured that the Canadian Forces worked harmoniously with their American counterparts in Haiti, Bosnia, and Kosovo. Following September 11 2001, the CF fought with the United States military in and around Afghanistan for nearly three years. Though some Canadians are uncomfortable with the logic of interoperability, it can be argued that contacts to the American armed forces have allowed the CF to be a more effective and visible peacekeeping and war fighting force. As Elinor Sloan argues in her chapter, however, preserving interoperability with the United States military demands continued investments and doctrinal improvements. Given regular advancements in American military technology and force structuring, Ottawa cannot take defence cooperation for granted.

Continental defence has returned to the fore of Canadian defence policy after September 11 2001. Since the establishment of the Permanent Joint Board on Defence (PJBD) in 1940, Canadian officials have balanced the requirements of an effective continental defence with the protection of Canadian sovereignty. Current efforts to strengthen the bilateral defence of North America mirror these efforts. In January 2003, a Canada-United States binational planning group (BPG) was established to enhance land, intelligence, and coastal defence cooperation in light of the terrorist threat. The BPG is located in Colorado Springs next to NORAD and US Northern Command headquarters. Thus far, the BPG has agreed on consequence management collaboration, but with the BPG mandate expiring in 2005, the institutional structures and sovereignty protections of new bilateral coastal defence efforts are still unclear.

Alongside land and coastal defence cooperation, Canada is debating participation in the American ballistic missile defence (BMD) system. The government has been leery of BMD because of the system's destabilizing effects and possible weaponization of space. Missile defence critics worry that Canada's reputation as an advocate of arms control and disarmament will be undermined by a BMD role. Yet, given that the United States' initial plans involve only ground and sea-based interceptors, many in Canada are urging the government to join BMD and assert a Canadian role in the protection of North America from burgeoning ballistic missile threats. Moreover, a Canadian abstention from BMD might affect the NORAD relationship. As the command which supplies warning and assessment of ballistic missile launches, NORAD will play a vital role in the missile defence system. Recognizing NORAD's importance to BMD, Canada and the United States agreed in August 2004 that NORAD data can be transmitted to missile defence command and control. Whether this step inexorably ties Canada to BMD or not, the August agreement highlights the complex factors Canada must consider in discussing missile defence issues with the United States.

On 12 December 2001, the Smart Border Declaration, and its thirty-point Action Plan, was announced by John Manley, then Canada's minister of foreign affairs, and Tom Ridge, the US director of homeland security. While progress is being made on many aspects of border cooperation, serious structural problems remain, especially in the area of immigration controls. Furthermore, border management is still based on a system of controls that are directed at impeding individuals at the actual "physical" border; that is, strengthening points of entry and border patrols, rather than taking on the "virtual border" that resides in different national management and visa control systems of the two countries, as well as third countries.

Canada and the United States share many critical components in their energy and industrial infrastructures, including oil and gas pipelines, electricity grids, and vital communications and transportation links. These are all obvious terrorist targets. Consequently, there is a need for close collaboration to ensure that these systems are adequately protected and that intelligence is shared.

Intensified cooperation between and among Canadian intelligence and law enforcement agencies is clearly necessary to identify threats and risks at the border and to communicate them in a timely fashion to the United States. However, as a recent report of the auditor-general suggests, deficiencies remain, particularly in the area of information exchanges between different intelligence and law enforcement agencies within the Canadian government.[11] The 21 April 2004 announcement of $500 million for security gaps suggests efforts are being made to address these problems. Nevertheless, a real or perceived breakdown of intelligence sharing, especially in advising US authorities of Canadian-based threats would be disastrous, especially in the current political climate, where the first instinct of American authorities and politicians is to be suspicious of Canada's resoluteness on security issues.

SMART POWER

The subject of the volume's third part is smart power, which ties the choice of priorities to the amplification of Canada's influence in the world. Smart power suggests the mobilizing of the national experience in areas like water management, science and technology, and humanitarian intervention, and calls for a focussed Canadian leadership in the search for alternative forms and procedures of global governance. Smart power goes beyond a more concentrated use of knowledge and skills to demand better coordination between all the arms of foreign policy, as well as the renewal of Canada's military. The proponents of smart power do not sneer at the idea that Canadians have values they think important to protect and project, nor do they accept that Canada is a faded power.

A measurement of Canada's effectiveness in the world cannot be based solely on the amount spent on defence, development assistance, and diplomacy. Any calculus of a country's international influence must also take account of the strength and health of its economy, its cultural assets, its technological prowess, including its powers of communication, and its ideas, values, and powers of attraction. Canada has the eighth largest economy in the world, reckoned in US dollars. The gross domestic product (GDP) growth rate in the period 1997–2001 stood at 3.8 percent, one of the highest in the OECD. The

Bank of Canada predicts a continued pattern of moderate growth, even after the SARS and "mad cow" crises and the spike in world oil and energy prices.

Furthermore, Canada is moving to the forefront of crucial areas of economic innovation and growth, such as biotechnology. It is here that Peter Singer, Elizabeth Dowdeswell, and their University of Toronto colleagues see an opportunity for Canada to lead in the application of technological expertise to the health and environmental problems of developing countries. They ask that the government raise Canada's annual research and development expenditures for international developmental science and technology to 5 per cent of the overall development budget, as the prime minister has pledged to do. Starkly outlining the world water crisis, Margaret Catley-Carlson makes a similar request of the government: to bring together Canadian resources and proficiencies in water resource management issues into a coherent and deliberate international development priority.

Smart power also looks to the possibilities presented by communications technologies to distribute information and mobilize civil society. It seeks vigorously to promote Canadian interests and values, including the rights of citizens abroad when they come under attack or are trampled by authoritarian regimes. Noting the expert use of communications media by NGOs, journalism professor Christopher Waddell recommends that the foreign affairs bureaucracy seize the Internet as a modern way to do the ancient work of diplomacy.

Smart power can take on an important dimension in the management of the world's humanitarian crises, such as the disasters in the western Sudan, Uganda, Congo, and Burundi that have yet to capture the undivided attention of the international community. Canada is well placed to provide knowledge-based skills that will allow these societies to develop and engage their own capital in the tasks related to social, economic, and political reconstruction. Canada has direct experience in constructing civil society partnerships that can encourage local actors to take on the reconstruction and development process. The 3D approach, coordinating defence, diplomacy and development as a strategy to deal with state failure, must be fully incorporated into the decision making and planning process of all departments and agencies, and not just Foreign Affairs, National Defence, and CIDA. The British example of Conflict Prevention Pools (CPPs) is a model that Canada might use, so that objectives and mandates will be clearly understood by all participants.

In the continuing predicament of multilateralism, one of the central challenges of global governance is the need to educate governments, generate and disseminate knowledge, and collaborate in finding and executing remedial policies. Paul Heinbecker, Canada's ambassador to the UN during the run-up to the Iraq war, wants Ottawa to reinvigorate international debate and discussion about the challenges of humanitarian intervention and help devise principles of action that are centered around the "responsibility to protect." Canada can help the secretary general redefine the agenda of the United Nations by organizing a more effective global response to disease control, hunger, lack of education, and environmental destruction. It can also build bridges between a world that has come to distrust the US, and an America that has a sense of unique vulnerability. George Haynal, another recently-retired senior diplomat, fleshes out Paul Martin's G-20 concept, combining developing and developed nations as a means of taking practical action on a wide array of problems, from the conduct of the international economy to management of the biosphere, population growth, and global warming.

A SMARTER CANADA

The prime minister's advocacy of a leaders' G-20 and the Canada Corps are concepts, he proudly claims, that are "off the beaten track," and "so much the better" for that.[12] But he admits that he wants to revitalize the Canadian foreign policy tradition, not revolutionize it. Much of the Martin rhetoric is consonant with well-meaning Canadian internationalism as it has been practiced, nurtured, and explained since 1945. There is a dash of Axworthyian interventionism, too, as well as the former foreign minister's penchant for the employment of Canada's soft power skills and ideas to shape a better twenty-first century. Nor is Martin the first Canadian leader to boast of the country's special responsibility to lead, because of "who we are": tolerant, compassionate, diverse, democratic, multinational, powerful economically yet anti-imperial.[13]

Canada's internationalism isn't going anywhere, not least since the prime minister believes that Canada will be treated with more respect in the United States if it is influential in world affairs.[14] At the core of the Martin message is the promise that his multilateralism will tighten and intensify the beam Canadians shine on the world. The overall aim, as the Martinites put it in the Speech from the Throne inaugurating the third session of the thirty-seventh Parliament, was to find ways to "work smarter, in diplomacy, in development, in defence and in international trade – all of which have become profoundly interdependent and are increasingly touching Canadians in their daily lives."[15] Left not fully said, and perhaps not fully comprehended, was that a resolute government will have to set clear priorities and make hard choices if Martin's smarter Canada is to be realized.

NOTES

We thank officials from several government departments, notably Foreign Affairs and National Defence, for granting us interviews, and we are particularly indebted to Philippe Lagassé and Susan B. Whitney for their extensive commentaries on earlier drafts.

1 "Address by Prime Minister Paul Martin on the Occasion of his Visit to Washington, D.C.," 29 April 2004, http://pm.gc.ca/eng/news.asp?id=192; "Address by Prime Minister Paul Martin on the Occasion of a Luncheon Hosted by the CORIM, the CERIUM, the Institut d'études internationales de Montréal à l'UQAM, and the Montreal International Organization" 10 May 2004, http://pm.gc.ca/eng/news.asp?id=201; "Address by Prime Minister Paul Martin at CFB Gagetown, New Brunswick," 14 April 2004, http://pm.gc.ca/eng/news.asp?id=172.
2 Aileen McCabe, "Schooled, Well-Coiffed and Eager for the Job," *National Post*, 21 July 2004, A5.
3 Jonathan Manthorpe, "Foreign Affairs Will Continue to Suffer After the Election," *Ottawa Citizen*, 4 July 2004, A12.
4 Andrew Cohen, "Foreign policy, Martin Style," *Ottawa Citizen*, 20 July 2004, A12.
5 Quoted in Andrew F. Cooper, "Niche Diplomacy: A Conceptual Overview," in Andrew F. Cooper, ed, *Niche Diplomacy: Middle Powers After the Cold War* (Basingstoke, Hampshire, England: Macmillan, 1997), 5.
6 Bill Dymond and Michael Hart, "The Potemkin Village of Canadian Foreign Policy," *Policy Options*, 25, 1 (December-January 2004), 40.
7 Lloyd Axworthy, *Navigating a New World: Canada's Global Future* (Toronto: Knopf Canada, 2003), 92.
8 Michael Ignatieff, "Peace, Order and good Government: A Foreign Policy Agenda for Canada," O. D. Skelton Memorial Lecture, Ottawa, 12 March 2004.
9 See Norman Hillmer, "Canada, the North Atlantic Treaty Organization and the Boundaries of Alignment," in Ann-Sofie Dahl and Norman Hillmer, eds, *Activism and (Non)Alignment: The Relationship Between Foreign Policy and Security Doctrine* (Stockholm: The Swedish Institute of International Affairs, 2002), 55–70.
10 Pollara, Inc, "Canadians' Attitudes Towards Foreign Policy," a report prepared for the Canadian Institute of International Affairs, April 2004.
11 *The March 2004 Report of the Auditor-General* (Ottawa: Government of Canada, 2004).
12 Prime Minister Martin's speech at Montreal, 10 May 2004, 5.
13 Ibid., 3.

14 Campbell Clark and Drew Fagan, "PM Hopes to Rule at Age 75," Globe and Mail, 19 December 2003, read on unac-discuss@unac.org, 22 December 2003.

15 "Speech from the Throne to Open the Third Session of the Thirty-Seventh Parliament of Canada," 2 February 2004, http://pm.gc.ca/eng/sft-ddt.asp.

PRIORITIES

2 The Making of Hard Choices in Canadian Foreign Policy

DENIS STAIRS

It has become increasingly fashionable in recent years for observers of Canadian foreign policy to argue the case for economizing on Canada's commitments abroad, and hence for clarifying priorities and using them to make hard choices. The items on the international agenda at large have multiplied dramatically over the past few decades, and many of them invite Ottawa's active, and sometimes very expensive, participation. But at the same time the resources available for making a Canadian contribution have seriously declined in response to the combined forces of fiscal prudence on the one hand, and the principle of "health care first" on the other.[1] In such circumstances, and in the absence of a carefully-led consensus on what matters most, Canadian involvements overseas have become more thinly distributed. The consequence, as some are inclined to assert, is token participation everywhere (almost), without much evidence of decisive impact anywhere (almost). Hence the case for "niche diplomacy," and for a more strategic approach to the focusing of the government's efforts abroad.[2] If there are fewer bucks to go around, perhaps they should not "go around" at all, but be spent instead where they can do the most good.[3]

In practice, of course, Ottawa *does* 'focus' on at least *some* things. It focuses heavily, for example, on the United States. It could hardly do otherwise. Whether Canadians like it or not, the relationship with the Americans is where the most vital of Canada's international interests really lie. Overseas there is greater room for choice, if only because most of what Canada does outside the North American continent is elective and voluntary. It can bring rewards, rewards that Canadians, including the professionals that populate the foreign policy community, often like. But they are not rewards they really have to have. They could live comfortably enough without them. In this circumstance, as in others, policy-makers in Ottawa naturally take various (and sometimes competing) considerations into account when deciding what to do. Yet such considerations are usually just that: "considerations." They do not compel. The government can take them or leave them, and which of them it takes, and which of them it leaves, is determined as much by combinations of casual preference, ingrained habit, and political or diplomatic convenience as by *force majeure*. Canadians, as Thomas Hockin astutely observed decades ago, are voluntarists abroad.[4] They have the luxury of choice, the freedom to choose.

Freedom of this sort can be a parent of opportunity. It can also be a burden. Making constructive use of it is hard work, especially when imperatives are absent. Imperatives, after all, make the choosing easy, even if the cost of the policy that results is high. But when genuine alternatives are available, they can trouble the political mind. They can do so especially when the potential consequences of the options in play are uncertain and obscure. They can do so even when they are clearly understood, if their probable effects happen to present themselves in inconvenient combinations of 'good' and 'bad.' In such circumstances, the temptation is to let things drift. Nothing awful happens, even if nothing very useful happens, either. No one has to pay the price of setting priorities that always comes in politics from letting some folks down while lifting other folks up. From the vantage point of the politicians, the silent thanks of the ones who win are buried every time by the angry lamentations of the ones who lose. It may not be surprising, therefore, that Canadians talk a lot about the need for focusing their efforts, and for emphasizing some things at the expense of others, but seem in practice to do it very little.

In sum, setting priorities in politics is risky business, and in a democratic environment especially, the most powerful of the incentives yield a preference for risk-avoidance, rather than for risk-taking. It is largely for this reason that 'incrementalism' is the preferred pattern of policy development. For a time, at least, it is often the safest way to go. But if left to its own devices too long, a sensibly incremental process can turn into a self-perpetuating habit of drift, and contradictions can result. Among them are the contradictions that can develop between what is *said* and what is *done*, between what is wished for and what is accomplished. Such patterns are sometimes broken by exogenous events, like a great depression, or a great war, or perhaps, as we might now be tempted to assert, a truly terrifying 'terrorist' attack. It is much harder, perhaps, to break the established mode of action simply by working through a policy update with the help of nothing more than some careful thought. The chances are sometimes better when there is a change in government, and a new prime minister is determined to eventually leave behind some distinctive traces of his or her time in high office. Whether the task is easy or difficult, however, making changes simply by "thinking them through" is what the argument for hard choices is designed to encourage in the end, and the internal politics of such an endeavour therefore warrants a closer look.

The discussion that follows is organized (like the government's forthcoming international policy review) with the help of the currently fashionable concept of the "three Ds," defence, diplomacy and development,[5] and begins in each case by asking in more detail why Canada has allowed itself to become over-extended in relation to its real capabilities (or at least to the capabilities that it has been prepared in recent times to mobilize for foreign policy purposes). In each of these cases, as well, it attempts to identify some of the generic obstacles that stand in the way of jettisoning some of our existing commitments in order to focus more efficaciously on the ones that remain. It then considers one or two of the criteria that, in principle, might be brought to bear in trying to engage in 'hard-choice' decision-making. The challenge that emerges is clearly a daunting one, and some might think it insurmountable. But a few observations on how to meet it are nonetheless offered at the end. Call this last part of the exercise "academic risk-taking."

GETTING OVER-EXTENDED IN DEFENCE

In the case of defence policy, it is useful to remind ourselves that Canada emerged at the end of the Second World War with roughly a half-million personnel in uniform, but with the conviction, too, that war itself was aberrational, that peace had been restored once again, and that demobilization could speedily follow. The Second World War, like the First World War, had been regarded as a 'total' war, appropriately aimed at defeating a fundamental challenge to liberal civilization. Certainly it was much more than a classical exercise in the application of military force to the pursuit of pragmatically defined and substantively limited interests of state. Limited wars prosecuted for limited ends had gone out of intellectual and political fashion. Nice states, *liberal* states, simply did not (certainly it was thought they *should* not) do that sort of thing. And Canada *would* not – except, perhaps, in the context of acting collectively with others to bring outlaw aggressors to heel. Since the 'posse' principle upon which the collective security system of the United Nations (UN) was based assumed that such outlaws would be confronted by the overwhelming force of the international community as a whole, or at the very least by the combined capacities of its most powerful members, having large armies at the ready seemed unnecessary. Small armies would do. Obviously there was little in such reasoning to constrain the contraction process, and in the politics at home there was nothing to constrain it at all. Quite the contrary. So demobilization did, in fact, quickly follow.

There soon materialized the Cold War. At first it did not lead to rearmament, although it did lead to alliances. In the case of the North Atlantic Treaty Organization (NATO), the underlying premise was that the Soviet Army would be contained in Eastern Europe by the menace of the American atomic bomb, the application of which to Western European security was the primary function of the alliance in the first place. The premise, however, did not last for long. With the outbreak of hostilities in Korea in June 1950, the fears of the most fearful seemed to be confirmed. The Cold War could conceivably go hot, and atomic weapons were too blunt an instrument to be suited to putting out fires in peripheral locations. More conventional capacities were therefore required as well. A massive rearmament effort ensued in order to deal with what was now regarded as a much more variegated security threat. For Canada, the effort was manifested in greatly expanded defence expenditures, first introduced in the February 1951 budget.

As it turned out, the Cold War, while in one sense a low-level contest, was not to be a short-term phenomenon. It lasted a long time, and the military capabilities that were constructed in response to it became a kind of benchmark against which capacities in the future would be measured. As a side-effect of the capabilities that Ottawa had developed for dealing with Soviets in potentially aggressive temper, moreover, it became possible for Canada to respond to other kinds of military challenges, as well, notably the ones involved in peacekeeping. Canada had the capacity to do the peacekeeping job, and other governments knew it. Not too many other powers had comparable capabilities, and many of the ones that did had reputations abroad that made them politically unsuited to the task of dabbling, however benignly, in other countries' quarrels. Before Canadians realized what was happening, their *ad hoc* 'helpful fixings' had been transformed into the presumption of a 'role,' a presumption increasingly shared at home and in governments and international organizations abroad. Canadians were asked, and were expected, to do more. And more. Again. And again.

After a time the Cold War, while causing all manner of misery in various peripheries of the state system, appeared less and less threatening at its stalemated core. Canadians learned to stop worrying about it. And when that happened, the budgetary allocations (in real 'purchasing power' terms, at any rate) started to fall back. In the Trudeau period, as the government began spending more of the available public resources (and some that were not available, too, so that they had to be borrowed) on domestic programming, Canada's military establishments in Europe were cut almost in half. But in spite of the contrary expectations of the day, Canada's other military activities abroad continued to expand, a process that was greatly accelerated, to the surprise of many, in the 1990s, after the Cold War itself had finally come to an end.

With each repetition of the Canadian performance (the requirements of which grew much more onerous as traditional peacekeeping operations were displaced by what amounted to peace enforcement 'warfare'), the expectation that Ottawa would continue to make such contributions in the future became ever more deeply embedded. The result, which by the turn of the millennium had become transparent even to those who were only casually attentive, was a situation in which the operational requirements were going up, while the operational assets, under intensifying pressure from program reviews aimed at bringing government expenditures under control, were running down.

The obvious solution to this sort of dilemma was either to economize on the requirements (in this case, turn down and/or withdraw from operational commitments overseas), or increase the assets, or have recourse to some combination of the two. Given that increasing the assets was not an option while program reviews and budgetary constraints were in force, economizing on the requirements seemed to be the viable alternative.

At this point, however, a powerful array of constraints entered the picture. Indeed, they had been in the picture for some time. Some were, and still are, rooted in the international environment, in expectations at the UN, for example, or in NATO, or in Washington. Others were inherent in the politics at home, and most notably in the expectations (some of them a trifle romantic) of Canadians themselves, and hence also in the preferences of their elected politicians. But a lot of them resided as well (as they still reside) in the Department of National Defence and within the military establishment itself.

The professionals, after all, know very well that the future is uncertain, and hence that every economizing assessment of what may be needed most can only be a guesstimate, and nothing more. Hence they avoid the making of hard choices because they fear being caught with the wrong mix of capacities. They fear giving up their skills when they give up weapon systems. They fear the loss of professional status that can come from dropping out of bigger-league games. They fear that playing only in the minor leagues will result in smaller budgets, not bigger budgets, in the end. They fear, in addition, that capacities lost, in a world governed by the long leads and lags of training and procurement, could not be easily or quickly recovered should they later be urgently required. Perhaps above all, they fear making the choices themselves in any context in which their political betters have failed to give them clear and transparent instructions that everyone else at home can see and understand. They fear this because they know that the absence of clear direction from the top is the unmistakable sign of a political leadership in flight from its appointed responsibility for making the tough decisions, and that such a leadership will hang the uniforms out to dry if the priorities they set turn out to be misfires as the future unfolds.

It may be worth observing, *en passant*, that this leadership problem is not a partisan phenomenon. The Progressive Conservative government of Brian Mulroney produced a defence white paper in 1987 that said one thing, and later a budget that said something entirely different.[6] The Liberal government of Jean Chrétien did much the same in 1994–95.[7] Political hesitations have political roots, and all politicians learn quickly enough where the roots are planted.

Finally, there are incentives of a more self-serving sort that may also encourage the professionals to resist the case for specialization. One of them is that a policy founded on the argument for focusing on niches can lead to the abandonment of precisely the activities that, from the professional point of view, are the most rewarding and the most fun. The air arm will oppose a focus on transport at the expense of fighters partly because flying fighters is a more exciting challenge than flying freighters, and partly because the mystique of the "air force" is associated more with the gladiatorial history of aerial combat than with bombing runs and troop transport. Sailors, similarly, tend to like big ships more than small ships. The big ones, on the whole, can move more quickly, play more roles, deliver more firepower, and impart more prestige than their smaller counterparts. With more qualifiers, perhaps, much the same can be said for the "army," the size of the muscle on the ground being related among other things to the weight of the armour and the sophistication of the artillery.

Another, and similarly self-serving, source of inertia can be found in the competitive organizational politics of the military establishment. The various services vie with one another for the most favourable budget allocations, including the ones that are aimed at procurement. "Regular" units, moreover, will compete with "reserve" units. Helicopter squadrons may think fighter squadrons are getting too much attention, and transport squadrons may think the same of both. And so on, with the result that every specialization option tends to arouse in the system, if the system is left to its own devices, a wider array of adversaries than of supporters. That being so, it is easier to resolve differences and maintain bureaucratic peace by doing much the same this year as was done last year, than it is to face up to the consequences of trying to alter the pattern. From the latter, zero-sum games inevitably ensue, as aroused factions go to their battlements in defence of their turf.

The significance of these bureaucratic phenomena should not be over-stated, since the policy issues themselves are more fundamental to the policy debate. In any case, the excesses of organizational rivals can almost always be overcome, in Westminster-style systems of government, by a leadership that really knows what it wants and is determined to have its way. Besides, the rivalry itself is a sign of dedication. No one, presumably, would want to have an armed forces establishment composed of specialists who lacked commitment to their specialities. A passionate attachment to the unit, its gear, and its job is presumably one of the most fundamental of the prerequisites for being effective in the field. But obviously it makes the process of policy-adjustment a little more difficult.

It should be noted, too, that civilians are in no position to complain about the phenomenon, perennial though it may be, of bureaucratic politics in the armed forces. For they, too, pursue their vested interests, and with similarly deleterious effects. Canada, for example, has too many bases. Defence expenditures could be more usefully deployed if some of them were abandoned. Yet threatening to shut down a base, and with it opportunities for local jobs and profits, results at once in a political uproar that politicians are rarely willing to face. Constraints of a similar sort flow also from the procurement process. Exotic equipment can often be obtained at much less cost "off the shelf" and overseas, but civilian-driven political compulsions lead to the demand for "offsets." They lead to the insistence that suppliers produce (or assemble) on Canadian soil much of what they sell, even if this is a far more expensive way to go.[8]

The bottom line: Canada is over-extended in defence, and everyone who cares to pay attention now knows it.[9]

GETTING OVER-EXTENDED IN DEVELOPMENT ASSISTANCE

Interestingly, in the case of development assistance there was a self-conscious and surprisingly determined attempt at the beginning of Canada's involvement to economize quite explicitly on the priorities, and hence on the targeting. This was partly because the government was not initially very enthusiastic about getting into the "foreign aid" game at all, knowing as it did that the requirements (if the job were taken seriously) were massive, and the potential needs unlimited. The Canadian delegation at the Colombo Conference in the winter of 1950 was tightly constrained, in responding to the importunities of the Indians (supported by the Australians) among others, by the firm instruction it had received from the Department of Finance, which had a warily jaundiced view of what might be entailed in trying to relieve poverty in South Asia.[10] Economic deprivation might well be a stimulus to radical politics, more specifically, to "communist" politics, but trying to head off the latter by moderating the former was a daunting aspiration.

The basic Canadian strategy, therefore, was to give as little as possible. Most of the effort at the beginning was devoted to the preliminary and non-committal task of thinking systematically about the nature and dimensions of the problem itself. Canada also urged, quite successfully as it turned out, that the Americans be brought into the process on the very sensible ground that only Washington had at its disposal the kinds of resources that might, if appropriately applied, have a significant impact. The Americans, motivated as they had been in the Marshall Plan by the thought that prosperity is the enemy of revolution, took the bait, in return for agreement that a selection of non-Commonwealth countries might be added to the original Colombo list of Commonwealth recipients.

Thereafter, for over a decade, the economizing principle for Canada, apart from keeping the size of the Canadian contribution itself in what was thought to be reasonable check, was to assert that Ottawa could not help everyone. It had therefore decided for obvious and understandable historical and related reasons to focus on the most needy of its Commonwealth partners. Impoverished Latin Americans, among others, might not like this very much, but it was hard for them to deny the cogency for Canada of Commonwealth membership as a target-selection criterion.

After the first decade, however, Canadian development assistance programming overseas grew like Topsy in response to a multiplicity of diverse pressures. Decolonization broke up the British Empire, generating a large battery of new Commonwealth claimants in the process. The requirements of domestic Canadian politics led Ottawa in the 1960s to add to its roster of foreign aid recipients a similarly expanding list of countries in *la francophonie*. Québécois needed to know that Canada's foreign policy had francophone as well as anglophone dimensions, and that it included opportunities abroad for French-speaking as well as English-speaking Canadians (teachers, for example). The recipient governments, occasionally pressed by France to play inconvenient games of symbolic politics by making more of Quebec City than of Ottawa in their Canadian dealings, needed to be reminded, with the help of practical demonstrations, that the biggest development assistance budgets in Canada were in federal hands, not provincial ones.[11]

The development assistance programs of various international institutions also began to expand as the post-war period wore on. Canada, anxious as always to pay its multilateral dues in order to amplify its diplomatic influence, found it hard to avoid putting money on the table wherever money on the table was expected. Itinerant Prime Ministers and other notables of government often found it convenient to leave gifts of development assistance in their wake whenever they travelled in the "third world," gestures that had short-term diplomatic purposes, but long-term programmatic implications. Such commitments added up.

The substantive objectives abroad of Canada's overseas development activities grew more ambitious in the 1980s, and at the same time were more frequently exposed to shifts of emphasis. It became increasingly popular to think of development assistance as a source of external leverage, and as a vehicle in particular for re-engineering the societies and polities, as well as the economies, of the recipient powers. With luck, it would help to relieve suffering and misery in the short term while promoting economic growth in the long term. It could also be used to serve other kinds of "social justice" and "economic management" purposes in the target countries, by encouraging democratization, for example, or advancing human rights and the rule of law, or promoting gender equality, or liberalizing markets, or embedding habits of "fiscal responsibility" in the administrative practices of recipient regimes.

In varying combinations, such aspirations were reiterated in the recurrent reports of parliamentary committees and the like. Driven in part by passing fads and fashions in the World Bank and elsewhere, they were dutifully regurgitated in the official documentation of the Canadian International Development Agency (CIDA) and other accounts of the pertinent government policies. Sometimes the implications of such outpourings were more rhetorical than real, but they nonetheless opened up the agenda even more, and hence increased further the pressure on the CIDA budget. This process may have been accelerated in the 1990s, moreover, by the flirtation in Foreign Affairs and International Trade with the concept of "human security" and the growing recognition that the perils created by failed and disrupted states might require developmental as well as "law and order" remedies.

As time went on, a kind of "domestic politics escalator" emerged. It resulted on the one hand from the increasing diversity of the Canadian population, and on the other from the growing importance of the role played by non-governmental organizations (NGOs) as both policy drivers and program deliverers. From the standpoint of winning political favour at home, it was harder than ever before to concentrate on anglophone and francophone targets in the Commonwealth and *la francophonie*. It was also harder than ever before to resist the sometimes carefully orchestrated representations of the pertinent interest groups, with which CIDA often cultivates a deeply rooted mutually interdependent relationship. Delivery contracts that have been concluded with such organizations can become institutionalized over time, and are then frequently buttressed by habit, familiarity, comfort and trust, and hence also in the end by inertia. Dependencies build up in both directions. CIDA needs the professional capacity that the NGOs can provide in the field. The NGOs need the money that CIDA can provide to keep their overheads covered and their operations on-going. Once such connections are fully established, dismantling them in order to rationalize the effort becomes a much more onerous enterprise, both psychologically and politically.

Nor are the NGOs the only voices that intrude on the decision-making from the domestic environment. They are joined by those of others who also stand to gain: business enterprises, for example, and wheat boards, along with their respective clienteles.

The problem is complicated even further by the fact that different departments within government itself are constantly attempting to have their own ends served by development assistance expenditures, or at least by the terms that govern the way the expenditures are made. Industry Canada wants industry to benefit. International Trade wants trade to benefit. Agri-foods and Agriculture Canada wants food producers and processors to benefit. Foreign Affairs wants Canadian diplomacy to benefit. Treasury Board wants to see a real return that looks like the promised return, whatever the promised return might be. The Finance Department, eventually, wants to see the money come back. And so on.

Given all these circumstances and the pressures they impose on the decision-makers, it is hardly surprising that Ottawa seems to be trying to do more with less, and in more places, too, so that the real impact of its programming conveys an impression of thinning out. As in the case of defence policy, moreover, the tendency for commitments to proliferate is matched by obstacles that prevent the excesses from being easily brought to heel. Some of these, as will be evident from the foregoing discussion, are inherent in the workings of the bureaucracy itself. CIDA has inertias of its own, and they are compounded by inertias elsewhere in the government apparatus. Once a cognate department has won a policy concession, it will be loathe to let it go.

In addition to these internal sources of opposition to the idea of pruning the effort, so as to focus it, there are obstacles elsewhere. Among them is the scope, urgency and persistence of the development challenge itself. The needs are real and they arise in a lot of places. In any particular case, Canada may not be able to do very much, but doing even a little may seem better than doing nothing at all. Concentrating the effort so as to be more effective in Country X may not compensate for abandoning the cause entirely in Country Y. This may reflect a genuine moral dilemma. Certainly it reflects a diplomatic one. Of the more than 100 countries on Canada's current list of recipients, it might not seem unreasonable in principle to drop a few in order to have a more discernible impact on the ones that remain. But the losers would still have lost, and their friends in Canada (expatriates among them), to say nothing of their representatives on the diplomatic circuit, would be sure to notice and complain. So would the NGOs and others who serve them. The short-term costs of making the change may thus seem considerably higher than the value of the advantages, as measured by visible impact, that might ultimately ensue, particularly since the aggrieved, both at home and abroad, will make a lot more noise than the parties who benefit and hence approve.

In practice, not all of the countries that might be identified as priorities on the potential list of recipients will have unlimited "absorptive capacity," even if they seem to have unlimited needs. Their circumstances may be so dire that they are unable to make optimal use of the resources they are offered. In cases of this sort, an attempt to concentrate the effort may result, not in a bigger bang for the buck, but in greater waste.[12]

Constraints on the capacity to initiate useful change may come as well from the representations of other donors, and more particularly from the multilateral institutions within which they often try to reach some sort of consensus on what works best. In such environments, the "conventional wisdom" that results from epistemic talk is sometimes surprisingly short-lived, but in any particular phase, the ruling fashion can have powerful effects on decision-making in donor capitals as well as on the policies of the multilateral agencies themselves. It may be hard to go against the grain.

The bottom line: Canada is over-extended in development assistance, and everyone who cares to pay attention now knows it.[13]

GETTING OVER-EXTENDED IN DIPLOMACY

A somewhat similar pattern, albeit more difficult to measure, applies also in the case of the third "D," as reflected in the expansion of Canada's representational commitments abroad, and in the obstacles that stand in the way of redeploying them in more focused style.

Here, too, the historical tale is familiar enough. In 1939 the fledgling Canadian foreign service was represented in only seven posts abroad, and as late as 1937 there were only eleven officers at headquarters in Ottawa.[14] This was hardly surprising in a context in which Canada's capacity to conduct a foreign policy independently of the British Empire had been acquired only recently, and even then by an almost surreptitious, incremental process that some would argue did not finally play itself out until the independent declaration of war against Germany in September 1939. The Second World War itself, however, had the effect of knocking some of the traditional great powers down, while raising other powers up. In 1945, even by the measure of raw military capacity, Canada could be credibly ranked fourth in the international hierarchy. Partly with this in mind, its foreign service professionals had determined in their post-hostilities planning that Ottawa should play an active role in post-war international affairs. Among other things, this would help to head off the prospect of a world governed solely by a great power cabal, and encourage a multilateral approach to the maintenance of the international order. Such an approach might even serve in some degree to obviate the danger of Canada becoming continentally confined, and hence subordinated to the United States.

It followed from this basic operating premise that Ottawa was inclined to think that Canada should be represented in almost every major multilateral forum, as well as in almost every national capital. The multilateral fora multiplied over the post-war period in response to new issues on the international agenda and to demands for the development of new instruments of international "governance." As decolonization advanced and as unwieldy concoctions like the Soviet Union, and later Yugoslavia, broke up into smaller bits and pieces, the national capitals proliferated. At its birth in 1945, the United Nations had 51 members. By 2002, with a total membership of 191, it had 140 more.

Canadians thus came to be counted among the most enthusiastic of the diplomatic "joiners," and the proliferation of their representatives abroad was given further encouragement by accelerating diversities at home, and by the consequent ambitions of Canada's political leaders. These included a tendency to revel in diplomacy at the top. While the

Cold War was in its most dangerous phase, chatter at the summit was often discouraged on the ground that foreign relations could be conducted in a more measured and less impulsive style if the bargaining was left to the professionals. The last-say decision-makers were better placed in reserve, to be mobilized only on special and symbolic occasions (usually to legitimize understandings and agreements already reached at lower levels). But in recent years summit diplomacy, much of it, but not all of it, multilateral, has become routine. Its practitioners give every evidence of taking pleasure from their game. Prime ministers have become itinerant. They enjoy leading their "teams" from Canada. And when they travel, they like to find an ambassador on deck wherever they go, a preference not entirely compatible with reducing the number of diplomatic missions overseas.

The problem of having too much to cover is compounded for the foreign service by the growing eclecticism and intricacy of the items on the foreign policy agenda itself, as well as by intensifying demands on foreign service officers to engage in ancillary busy work: "consulting with Canadians," for example, and responding to Treasury Board demands that they comply with passing fads in the organizational gimmickry of public administration. The difficulty, in short, comes not only from the need to cover an expanded array of geographical bases abroad, but also from having more to do.

Yet here, as in the case of defence and development assistance, any prospect of focusing the effort immediately concentrates the minds of defenders of the *status quo*. In this context, some of these lurk in the bureaucracy (not in Foreign Affairs alone, but in other departments and agencies), some are in the domestic constituency, and some are resident abroad. It is unnecessary to go through the mechanisms once again, for the behavioural pattern is essentially the same and it derives from similar incentives. As elsewhere, the structure within which the players operate has a lot to do with how they play the game. Here, too, the forces that favour inertia are immensely powerful, and here, too, they discourage the making of the hard choices that a concentration of effort would really require. Caution and interest alike produce instead an attachment to the values of prudence, and to the cautious decision-making habits of the incrementally disposed.

The bottom line: Canada is over-extended in its diplomatic representation abroad, and everyone who cares to pay attention now knows it.[15]

The practical conclusion that follows from all this is clear enough. Making "hard choices" is not an easy enterprise. It may even be close to impossible. Even if possible, it may not be worth the effort in the end. Given their own interests and the environments they face at home and abroad, the organizations of government do not easily warm to the task of giving up parts of what they do, even if there is compensation in the form of resources that will allow them to deal more effectively with the parts that remain. They therefore have to be pushed, nagged, bullied and cajoled into doing the job, and the pressure applied to them needs to be on-going. There is little joy in such a process, but there is no escaping it if the choices are to be explicitly made and reliably executed.

In the real world of government, this can happen only if direction comes clearly and persistently from the top. "Clearly," so that the apparatus cannot waffle, or find refuge in calculated ambiguity. "Persistently," so that it cannot get away with prevarication, or with simple stalling, in the expectation, born of long experience, that "this, too, will pass." The leadership, harried and distracted though it may be, thus cannot hope to succeed unless it pays close attention to the game and finds ways of seeing it carefully through.

It must begin, however, by deciding what it wants to do in the first place. And that may not be easy, either.

MAKING HARD CHOICES IN FOREIGN POLICY: THE CRITERIA PROBLEM

A political leadership that genuinely wishes to establish some priorities so as to render more effective the Canadian effort abroad will require some criteria with which to work. In that context, it may be useful to begin by reiterating that most of the available manoeuvring room arises in the context of operations overseas, and not in North America. The relationship with the United States is too important to Canadian interests to warrant a net transfer of foreign service resources from US locations to targets farther afield. On the contrary, there may be a strong case for moving at least some of the representational assets in precisely the opposite direction, a notion recently manifested in the decision announced in September 2003 to increase the number of Canadian consular offices in American cities from fifteen to twenty-two, while upgrading two of the existing consulates to consulates-general.

As noted earlier, the situation overseas is potentially very different, if only because Canadian activities there, while driven by powerful forces, are for the most part optional, elective and voluntary in the end. With this luxury of choice, in a world of perpetually limited resources, there ultimately comes not merely the ability, but perhaps also the need, to choose.

In that context, it might be assumed at the outset that identifying the criteria upon which to base the pertinent decisions would be a relatively easy and straightforward exercise. Presumably the way to start is to consult Canada's own needs, interests and preferences. Call them "values" if you must. This exercise will presumably be mediated by the government's own philosophy and priorities of rule. Then draw from the resulting analysis a sense of what matters most, and where, and what matters least. In practice, however, the process can never be quite so simple as this, if only because policy-making in government is always coloured by political forces of one kind or another. In effect, an escape from the various obstacles to change that have been described in the previous sections *can* never, and probably *should* never, be complete. Not all of the operational barriers, in other words, can be overcome by acts of will, even if the will at issue be that of the prime minister.

In any case, trade-offs will be required, some of them trade-offs of the existential sort that politicians have to make themselves because civil servants cannot be expected to do the job for them. A development assistance program mounted on the assumption that development aid is an instrument of foreign policy, will look rather different from one that is founded on the notion that the primary purpose is to fulfil a humanitarian obligation. The conduct of Canadian foreign policy more generally is bound in large measure to be reactive, a form of adaptive behaviour, and this inevitably entails *some* loss of control.

But when all such caveats are taken into account, there may still be some useful rules of thumb to consider. One of them might be that making the hard choices will be easier if the criteria are more functional than geographical. It might be tempting to suggest, for example, that Canadian policy need not be much concerned with sub-Saharan Africa, and that the resources currently deployed there could be more sensibly assigned somewhere else. Sub-Saharan Africa is not, after all, a region in which Canada has significant political or economic interests. On the other hand, it *is* an area in which the problems at issue are massively large, and therefore capable of absorbing unlimited resources with negligible effect. Clearly, however, a "hard choice" strategy based on such an assessment would carry an unacceptably high cost, both diplomatically in the UN and elsewhere, and politically at home. The idea is too "raw," too callous, too brutish on its face, to sell.

By contrast, a choice based on the principle that Canada *will* do "x" kinds of things (fight AIDS and other treatable diseases, or engineer clean water supplies), but *not* do "y" kinds of things (intervene in local "civil society" politics, for example) might be quite workable, and end up being as popular a specialization in the field of development assistance as peacekeeping has proved to be in defence policy.[16]

Similarly, in paring down the number of development assistance recipients and the number of overseas missions, it might be better to act on the basis, not of who or where the recipients are, but of how they are doing things. When the targets are excessively autocratic, for example, and too often bleed their public resources off to private bank accounts abroad, they could be excised from the list. Such "sanctions" (diplomatic and economic alike) are unlikely in themselves to persuade them to be more democratic and less corrupt, which is the most commonly articulated but absurdly optimistic reason for advocating such a policy, but they *would* allow the government to reduce its roster of overseas embassies and development assistance clients on politically defensible grounds.

To this, there are obvious counter-arguments, and some of them pull at the heart strings. Unless one assumes that the victims of autocratic regimes are entirely responsible for their own oppression, for example, it might be held that such a policy would contribute even further to the misery of those who are already among the most miserable. If such a view were thought to be persuasive, however, the conclusion presumably is not that priorities cannot be established at all, but only that they should be somewhat different. It might be concluded, for example, that the emphasis should be placed instead precisely on the polities in which autocracy and corruption are most rampant, and precisely on the jobs that the indigenous authorities should be doing themselves, but are not. Either way, it should be understood that the entire point of the exercise is to magnify the results by concentrating the effort, a process in which some are bound to lose (albeit not by very much) so that others may gain. Such is the price of economies of scale. Resources cannot be re-allocated, after all, without their being, well ... re-allocated.

Similarly on the defence side, it seems quite possible, assuming a reasonable level of funding, to make some hard choices that would yield constructive results. In principle, it would be possible in this case for a quite specific geographical criterion to take over, so that the military commitments of the Canadian Forces were confined entirely to what the Americans call "homeland security" and to co-operation with the United States in continental defence. But this would involve a truly dramatic retreat from past practice, and from the aspirations (or so it would appear) of attentive Canadians at large. It would also remove a vital prerequisite for the effective conduct of Canadian diplomacy in the United Nations and elsewhere, as well as in the context of a variety of bilateral relationships. That being so, it seems safe to assume that

Ottawa will want instead to maintain Canada's presence as a modest player in the security affairs of the world at large.

Given that assumption, the practicable criteria of choice are once again likely to be more functional than geographic. This is partly because the geographical criterion makes little sense in an era in which threats to security are globally rather than regionally distributed. At such a time, even a geographically-based alliance like NATO finds it necessary to do its military business "out of area." The special case of the North American environment aside, therefore, the policy issue is not a matter of deciding *where* to engage, but *how* to engage: in what degree, and with what capacities.

At the time of writing, it would appear that the Martin government is moving in the direction of wanting to specialize overseas in certain kinds of multi-faceted stabilization and nation-building enterprises in failed or disrupted politics, while abandoning the attempt to maintain a significant capacity for engaging in large-scale conventional military campaigns of the traditional sort. This conception may be derailed by the 2004 election results, or by the domestic politics that continually play themselves out in rival policy fields. But if not, and if it also survives the scrutiny of the international policy review, it could well result in major economies in certain areas of procurement, as well as in on-going operations.

These economies could then make it possible to invest much more heavily in the capabilities that remained. Getting out of heavy battlefield armour, for example, obviates the need to invest in new tanks and long-range artillery. It also undermines the case for purchasing heavy-lift transport aircraft in order to make it possible for Canada to carry such weighty equipment to and from locations overseas, and thereby escape the problem of being excessively dependent for this purpose on allied assistance or on the availability of alternative carriers on the "commercial" market. Similarly, a decision to abandon the attempt to maintain a fighter capability for deployment overseas – that is, a capability beyond the requirement for interception of aircraft heading into Canadian airspace – would ease very substantially the burden of fighter replacement, remove the need for an aerial refuelling capability, and generate on-going savings in maintenance, training and the like. All this would presumably make room for a reinvigoration of the infantry and other components of localized peace-enforcement operations, together with the (already announced) procurement of a new generation of multi-purpose naval supply ships with "troop transport" capabilities.

These sorts of decisions, if carried through, would certainly demonstrate the advantages that can come from the making of hard choices.

In this case it would be a choice that would leave Canada, naval forces possibly excepted, without any discernible capacity to engage with others in "big-war" operations in overseas theatres, but which would strengthen very considerably its ability to contribute to precisely the sorts of engagements that have dominated its active military agenda over the past decade and a half. Such a focus may in the end require that some diplomatic energy be expended on persuading the Americans, in particular, that this is actually the most constructive way in which Canada can "make a difference" that is genuinely helpful to them as well as to others. The argument may not be difficult to sell, however, given the Americans' own lesson-burning experience in Iraq, and the high value they have already come to attach to the Canadian performance in Kabul.

Obviously there are other possibilities. The point of the present discussion is simply to show that clear direction from the top, in spite of all the obstacles, can sometimes bring "drift" to an end, and replace it with a coherent policy result. The job, it is true, may be a little easier in the case of defence than in development assistance, where the problems at issue are multi-faceted, on-going, and in many cases apparently resistant to policy-driven remedies. Here the Martin government seems to be placing considerable emphasis, like its predecessor, on the epidemic of HIV-AIDS, especially in Africa, an option which is both appealing and workable.

In addition, however, the prime minister has attached special weight to the notion that Canada should focus on encouraging the development of "stable, strong and honest public institutions," on the ground that "[w]ithout solid public institutions, operational government ministries, a good legal system, honest police forces, independent courts, human rights commissions, schools, adequate hospitals and competent public services, the stability brought by peace-keeping forces can be fleeting at best."[17] This may prove more problematic, since the strength of public institutions of this sort depends on a host of other complex, inter-related and deeply imbedded variables: the level of economic prosperity, the distribution of the available wealth, the demographic composition of the society at issue, the tenets of the local political (and often religious) culture, the collective interpretation of past political events, and the indigenous mechanisms of "socialization" not least among them.[18] But if the policy analyses are properly done, the targets carefully selected, the other prerequisites successfully put in place, and the overtones of self-congratulation typical of Canadian rhetoric at home tactfully separated from the delivery, there may be possibilities here.

The final bottom line: The job, not completely, but in part, can probably be done, but only if the political leadership cares enough to find the time, and the mechanisms, to see the process through. Paying only sporadic attention will not be enough. But paying more than sporadic attention may be very difficult.

NOTES

1 "Health care," along with education, the social safety net, and almost every other domestic public policy purpose that enjoys a significant array of defenders at home.

2 The leading author of the "niche diplomacy" argument in the Canadian context is Andrew F. Cooper, who raised the issue nearly ten years ago. See, for example, his "In Search of Niches: Saying 'Yes' and Saying 'No' in Canada's International Relations," *Canadian Foreign Policy*, 3, 3 (Winter 1995), 1–13. A similar case has been made from time to time by Evan Potter, as in his "Redesigning Canadian Diplomacy in an Age of Austerity," in Fen Osler Hampson and Maureen Appel Molot, eds, *Big Enough to be Heard: Canada Among Nations 1996* (Ottawa: Carleton University Press, 1996), 23–55.

3 The phrase begs the question of doing the most good *for whom* and *for what*. For present purposes, however, it does not matter whether the intention is to do the most good for others, or for Canadians, or for both, although the issue becomes relevant when the hard choices start being made.

4 Thomas A. Hockin, "The Foreign Policy Review and Decision Making in Canada," in Lewis Hertzman, John Warnock and Thomas Hockin, *Alliances and Illusions: Canada and the NATO-NORAD Question* (Edmonton: M.G. Hurtig, 1969), esp. 95–110.

5 Some add a "T" (for trade) to the faddish phrase. Trade policy, however, will not be considered in the following discussion.

6 Canada, Department of National Defence, *Challenge and Commitment: A Defence Policy for Canada* (Ottawa: Supply and Services Canada, 1987). See also Norrin M. Ripsman, "Big Eyes and Empty Pockets: The Two Phases of Conservative Defence Policy," in Nelson Michaud and Kim Richard Nossal, eds., *Diplomatic Departures: The Conservative Era in Canadian Foreign Policy, 1984–93* (Vancouver: UBC Press, 2001), 100–12.

7 Canada, Department of National Defence, *1994 Defence White Paper* (Ottawa: Supply and Services Canada, 1994).

8 Government accountants may argue that this is not really true for the government as a whole, since the increased costs of production involved may be made up in whole or in part by the tax-dollar return that comes from the paying of Canadian wages and the earning of Canadian profits.

That, however, lends poor comfort to the Department of National Defence and the Canadian Forces, since the additional revenue that results does not accrue directly to them.

9 This conclusion has been asserted in umpteen reports of parliamentary committees, think tanks, defence-oriented interest groups and independent scholars over the past two or three years. Perhaps the most readable and best-known account is the one contained in Andrew Cohen, *While Canada Slept: How We Lost Our Place in the World* (Toronto: McClelland & Stewart, 2003). See esp. chapter 3, 37–71.

10 For a first-hand account, see Lester B. Pearson, *Mike: The Memoirs of the Right Honourable Lester B. Pearson: Vol. II – 1948–1957* (Toronto: University of Toronto Press, 1973), 107–12.

11 The most explicit manifestation of this calculus at work was the so-called "Chevrier Mission" of 1968. See John P. Schlegel, *The Deceptive Ash: Bilingualism and Canadian Policy in Africa: 1957–1971* (Washington, D.C.: University Press of America, 1978), 261–6.

12 Having said that, it should be understood as well that this is precisely the sort of argument that will be mounted by those in CIDA and elsewhere who are opposed to fundamental change. They have pride in what they do, think others grossly underestimate the complexity of the developmental challenge, and know that ALL their operations have defensible rationales. The natural conclusion, surely suspect, is that whatever *is* being done is the best that *could* be done, given the circumstances of the day. One of the hardest tasks of judgement that confronts a political leadership in relation to complex policy issues is to know when such arguments need to be taken seriously, and when they should be discounted. On this front, if not on others, seasoned hands usually know best.

13 For a succinct statement on this commonly held view, see Cohen, esp. 72–100.

14 John Hilliker, *Canada's Department of External Affairs: I – The Early Years, 1909–1946* (Montreal & Kingston: The Institute of Public Administration of Canada and McGill-Queen's University Press, 1990), 195–6.

15 See the excellent synthesis of the problem in Cohen, 118–56.

16 It will be noticed here that the emphasis in this discussion, driven by the basic question of whether Canada would do well to "specialize" more in the future than in the past, is on the allocation of representational and development assistance resources. In the case particularly of development assistance, some would argue that a much more fundamental "re-think" is required. Perhaps, for example, the emphasis should be shifted to trade and investment policy, and away from development assistance entirely, since there are reasons to think that changes in the trade and investment policies of the developed world could have a far greater impact on economic conditions in the developing countries than anything that might be

done to enhance the efficacy of traditional "foreign aid." An entirely new approach to working in partnership with private sector enterprises may also be warranted, and constitute a far more significant policy initiative than finding niches for CIDA to occupy with purely public funds. These kinds of issues, however, go far beyond the scope of the present article, the primary purpose of which is only to identify the kinds of constraints that inhibit the flexibility of the policy process within its existing framework.

17 "Address by Prime Minister Paul Martin on the Occasion of a Luncheon Hosted by the CORIM, the CERIUM, the Institut d'études internationales de Montréal à l'UQAM, and the Montreal International Organization," 10 May 2004, http://www.pm.gc.ca/eng/news.asp?id=201.

18 As imperial powers have discovered everywhere, and as the Americans are discovering now, meddling in such matters, particularly when the meddling is selective, can often do great damage. And whether damaging or not, the consequences are usually unanticipated. Well intentioned "developers" might do well to remember the first law of responsible medicine: "Do no harm."

3 Establishing Canada's Priorities

GORDON S. SMITH

There is always considerable constancy in Canadian foreign policy. This is hardly surprising since national interests and values tend not to change much and, when they do, only slowly over time. Both the Liberals and Conservatives are committed to a closer relationship with the United States, although that does not mean they would adopt the same policies. Both are committed to give higher priority to defence. But it is clear from their statements, probably reflecting Prime Minister Paul Martin's experience, that the Liberals are significantly more attuned to the need to meet global challenges and to strengthen multilateralism.

This chapter is about the likely changes in substance in foreign policy, as well as the desire to produce more synergy in the instruments of foreign policy. It discusses the three "Ds" – diplomacy, defence and development – which has gained a certain currency, both in Canada and abroad.

Paul Martin came into power as prime minister in late 2003 with two explicit, over-riding objectives in the international field: that the relationship with the United States had to be better managed, and that increased global interdependence was a reality requiring better governance. In the February 2004 Speech from the Throne, there was a clear message that globalization had to be better shaped to provide for more winners as well as support for the poorer people of the world. New rules were required to govern international actions when a government fails to protect its own people from tyranny and oppression. The government also wished to create a Canada Corps bringing together and strengthening the various activities of Canada and Canadians to build capacity for governance in developing countries.[1]

The prime minister also stated his belief that Canada needed to do much better in integrating our main resources in the international arena: the "three Ds." A foreign policy review was underway at the level of officials, and the prime minister made several major foreign policy speeches, the most important being the one in Montreal on 10 May.[2] This chapter will review progress to date and set out some of the challenges that need to be overcome.

THE UNITED STATES

Canadians know that their country is becoming economically more and more deeply integrated with the United States. Many may not particularly like it, but they know it nonetheless. Canadians, however, see themselves as disadvantaged by the unequal nature of the relationship, and the feeling that the United States is only prepared to play by the rules of the international system when it wins, for example, in the North American Free Trade Agreement (NAFTA) and the World Trade Organization (WTO) on softwood lumber. The facts may or may not be different, but the perceptions are as they are. Nonetheless the facts do indeed tell us a great deal as, for example, set out by former senior US official and Nobel laureate Joseph Stiglitz in his new book *The Roaring Nineties: Seeds of Destruction.*[3] On international economic questions, the US plays hardball, including brushing off the batters of the opposing team when they get too close to the plate.

Canadians see the United States as becoming increasingly unilateralist. This is, in part, a reflection of the current George W. Bush Administration, but there is more to it than that. There is also a worry that, as we deal file by file with the US, albeit in the context of NAFTA, our neighbour feels a certain "droit de regard" about what happens to our precious resources, from energy to water. Canada has not really had a serious debate as to whether we would be better off selling available resources at market rates or instead conserving them for future generations. Nor has there been a real debate on whether we are better to proceed file by file or instead to look at a larger "package deal" or "grand bargain," involving politically explosive trade-offs. The discussions, such as they are, tend to be highly emotional.

The attacks on New York and Washington of September 11 2001 changed the world in many ways. The attacks, however, changed the world in different ways; where one lives has a major impact on perceptions on this attack. In the United States a new organizing principle rapidly developed for relations with the rest of the world. The principle was the need for absolute priority to be given to the global war on (largely Islamic) terrorism. The feeling seemed clearly to be: "You are with us or against us. We have the right to take whatever and whenever action that we need to protect our security."

The United States felt and feels profoundly vulnerable to future attacks, particularly from Al Qaeda or other groups associated with Osama bin Laden's network. That is hardly surprising, given what these terrorist groups have said – they do not mask their intentions – and what they have done. The probabilities of further attacks increase as the US pursues policies in the Middle East which fan the flames of hatred for that country. The appalling photographs that appeared in May 2004 of Iraqi prisoners being tortured by the US military had serious impacts in that region and beyond. The likelihood of terrorist use of weapons of mass destruction (WMD) was and is rated by many experienced observers as just a matter of time – not whether but when. Ward Elcock, the outgoing director of the Canadian Security Intelligence Service, has warned that Canada is equally vulnerable, and declared an attack is only a matter of time.

After September 11 American and coalition attacks on Afghanistan were aimed at destroying the bases for Al Qaeda operations as well as overturning the Taliban government. Canada was in the mountains of Afghanistan early and is now the leader of the Afghanistan mission run through the North Atlantic Treaty Organization (NATO).

The response to September 11 did not, however, stop with Afghanistan. Iraq was next on the list, and indeed some would argue had been on certain lists even before September 11. The decision to attack Iraq exacerbated the division between the US and much of the rest of the world, importantly including much of Europe. Iraq was early on joined by Iran and North Korea as part of an "axis of evil," as described by President Bush. The US secretary of state, Colin Powell, however, made it clear that Iran and North Korea were not earmarked for a military response, at least not yet. In Iraq, however, the United States was not prepared to let the United Nations process of inspections and resolutions run its course. President Bush invoked the doctrine of preventive attack, asserting Saddam Hussein's regime not only had weapons of mass destruction but ties to Al Qaeda.

These connections have yet to be proven in a very convincing way. Indeed, Richard Clarke's important book suggests strongly that Bush and senior colleagues like his vice-president, Dick Cheney, and the deputy secretary of defense, Paul Wolfowitz, were looking, almost desperately, for a link to Iraq.[4] Clarke was in a position to know, with his senior position on the National Security staff. That Iraq had had both chemical and biological programs and the capability for making weapons is undeniable, but that is different from actually having the weapons in recent times. That Iraq had tried to build or obtain nuclear weapons is also undeniable, but it did not have them in September 2001, and was some distance away from having them. Enquiries have been launched as to why the intelligence was so wrong. Or was it less the intelligence than a political determination to bring about "regime change" in Iraq?

The Canadian government made clear publicly it was unconvinced of the Al Qaeda connection, and constantly supported the UN-led inspections as necessary and sufficient to determine if Iraq had WMD. Appropriate action could then follow. When the US decided to attack Iraq, Canada did not join George W. Bush's coalition.

As the war in Iraq unfolded, the rationale for it manifestly changed. US rhetoric increasingly focused on the murderous actions of Saddam against his own people. Daalder and Lindsay, in their book *America Unbound*, argue convincingly that there were two camps in the Bush Administration, often confused as if there were only one – they are not all "neocons," the expression used for neo-conservatives.[5] Daalder and Lindsay distinguish between "assertive nationalists" and "democratic imperialists." The former want to use US power as and when necessary to defend US interests; the latter want to remake the world in the US image, a goal that is much more sweeping. Daalder and Lindsay further argue that the Iraq operation has been an uneasy compromise between the two groups, with some "liberal internationalism" periodically thrown in. There are increasingly real questions about the adequacy of public support in the US, as well as about the feasibility on the ground in Iraq for creating a liberal, democratic, market economy oriented polity. This is particularly so, both if the killings go on and include more and more American civilians, and if the growing crisis arising from the taking of hostages does not somehow get resolved.

Canadians, and many Europeans, did not like the way the United States dealt with Iraq. The swaggering style of George W. Bush also continues to aggravate seriously the negative perception of US policies in the eyes of many Canadians.[6] Nonetheless the reality is that the perception of the United States being under attack is not just held by the president and his "neocon" supporters. The perception of a substantial threat of further devastating attacks is quite widely held in the United States, including by many senior Democrats. There is, for example, no real resistance in the US to heightened levels of airport and aircraft security. And the one Democrat who tried to distance himself most from the war on terrorism, Howard Dean, is history. Senator John Kerry has actually promised more resources for defence and homeland security. The threat is real, although the US is not meeting it in the way it should. Provided we are sympathetic about the threat of terrorism and supportive of counter-measures, it does not follow that we cannot pursue an independent Canadian foreign policy in response.

Most Canadians and Europeans do not understand how very differently the perceptions of threat have emerged among traditional NATO Allies. This is dangerous. While in NATO there have been serious differences among allies, it always at the end of the day held together because of the glue provided by the threat of the Soviet Union. That glue has disappeared. The only people who really worry about Russia now are the new members of NATO, ex-Warsaw Pact nations. NATO is now in danger of serious splits, or more likely irrelevancy, because of the differences that exist. NATO needs more missions of the kind it has undertaken in Afghanistan if it is to stay relevant. It may be possible to paper over the cracks; it is in everybody's interest to do so. But there are many Americans who share Robert Kagan's views that, on fundamental issues, the US is from Mars and Europe is from Venus.[7] And on the other side there are many Europeans who see the US as an increasing threat to peace as a result of its unilateralist behaviour. The US is also seen as blindly allied with Israel, the government of which is considered by many in Europe, according to public opinion polls, to be a major threat to peace.

The Canadian pollster Michael Adams has recently written a best-selling book called *Fire and Ice*.[8] It is about the increasingly different values and attitudes in Canada and the US. He notes these differences do not just date back to September 11 or the election of the current US Government. In the US, there is a greater sense that the world is a nasty place and that violence is not only appropriate but also necessary to deal with that harsh reality. Canadians do not feel this way. The book is controversial and some question its hyperbole and even methodology, but I believe its central thesis is accurate.

Prime Minister Jean Chrétien created the impression in the US that Canada was not there for our American neighbours when we were needed. It was not just about not sending troops to Iraq.

Rather, one had to go back to the slowness of his response on and in the days just after September 11. The impression was created both in this country and south of the border that Canada saw the threat to the US as a problem for the US, not one that we held in common.

Security trumps even the economy when society at its core is threatened. That is the case in the US, but not Canada. One of Prime Minister Martin's priorities should therefore be to explain to Canadians how and why the sense of current threat south of the border is what it is. We are not ourselves without a threat in Canada, as Stewart Bell has argued in his recent book.[9] Another, much more complex, objective should be to ensure he has a relationship with the US President such that they can discuss the pros and cons of various strategies to deal with the combined threats of global terrorism and WMD. The reality is that Canada will never be a big player on these issues; Canada simply does not have the military muscle or the economic strength. Soft power is not no power, but it is limited power if not combined with real hard power. Canada has some, albeit limited, hard power, and likely will acquire more.

In the bilateral economic dimension to the Canada-US relationship, the capacity to communicate and bargain is critical. Canadians have to appreciate, however, that the power that lies in Congress frequently means the president, powerful though he may seem, cannot deliver in the same way as a prime minister can in a parliamentary system. We need to think through where we wish to go in our relations with the United States. What are the choices and what are the tradeoffs? What will the future agenda look like? When is linkage helpful and when is it not?

Later in this chapter, I shall discuss some of the global challenges stemming from living in an increasingly interdependent world, but one in which the discrepancies between "haves" and "have nots" become more and more important. If we are to build a world in which we can better shape globalization and meet other global challenges, the necessary governance must include the United States. This too requires that the prime minister of Canada have an open and productive relationship with his American counterpart. He needs to be able to persuade President Bush that multilateral solutions can work, and are in the US interest.

GLOBAL CHALLENGES

During his period as minister of finance, Paul Martin was deeply conscious of growing global interdependence and inequality in the world. He was conscious of this in the economic area, but beyond as well. His long time friend, Maurice Strong, has for more than three decades drawn attention to global environmental challenges and the need for global responses. Another good friend dating back from their years together in Power Corporation, Jim Wolfensohn, was president of the World Bank during the period Martin was in the Finance Department. Wolfensohn attempted a number of reforms, but found the institution difficult to change. It is reasonable to assume Martin and Wolfensohn have discussed more than once the reform of global institutions. Martin was also very close to his father who was Canada's internationalist foreign minister for a number of years.

Martin was one of the G-7 finance ministers for almost a decade. He considered it an effective body because it brought people together around a relatively small table. Conscious of the fact that the G-7 was composed entirely of developed countries, and working with Larry Summers, the US treasury secretary at the time, he was deeply involved in first creating, and then leading, the G-20 group of finance ministers. This added key developing countries, such as China, India, South Africa, and Brazil, to the G-7.

As prime minister, Paul Martin has said he would like to see a G-20 at the level of government leaders.[10] He raised this possibility at the World Economic Forum in Davos in January 2004. The membership of the G-20 might or might not be constant.

One could have part of the membership floating, according to the subject to be discussed. Martin is strongly of the belief that the way to bring about change is for leaders to engage face-to-face. If they can reach consensus, they can make things happen.

The Centre for Global Studies at the University of Victoria, together with the Centre for International Governance Innovation in Waterloo, have held two meetings on future possibilities for a G-20, both attended by Martin, one before he became prime minister and one after. The consensus at the second meeting was that challenges in the global health, water and climate change areas were particularly ripe for action by G-20 leaders. The sense was that Canada should lead in proposing a pilot meeting that would address one of these issues. If there was success, one could regularize such meetings. The feeling was that this could lead to major improvements in global governance, building on democratically elected and accountable governments at the national level, through the creation of transnational networks.

During Paul Martin's time as finance minister, the protests against globalization and global institutions were growing. Civil society, sometimes with uncivil behaviour, wanted its voice heard. Martin has indicated that he is leery of direct engagement of civil society in international organizations, certainly if it goes so far as to be regarded as part of the process of accountability. Rather it is elected governments which must be accountable to their electorates for their actions, including those taken in the context of international institutions.

Prime Minister Paul Martin would like to help lead a process that will bring about needed reforms to the International Monetary Fund and the World Bank. He also has a deep commitment to the United Nations, not one that is starry eyed, but instead based on a firm belief that the world's most universal organization must be strengthened to meet the challenges that are now evident and those that lie ahead. Earlier this year he produced, together with Ernesto Zedillo, the former President of Mexico, a report to the secretary general of the United Nations on what should be done to ensure more private investment is made in developing countries. At Davos, he extended an invitation to Kofi Annan to address the Canadian Parliament in March 2004. The UN secretary general was the first major international leader to visit Ottawa in the period after Prime Minister Martin took office.

It is interesting that Prime Minister Martin has picked up on the need for follow through to the report of the Evans/Sahnoun Commission, entitled *Responsibility to Protect*. This Commission was launched by the former foreign minister, Lloyd Axworthy, and its report was presented to the UN secretary general. It neatly turned on its head the question of the right to intervene into a responsibility of states to protect their citizenry. The report went a substantial distance to defining at least some of the circumstances that would permit intervention when all else failed. Kofi Annan clearly wanted to see the report kept under international discussion, and the Martin government has agreed to assist in doing so.

Martin sees a relationship and necessary balance between the increasingly deep relationship with the US and an active presence on the world scene. Canadian internationalism helps to assure the country that our foreign policy is independent.

CANADA'S RESOURCES AND MACHINERY OF GOVERNMENT

Canada may be a large country geographically with a relatively high standard of living, but that does not translate automatically into being a major power. We may be part of the G-8 and members of more international bodies than virtually any other country, but it would be a mistake to read too much into this. There have been significant reductions in real terms in the budgets devoted to the armed forces and to development assistance, with the consequence that we have relatively fewer resources at our disposal in the world than we had in the past. We have also seen major cuts in the Foreign Service at a time when demands on it have increased.

This is not to argue that more money gives greater results. It depends on how it is spent. For the armed forces, it is quite impossible to have a first rank capability in all areas. We thus need a clear sense of what kinds of conflict the military might engage in. This should recognize the low probability of traditional inter-state conflict and the rise in intra-state conflict and in the capability of non-state actors. It is also likely that this and future Canadian governments will wish to engage in the sort of counter-terrorism activities with which the Canadian Forces have been engaged in Afghanistan. The prime minister, indeed, stated in Gagetown on 14 April that "The real security challenge of the 21st century is centred on terror cells. Today's front line stretches from the streets of Kabul, to the rail lines in Madrid, to cities across Canada."[11] It has already been announced that the Special Forces unit, JTF2, is being expanded; an important policy question will be by how much. The Kabul-centred role of the remainder of the Canadian Forces activity in Afghanistan has shown that even security patrols are at risk, and this requires a substantially higher degree of protection than, for example, light peacekeeping.

For development assistance, the key is having an impact on poverty alleviation on the ground. There is no point in pouring more money into overhead or into the pockets of corrupt foreign officials. Choices need to be made about which countries we should be involved in and to do what. Indeed the "to do what" question should perhaps have a determining effect on where we operate. The likelihood is that the Canadian International Development Agency (CIDA) will be restructured in some way and that Canada Corps type activities will be increased.

For the Foreign Service, extra money needs to be well targeted in places where it will make a difference. Canada cannot be chasing all of the rabbits all of the time. Priorities need to be set. That means we cannot try to do everything. What is worse, we have not had "our act together." This is where the 3 Ds come in. People in CIDA have had a strong sense of their independence and role in poverty alleviation and other worthy goals. People in the Department of National Defence feel they have the best sense of where Canada's security interests lie. The Department of Foreign Affairs often has difficulty speaking with one voice and, when it does, exerting leadership with other departments. We have difficulty speaking about interests, and there is often confusion about promoting Canadian values. We need to do much better.

There were signs in early 2004 that this situation was starting to change both at the ministerial and senior official level. Foreign Affairs is consulting intensively with the other major international departments, CIDA, DND, and now Trade. Foreign Affairs is also consulting extensively with the large suite of "domestic" departments engaged internationally, from Agriculture to Environment. The domestic departments are being asked what they would like to see as Canada's objectives. These will then be discussed and stitched together, thus assuring a higher degree of buy-in than there has been in the past. This is important, and should be encouraged. Canada simply does not have, and nor will it have, even if and when budgets go up, sufficient resources for the "three Ds" to go their separate ways.

What does this mean in practice? It means that, if we are going to engage our military in a country like Afghanistan, we need to be there with our development assistance and a strong embassy. That is what is now occurring in that country, but it has not always been the case. Too often our priorities for military deployment, development assistance and diplomacy differed.

Paul Martin has recognized the need to bring together our resources in the international area. Indeed, he has called for a review of our international policy that would integrate the three dimensions. That review is being led by the minister of foreign affairs.

Trade and Investment is becoming a separate department, again, with common administrative services with Foreign Affairs. This could turn out to be a serious error. Just as diplomacy, defence, and development are coming more together, trade and investment is being broken off. No matter what people say, ministerial loyalties will determine how officials feel and act; the separation into different departments will create new loyalties.

For many countries, development is the biggest dimension of the relationship for Canada. And for many developing countries, their priority is for a more liberal trade regime. That is why CIDA, Foreign Affairs *and* Trade need to be closer together, something that is being recognized in a number of other countries. For many other countries, the key to our relationship is trade. There are likely to be more questions (and there already were many) about from which group does the ambassador come, who can task whom (if they are part of a separate department), and the like. Moreover, government reorganizations are expensive, above all in time lost but also in money, and rarely solve problems without creating new ones.[12]

There is an additional issue, one which confronts all foreign ministries, and most aid agencies. Foreign ministries, and this is the case in Canada, are typically organized geographically and functionally. The functional branches are generally able to come up with a reasonable set of priorities. The geographically organized branches, by their very nature, cannot. Human nature says if you are responsible for Canada's relations with Italy, or Indonesia, you think those relations are terribly important and under-resourced. It doesn't get better at higher levels. No assistant deputy minister responsible for Europe will see resources willingly transferred from his or her region to Asia. This way of organizing foreign ministries helps explain why at inter-departmental meetings other departments can send one person, but there may be five from Foreign Affairs. From my experience, this is not a uniquely Canadian phenomenon. Unfortunately, it frustrates others in the room as people seemingly from one department argue with each other. And it creates the impression Foreign Affairs has more people than it needs.

Coming to ministerial leadership, a key element, there is good news. The decision to recreate the Cabinet Committee on Priorities and Planning is an excellent one. There needs to be a forum capable of looking well beyond the day-to-day to longer term issues. The prime minister has also created a Committee on Canada-US Relations. While there will be questions as to what issues go where (the secretary to the Cabinet is the traffic cop when it comes to routing Cabinet documents), this is an excellent innovation. Finally, Paul Martin has created a Cabinet Committee on Global Affairs. The name of this Committee is interesting, and hopefully reflects a perception of a world in which global challenges are crucial and lead to a need for better forms of global management. The fact that the prime minister will chair all these committees may look very centralizing to some observers, but the fact is that experience has shown that the foreign minister in the past just has not had the influence to do it. There is no choice but for the prime minister to carry out this function himself, at least in the initial stages and on major issues.

Prime Minister Martin signalled some important changes as he structured his first Cabinet. After acknowledging the importance of global terrorism, as well as international crime, threats of disease and state failure, he created a new post of minister of public safety and emergency preparedness. He added immediate clout to the position by giving the post to the deputy prime minister. He showed recognition of the critical nature of border security for both Canada and the United States by creating a new Canada Border Services Agency. Finally, he indicated that a much-needed reform of the refugee determination process would be undertaken soon.

CONCLUSIONS

Foreign policy is made more in the doing than in the philosophizing. Paul Martin's priorities and interests are well known, and priority areas have really already been addressed. So far, the indications are that his government will be different than its predecessor in foreign policy. It will be more conscious of the degree of integration with the US and the consequent need to make strategic choices and trade-offs. It will also be more conscious of the need to improve governance of global challenges and act accordingly. Finally, it will do more to bring the "three Ds" together. One must hope that the "T" (Trade) will not now go off more on its own.

RECOMMENDATIONS

- Understand that our neighbour, closest trading partner and only remaining superpower believes it is at war with global terrorism and will act accordingly;
- Co-operate with the US on North American security issues and try to encourage both a more multilateralist response from the US, as well as more balanced policies in the Middle East;
- Give priority through the G-20 and the Canada Corps to Canadian leadership in improving global capacity to deal with challenges to our security, environment and prosperity;
- Invest money in a targeted way, using the 3D approach, to improve our international presence as well as co-ordination in policy;
- More specifically, increase military spending to give the Canadian Forces the capacity to conduct and support the sort of anti-terrorist/guerrilla fighters that are now encountered in Afghanistan;
- Increase international development assistance in a way that it responds to foreign policy priorities, including the need to meet global challenges such as climate change and the scourge of failing/failed states, by being more focused so that Canada can make a difference;
- Provide Foreign Affairs with resources to enable leadership, priority setting, co-ordination and service to Canadians.

NOTES

1 To avoid any appearance of conflict of interest, it should be known by the reader that I have been asked to co-chair, with astronaut Julie Payette, the board of the Canada Corps.

2 See http://www.pm.gc.ca/eng/news.asp?id=201.

3 Joseph Stiglitz, *The Roaring Nineties: A New History of the World's Most Prosperous Decade* (New York: Norton, 2003).

4 Richard Clarke, *Against All Enemies* (New York: Free Press, 2004).

5 Ivo H. Daalder, and James M. Lindsay, *America Unbound* (Washington: Brookings Institution Press, 2003).

6 See Anne-Marie Slaughter, *A New World Order* (Princeton and Oxford: Princeton University Press, 2004).

7 Robert Kagan, *Of Paradise and Power: America and Europe in the New World Order* (New York: Knopf, 2003).

8 Michael Adams, *Fire and Ice: The United States, Canada and the Myth of Converging Values* (Toronto: Penguin Canada, 2003).
9 Stewart Bell, *Cold Terror: How Canada Nurtures and Exports Terrorism Around the World* (Toronto: Wiley, 2004).
10 See the chapter below, by George Haynal.
11 See http://www.pm.gc.ca/eng/news.asp?id=172.
12 The author was responsible for machinery of government in the Privy Council Office for a number of years.

4 International Policy Reviews in Perspective

ROB McRAE

Foreign policy reviews, whatever we might think about their usefulness, have become a staple product of most Western foreign ministries in recent years. In Canada, they are frequently associated with the arrival of new governments, perhaps responding to the natural desire to take stock and chart a new course on the international scene. But the pattern in Canada has not been particularly successful, if looked at from the standpoint of introducing real change in our relations with the world.

Reviews have often satisfied themselves with describing the world of the present, or even the past, rather than focusing on the future. Admittedly, anticipating the future and adapting accordingly is difficult at the best of times, and involves a degree of risk-taking if significant resources are at stake. Committing resources against anticipated needs, rather than the needs of today, is often difficult to justify in domestic terms. It is well nigh impossible to gain public agreement when resources are geared to anticipated international developments.

Hence reviews have rarely, if ever, presented real choices to the Canadian public. Nor have reviews been crucial to a government's decisions about how we manage our international engagement at home.

Should we conclude that all such reviews are therefore doomed to failure, and that the process ought be abandoned for good? On balance, the answer is no, though we need to be much more explicit in the future as to what a review should seek to accomplish. In other words, we need, at the start, to be clear about the "bottom lines" for any review, together with a sense of "desirable outcomes," if circumstances permit. Only in this way will we be able to judge our relative success in exercises that often tend to temporize rather than to lay out difficult issues for what they are.

Beyond process questions, this paper also looks at the changed context (both domestic and international) for reviews, and how that changed context necessarily influences the potential outcomes of any review. Finally, based on an analysis of longer-term trends, the paper sets out key strategic interests for Canada that future reviews will need to address.

PRELIMINARY CONSIDERATIONS: MEASURING SUCCESS

The following is a check-list of "bottom lines" for any review, if it is to attain a modicum of success with its principal audiences. Those audiences or "clients" are three-fold: the Canadian public, the experts, and the bureaucracy in Ottawa. Unless there is something for each of these, the review will fail to deliver real change. Here is my list of key ingredients for a successful review:

Rooted in the Domestic Today, a public document that sets itself up as a review of foreign policy can no longer pander only to the pundits and experts of international policy if it wishes to exert change. The review needs to be seen as relevant to the government's domestic agenda if it is to have a chance of obtaining new resources for the priorities it identifies. In fact, in a globalized world, virtually all domestic issues have an international dimension, and the distinction between domestic and international issues is fading in reality if not in the public mind. The review therefore needs to make clear that an international strategy is essential to delivering on domestic priorities.

Relevant to Current Issues Reviews must be seen to be grappling with the major international issues of the day if they hope to be seen as relevant to the public. Clearly, in our own time, this means we must have strategies that deal with international terrorism, failed states, various regional conflicts, international health crises, environmental concerns, humanitarian assistance, and of course trade issues, especially in the context of Canada-US trade. Canadians also expect that the government set out our views of issues central to US foreign policy, whether for or against. Iraq is the latest example, but it is the last in a long line.

Analyses Trends and Anticipates Developments There is a tendency among policy-makers to weave analyses of trends and current events out of their personal impressions of the world. These can be convincingly portrayed, as they often are in Ministerial speeches. But policy-makers are no less likely to harbour myths about the world than is the public, unless they are forced to confront inconvenient facts. There are lots of myths about the nature of Canada's role in the world, whether the generosity or poverty of Canada's contribution to development in the poorest countries, for example, or whether Canadians are more engaged internationally than any other people. The facts that lie behind the slogans are frequently more complicated than can be summed up in a winning phrase. It is crucial that any review conduct a reality-check on the assumptions behind our foreign policy, if it is to be not only credible, but useful. Though reviews cannot predict events, they can demonstrate an awareness of long-term trends that will affect us as a nation.

Three-dimensional International policy-making in the age of globalization is like playing three-dimensional chess: it is necessary to understand how virtually every development on one level say in international security, is connected to others, on an entirely different board, such as the international economy board. Not only is three-dimensional thinking required, the boards are often being played on different sides of the planet. This places new demands on foreign ministries everywhere, more used to playing two-dimensional strategies on separate economic, military, or development boards. Not only will these approaches fail, they will create unintended consequences that in a globalized world will change the game for everyone. Reviews therefore have to demonstrate three-dimensional thinking, and an understanding of the integrated nature of many of today's complex problems and opportunities.

Focused on Priorities There are a lot of things going on in the world that merit interest, but a review has to focus on issues of concern to Canada. This means demonstrating a sure grasp of the national interest, and of those principles we hold that might motivate us to take action even when our interests are not engaged. But not only must a review focus on issues of concern to Canada, it needs to show how we can leverage change in our favour internationally, and what capacities are required to effect it. In other words, where are (or will be) our interests or principles engaged, what is the strategy to obtain our objective, with whom must we partner, and what capability do we require to take the specified action?

The bottom lines identified above are already a tall order, if past reviews are any guide. Achievement here would already produce a significant review. But there is one other element, if incorporated, that would make the review more effective.

Long-Term Impact An international policy review will be still-borne unless steps are taken to make it sustainable over time. These steps include the engagement of the public, parliament, provinces, and the bureaucracy. Public support will be required if new policy directions are to be undertaken, especially if new resources are required. Parliament not only needs to debate the changes proposed, there should ideally be regular parliamentary involvement in the follow-up. Provinces and cities are in many ways the first line of engagement with globalization, for example, whether in terms of foreign investment or the new health threats. The proposed changes coming out of any review will require both the provinces and cities to be on board if those changes are to be more than cosmetic. Finally, if the review is intended to change the way we do things internationally, then the whole federal government should be engaged, since virtually every department plays an international role. This will require not only the establishment of policy coherence across government, it will require culture change to support new habits of collaboration.

CANADIANS IN THE WORLD

The above set out some generic markers for a successful review. However, what would these requirements mean in practice? For example, how is the international agenda rooted in our domestic agenda? What societal characteristics potentially can contribute to our success internationally? Which international trends and developments have implications for our national interests or our values?

The Domestic Roots of Our International Policy

It is increasingly apparent that, as Canadian society changes, those changes are shaping our international agenda as a nation. In turn, our international agenda is influencing the kind of Canada that is growing into maturity. Here are some key factors that illustrate this new reality.

Canadian Demography Our most relevant demographic statistics are telling: fully 18 per cent of Canadians were born outside the country (over 26 per cent in Ontario and BC); in recent years, immigration accounts for more than 50 per cent of population growth; over 45 per cent of principal immigrant applicants possess a BA degree or higher; and by 2011, our labour force needs will have to be met almost entirely through immigration.

Rather than creating ethnic tension, the pace of immigration appears to be more exhilarating than worrying in the minds of many Canadians. When Canadians are asked what makes them proudest, multiculturalism tops the list in recent polls. Pride in multiculturalism is particularly strong among young Canadians, who are also committed to the Charter of Rights and Freedoms, and to bilingualism. A majority of Canadians say we should accept either the same number of immigrants or more in the future. In other words, support for multiculturalism and immigration is growing as the country becomes more ethnically diverse.

The Economy This pattern finds a parallel in our economy. There is a deepening dependency on international factors: over 40 per cent of our GDP is exported (the G-8 average is 17 per cent); fully 37 per cent of our GDP is imported (the G-8 average is 14 per cent); the export of manufactured products (57 per cent of the total) now out-ranks the export of resource-based products (43 per cent); 85 per cent of our exports goes to the US, followed by Japan (2 per cent), UK (1 per cent), etc; our top five sources of Foreign Direct Investment (FDI) are: US ($224 billion), France ($32 bn), UK ($26 bn), Netherlands ($14 bn), and Japan ($9 bn); and approximately 22 per cent of Canadian firms' assets are controlled by foreign firms.

Reflecting the high degree of our economic integration internationally, a majority of Canadians see their country as a technologically-advanced major trading nation, and 80 per cent believe international trade is increasingly important to our economy. Over 70 per cent support continental free trade. As Canadians have become free traders, support for international trade has increased.

This fact is crucial when the economy continues to figure as the top public policy priority for Canadians after healthcare. Education, national security and defence, and the environment follow in terms of top-tier concerns. In other words, of the top five public policy concerns of Canadians, three have significant (and well-recognized) international components.

Health But Canadians are increasingly cognizant of the international dimensions of health too. The SARS epidemic revealed the extent to which serious health threats are only a plane-ride away.

When seen against the backdrop of our immigrant society, and the fact that more Canadians travel and more wish to live in two countries at once, it is clear that our society will be subject to the increased risk posed by new communicable diseases. Hence we will have a direct interest in the international machinery that manages those risks, particularly in terms of preventing or controlling future outbreaks. That interest will extend to the way in which those same international organizations measure the efforts of affected countries, given the potential collateral impact on travel, tourism, and trade. Finally, both human rights and development strategies are relevant to the outbreak of epidemics in the developing world, and these need to be seen through the health lens.

Education In a knowledge-based society, ideas and expertise flow across borders, and innovation is as much the product of international partnerships as it is of domestic development. Investment in education at home is vital to ensuring that we have the right capacity to participate in the global knowledge economy. This has real implications for our immigration policies. Already comprising 70 per cent of labour force growth in the last decade, Canada's labour force needs by 2011 will have to be met almost entirely through immigration. Our ability to attract and retain high-quality immigrants will be crucial, as will be our recognition of foreign credentials. In short, the prospect of an ageing workforce and a serious skill shortage will tend to increase the interconnections between immigration and international education. Our interest in attracting foreign students to our universities, and retaining a percentage of them, will require Canada to compete in the international educational market as never before. As with foreign investment, our perceived quality of life and equal opportunity will be more important than ever.

Homeland Security Since September 11 2001, Canadians recognize that international security is not something that only happens "out there." Security, whether national or international, is becoming in Canada a "community" affair. This reflects not only an appreciation of how terrorism can reach around the world. Ethnic communities in Canada potentially can become entangled in the disputes of distant homelands. Canadians understand as never before that security is a single spectrum linking national, continental, and international aspects. But they also have a broader appreciation of security, and see traditional security as intersecting with other issues too, such as human security, health risks, and our economic welfare.

Our Societal Strengths and Vulnerabilities in an International Context

Just as Canadians appreciate how our domestic goals increasingly have international dimensions, so too are they more aware of how our social make-up creates for us new opportunities and challenges internationally. When looked at across the spectrum of nations, Canada is not and has never been a "middle of the road" country. Our natural and social assets have always placed us at the extreme end of any international spectrum, whether in terms of wealth or quality of life, rights and freedoms, or security. In many ways we are unique: our multicultural make-up, our linguistic profile, our natural endowments, our privileged position vis à vis the US. At this most basic level, we need to be more self-conscious of what we bring to the world, what we might call our international assets.

Some of those assets are obvious. For example: we are an open, advanced society, with a modern developed economy; our geographic location favours us as a nation, providing a privileged relationship with the US and a window on Europe, Asia-Pacific, and Latin America; our historical roots facilitate interaction with the anglophone and francophone worlds, while our multicultural make-up offers direct links with countless homelands, and provides appeal as a model of diversity and governance; we have a distinctive role in the multilateral and regional forums that matter; and we are without colonial baggage, and possess international credibility on the basis of a record of fairness and equity in dealing with global concerns.

Since September 11, however, many of these assets are now perceived as vulnerabilities, if not in Canada, then elsewhere. Our openness, our dependence on the US market, the many ties of our citizens to distant and sometimes troubled homelands, bring concomitant risks, from terrorism to infectious disease. These risks are not lost on the US, and American pressure to reduce those risks can sometimes affect our soft power assets, our appeal as an open post-modern society. In other words our particular strengths as a nation are potentially our weaknesses.

International Policy and Canadian Values

Canadians, partly because of their geographic isolation, have traditionally been comfortable with a substantially values-driven foreign policy. This is also due to the immigrant origins of our society, where human rights or humanitarian issues naturally find resonance.

However globalization means that our economy, security, even our health, is increasingly dependent on others. We live in an interdependent world. This growth in interdependence leads us to be much more conscious of where our national interests are engaged, if we are to protect our citizens and our society. Indeed, our future as a country depends on a more sophisticated understanding of when our interests are at stake and how to promote them. This does not mean that we will cease to take action on the basis of our values, but a clear-headed assessment is required to tell the difference and propose strategies accordingly.

Opinion polls consistently show that Canadians expect our international policy to reflect "Canadian values." The issue of values dominated the government's 2003 Dialogue with Canadians process, affecting the way every discussion was framed. Yet much of this discussion was vague, even misplaced. There was justified pride in our version of liberal democracy, precisely because it not only tolerated, but actively affirmed, diverse values within our multicultural society. Canadians are attached to that diversity of values. Hence we would have a hard time in any international outlook to say what specifically Canadian values are. The same holds true for identity. Though we increasingly talk about a Canadian identity, there is no monolithic identity that would lend itself to the straight-line deduction of values and interests. What Canadians wish to share with the world, and this has become clear, are the particular balances that have been struck in our form of liberal democracy, balances which are reflected in the Canadian way of life.

This is why the debate over American values and European values, or Islamic values and Western values, should make us uncomfortable. Debates about collective morality tend to be reductive, and lend themselves to nationalism, often clothed in patriotic fervour. The promotion of values through foreign policy can find itself providing support to a "clash of civilizations" view of the world, a view which is inimical to the very essence of our polity. Rather, our international policies should reflect a clear sense of the political principles which animate our society, and offer useful lessons for newer democracies. This is where our support for governance in other countries should begin, not with an amorphous concoction of Canadian values.

Similarly, we can be much more clear about our vital interests. Though the nature of those vital interests can be debated, these are interests that are essential to the continuation of Canada as a country. They are indispensable to the exercise of sovereignty and the survival of our institutions. Vital interests are not created by political agendas or by public opinion. By this definition, Canada's international role should serve our vital interests as its starting point. There may be others, but clearly an open and secure border with the US is a vital interest, as is the prevention of an attack on Canada or the US by terrorists or by another state. There may be other vital interests, such as the protection of our ecosystem, but the point is that we need an open discussion of our interests as well as of the principles which should animate our international engagement.

STRATEGIC CONSIDERATIONS

Canada's Long-Term Interests

The question as to whether Canada should pursue a global or a regional international policy, much loved by the pundits, has not really taken off at the political level. This is no doubt due to the fact that this is essentially a false dilemma. Canada has no other option but to run both a continental and a global foreign policy. Our global role is, among other things, an investment in Canada-US relations. It strengthens our hand, and our credibility, in dealing with the US. It explains US disappointment over our position on Iraq, since that credibility (more than our hard power military assets) mattered most to the American Administration, especially to the purveyors of US hard power. This is not a substitute for the right mix of hard power assets, but Canada's global foreign policy reach counts for something in Washington and not only in Washington. A regional foreign policy can never be a real option for us.

In light of the above, our over-arching strategic interests as a nation include: a mature, self-confident relationship with the US, where the exercise of "smart sovereignty" underpins a friendly and predictable partnership in North America and beyond; the deterrence or prevention of any armed attack on North America, or on our Allies, including the threat or use of Weapons of Mass Destruction (WMD) by another state or by terrorists; rules-based systems governing the resolution of international disputes, trade, financial markets, energy, migration, and sustainable development, while preventing the collapse of existing regimes; international regimes that protect Canada's ecosystem, and so prevent uncontrolled environmental change, including the spread of infectious disease; and the progressive engagement of all countries and regions in the international system, including failing and failed states, through international assistance.

Given these over-arching interests, what long-term regional and multilateral challenges and interests will occupy future reviews, if they are to be both relevant and forward-looking? There are many current issues (the "headlines" of the day) which any review in the coming years should and will address. But there are also vital geo-strategic questions that will frame those debates, and which will to some extent continue to colour the solutions proposed. The following is an overview of these longer-term geo-strategic concerns that will likely preoccupy Canadian international policy for some time to come.

Our Future in the West

Current trends among developed countries are presenting new challenges to Canada and, if they continue into the future, could have a serious impact on our interests. On the one hand, the US feels less constrained by the demands of solidarity among Allies that marked the Cold War period. On the other, the European Union grows in strength and maturity, and is already a significant power in the world (outside the military domain). The risk for Canada is that we get caught in a "squeeze-play": shut out of Europe, and ambivalent about an increasingly unilateral (or preoccupied) US. In this scenario, there is no "trans-Atlantic space" which Canada can occupy, and little opportunity for us to balance our interests among traditional Western partners.

Though the EU was divided over Iraq, and certainly European publics were, over the longer-term economic integration will gradually constrain the independent-minded foreign policies of the new members. Moreover, the enlargement of NATO will actually enhance European integration. In Asia, Japan and South Korean have revealed a continuing determination to demonstrate relevance to the US on defence and security matters, as has Australia. To some extent, this is in response to changes in the Asia-Pacific area, including the rise of China and the nuclear crisis on the Korean peninsula. The patterns in these two regions are different: a regionally powerful and heavily institutionalized Europe with nascent global ambitions, and US hub-and-spoke relationships across the Pacific that are becoming even stronger in an uncertain world.

Canadian Interests From this analysis, certain interests flow: avoid the strategic dilemma of having to choose between the US and other members of the West, whether across the Atlantic or Pacific; in the post-Cold War world, seek out common causes around which a new "Western consensus" can be built; promote the use of the G-8 for international crisis management when traditional forums fail; maintain NATO as a credible trans-Atlantic forum; and develop a strategic agenda to engage the US on Asia-Pacific issues.

Emerging Powers

Emerging powers like China, India, and Brazil can either stabilize or de-stabilize their neighbourhoods. Some regions, like sub-Saharan Africa or the Middle East, remain stalled by cycles of instability, requiring resource-intensive intervention (whether civilian or military) from outside. China and India have both managed to reduce poverty and develop sizeable new middle classes, while the Russian economy is showing signs of real growth following economic reforms. The views of the government in Brazil will be crucial to determining whether a free trade agreement of the Americas is possible. The US has shown itself extremely adept since September 11 in engaging China, India, and Russia in particular, on a new agenda that includes unprecedented security sector cooperation. Indeed, US relations with these countries compare favourably with the occasionally strained relations between the US and some traditional Allies in Europe. At the same time, the cooperation of emerging powers is crucial in preventing the spread of WMD, and in dealing with such regional crises as North Korea and Iran.

China, now the world's sixth largest economy, is becoming a manufacturing superpower, and is beginning to make strategic global investments (like Japan 40 years ago). The burgeoning Chinese middle class will soon represent an important new market for Western goods and services. Mexico is both an increasing factor in our North American economic space and becoming a model for reform in the rest of the hemisphere. Emerging powers like Brazil share some of the developed world's views and therefore can act as allies in dealing with North/South issues. Finally, emerging powers are important sources of expertise and possess educated workers, providing a pool of skilled immigrants for Canada. But they are also central to the spread (or control) of infectious disease, including SARS and AIDS, where public health practices are sometimes weak and uncertain civil liberties can lead to a lack of transparency about serious outbreaks.

Canadian Interests Canada's interests are to anticipate political, economic, security, and social changes in emerging powers, and position Canada to contribute and compete in trade, investment and migration; to support the positive, stabilizing role of emerging powers in regional disputes, and strengthen regional security arrangements; to promote full participation and responsible engagement of emerging powers in global institutions and agreements, including trade, security, environment, health, etc.; to use trade and investment to promote international economic integration, to project Canadian governance, and to diversify and mature relationships with emerging powers; to support the voices for reform and human rights within emerging powers and foster a rules-based approach to decision-making domestically and internationally; and to develop strategic partnerships with emerging powers that are geared to specific shared interests

A New Agenda for Development

Over the past ten years, development policy has been marked by a convergence of views across donor countries and the developing world. The key elements of this convergence are a series of targets for development cooperation, the Millennium Development Goals, and a related set of principles of development effectiveness. Partnership between developed and developing countries, based on mutual accountability and responsibility, is central to this convergence of views.

This spirit of partnership is reflected in the 2002 Monterrey Consensus, where developing countries agreed that they bear the primary responsibility to create conditions that will permit the mobilization of domestic and foreign resources (private and public). For developing countries, this means they must put in place improved governance, the rule of law and respect for human rights, market-oriented economic policies, macro-economic stability, and an end to corruption. Developed countries agreed to provide increased and more predictable financing for development and to improve the effectiveness of this aid, through support for country-led development, better coordination and harmonization, and untying of aid programs. Enhanced policy coherence, particularly on trade, is another key responsibility for developed countries.

The Monterrey Consensus lies at the heart of the New Partnership for Africa's Development (NEPAD), the G-8 Action Plan for Africa, and the Doha development round of the World Trade Organization (WTO). It is increasingly reflected in the programs and practices of donor countries, such as Canada, the United Kingdom, the Netherlands and the Nordic countries, and donor institutions such as the World Bank, the regional development banks, and the development agencies of the United Nations.

However, conflict and insecurity undermines development, an issue not addressed by the Monterrey Consensus. The range of expertise needed to confront complex humanitarian emergencies goes beyond the purview of aid agencies and must involve other arms of government, such as defence ministries and those charged with responsibility for maintaining peace and order in democratic societies. Most of the Department of National Defence's peace support operations take place in developing countries. Addressing security issues in the developing world necessitates a whole-of-government approach on the part of donor countries. This means we need to re-think what does, and what does not, count as Official Development Assistance (ODA). The Development Assistance Committee of the OECD, through its Conflict, Peace and Development Cooperation Network, is now taking stock of donor activities in the area of peace and security, and will review the current ODA definition.

Canadian Interests Canada's development interests are to integrate support for social and economic progress consistent with Canadian values; to build developing country support for rules-based systems that respond to their desire for increased access to industrialized markets; to develop integrated strategies to address conditions in failed and failing states, as a way of supporting stabilization efforts, preventing conflict and the spread of international terrorism, promoting democracy and human rights, and prosperity; to address living conditions and governance issues that are linked to the spread of communicable diseases; to contribute to industrial development policies in developing countries with a view to their impact on global environmental issues; and to develop a "whole-of-government" business planning approach to developing countries, integrating poverty reduction with trade, debt, immigration, environmental, and security capacity concerns, as well as the provision of technical assistance in such areas as governance (in order to improve coordination and to share best practices).

Renewing Multilateral Cooperation

Thousands of multilateral conventions and treaties have been signed over the last fifty years. The result of this effort is a growing body of norms and an evolving policy framework that has proved invaluable in regulating inter-state relations, on everything from trade and the environment to human rights and the resolution of conflicts. Canadian domestic departments are active in a variety of forums to deliver global public goods, including issues which have real domestic resonance, such as the international capacity to fight communicable diseases or global financial stability. For Canada, the outstanding challenges include the need to build greater coherence between these many initiatives, including between such often competing agendas as trade, development, and security.

While many of the technical agencies continue to provide invaluable service in regulating a whole host of international issues, multilateral organizations everywhere, including regionally, reflect the stresses and strains of the new world order. This is due to three factors: the sometimes lukewarm engagement of the US; the growing assertiveness of emerging powers; and the difficulty of adapting to a changing world. "Variable geometry" is therefore a growing feature of multilateral cooperation, and, when multilateral organizations fail to deliver results, member states seek ad hoc coalitions outside them in order to build consensus to advance policy (e.g., landmines). While such coalitions can sometimes catalyse action, institutionalization is almost always required to ensure coordinated action and follow-through, and the establishment of new norms. The main impediments to change in multilateral cooperation continue to be the need to obtain consensus, bloc voting, and antiquated veto practises. These can effectively blunt collective political will, the establishment of priorities, or budget reallocation.

But Canadian interest in multilateral cooperation remains strong, as the best way to regulate international disputes between nations, and to concert action on global issues.

Canadian Interests It is therefore in our interest to promote a rules-based international framework that is applicable to all; continue to champion effective multilateral vehicles for the resolution of differences and disputes; to decide which multilateral organizations or forums should be a priority, taking into account our domestic interests and the comparative advantages of the organization in question; and to build issue-based alliances with broad stakeholders first, as the foundation for consensus-building within international organizations.

A NEW INTERNATIONAL POLICY FOR CANADA

Two themes stand out against the back-drop of a changing Canada and a changing world: Canada-US relations not only intersect with most domestic issues, they are an integral consideration to almost every international issue that concerns Canada; and an effective international role in today's world depends on the coherence of both policy and process at home.

When and where we are engaged around the world increasingly affects our relationship with Washington. Much of our global engagement already accords with US interests, because similar impulses animate a good deal of our international policies. This is not a question of bending to US will, but a recognition that we do share much in the way of fundamental interests: the spread of democracy and human rights, the struggle to stop the proliferation of WMD, our shared anti-terrorism campaign, economic prosperity at home and in other regions of the world, the control of infectious diseases, and a healthy environment both in North America and for the globe. The list could go on.

In other words, Canada and the US are "aligned" on many of the pressing issues of the day. Where our interests meet, we need to develop shared agendas, even a division of labour. Again, this is not so much a question of fitting into a US game-plan, as influencing US engagement by being pro-active, by putting something on the table, and by leading through focused policy initiatives. We need to tackle head-on US concerns about multilateral organizations by adopting a "tough-love" approach to selected forums, as a way of re-engaging the US and delivering on Canadian priorities. Where existing multilateral forums fail to meet the needs of a changing world, or where none exist to do so, Canada should not be shy about proposing new forums and new agreements to deal with emerging issues. We will need to prepare the ground in Washington. In every Administration, there are those who recognize that the US cannot do everything nor should, that sometimes it is better for the US that a country like Canada should take the lead, especially when it is a question of over-coming old attitudes and old habits across the international spectrum.

Recognition of Canada's role, really a unique role in today's world, is tacit recognition in Washington of our "soft power" as a nation. Though not a substitute for hard power (military and economic might), soft power is our ability to attract others to our cause, to lead through policy insight and international credibility, to occupy minds rather than territory. Canada has often succeeded attaining its international goals because of our extraordinary reserves of soft power, because of our appeal as a fair-minded multicultural country that is committed to rule of law and cooperative solutions.

But our soft power appeal also depends on the perception internationally that we are prepared to follow our own lead on international issues, sometimes at odds with US positions. This is nothing new in Canada's international policy tradition. While we may agree with the US on many over-arching objectives, we can disagree on the best means to achieve them. Our approaches are different on some things, and occasionally we differ on the objective as well. Some in the US understand that this is actually a good thing, since it adds to our international credibility and preserves our unique role on other issues of concern to the US. Still, those differences need to be carefully managed and telegraphed far in advance, so that both countries can put those differences in the proper context without their affecting other areas of cooperation.

How can we lead, both in terms of our bilateral relationship with the US, and in terms of our shared international interests? With such a powerful neighbour to the south, it is easy to slip into reactive mode, into almost daily crisis management. But we do, at least potentially, have a singular advantage. Washington's inter-agency process can be cumbersome. Our parliamentary system of government, and coherence across the bureaucracy in terms of policy, process, and ultimately machinery, provides us with a comparative advantage. We should and can be more focused, more agile, and more effective in terms of bringing new ideas and initiatives to the table when dealing with Washington and in terms of heading off potential impacts that would have negative consequences for our interests.

Making Choices The effective management of the Canada-US relationship is a *sine qua non,* a vital interest for Canada. The nature of our commitment is not so much a question of choice, but one of means. We share a geographic, economic, and security space, and this has implications for the respective political, social, and cultural characteristics of our two countries. A fluid and secure border is an imperative, but our interests are broader, as this paper has argued. The choice for Canadians, and for any government, is what we wish to pursue in the world that goes beyond an interest-based international policy, narrowly defined.

A purely interest-based policy would put Canada-US considerations in the forefront of any decision-making process on any international issue. It would re-orient our defence and security policy to a wholly US focus, and put a premium on interoperability with US forces alone. It would recognize that trade "diversification" is ultimately a chimera, and concentrate trade and diplomatic resources regionally in order to ensure "made in North America" outcomes. A purely interest-based policy would take us beyond an exclusive focus on the US, to include multilateral trade liberalization, access to foreign investment, partnerships for science and innovation, and an immigration policy wholly concerned with our labour force needs. It would include defence and security policies that had as their principal motivation the prevention of a WMD or terrorist attack on North America. And it would orient our entire development assistance effort to the furtherance of our trade and security agendas. Almost as important, an interest-based policy would lead to a reduced profile or withdrawal from a number of organizations and groups.

The choice we must make is what we do beyond that agenda. Canadians have traditionally sought a "full-service" international role. They are only now coming to terms with what that costs in today's world. If anything, that cost may increase, if multilateral organizations cease to provide effective solutions to the problems Canada wishes to see addressed. Coalitions of the willing, whether on economic or security issues, are almost always more expensive solutions, as Iraq demonstrates. The G-8, which is in role closer to a coalition of the willing than a multilateral organization, carries with it a significant price tag. Can we still afford to be a "G-8 insider"? In a more fluid international environment, where interdependence is greater than ever, crisis management will incur serious national costs if we wish to be a player. On other occasions, those costs will be imposed by interdependence whether we wish to assume them or not, as SARS has demonstrated.

If we choose a full-service international role, we will need to review our existing engagement and reduce it in some areas in order to free resources to deal with new issues and crises. This will have to be more than a reallocation exercise, since it would necessitate some fundamental policy decisions about where we want to be and where we can no longer afford to be. It would also have to embrace virtually every department in government that devotes resources to the international. Those resources should be seen as fungible and as potentially liable to re-profiling under a new international policy framework. That policy framework, which should not be a one-off but an evolutionary policy tool, will require not only horizontal coordination but a collective policy capacity across government. If governance is our comparative advantage internationally, then there has to be much more capacity at home to pool resources and to bring the right expertise to bear on emerging issues.

New Canada in the World Canadians know the world is changing. They see it at home. They are engaged in that world more than ever. In some ways, through their individual experiences with trade or travel or their connections to their homelands, they understand how that world is changing better than do their governments. Any government will have to take account of this growing citizen engagement, both complex and wide-reaching, in shaping a new international policy for Canada.

For this reason, a narrowly-defined interest-based international policy is almost certainly not politically salient. The definition of a full-service international role is already changing. However some of the expectations of our new Canada are already clear: to exercise "smart sovereignty" when dealing with the US, being clear what you want and do not sell cheaply, and about what is not on the table, as well as understanding that in order to have political currency in Washington you need to invest first; to better reflect domestic priorities such as health and education in our international role, and lead international efforts where new issues affecting Canada's well-being require it; to go beyond trade negotiations to use international policies to enhance productivity and growth at home, leveraging partnerships on S&T, investment, knowledge, learning and education; to define our "fair share" of the burden when it comes to international crisis management, including in failing and failed states, demonstrating how a reinvigorated human security agenda (peace, order and good government) can contribute to our post September 11 world, and when needed participate in properly-focused peace support operations in order to provide political/military solutions; to invest in international development and governance as in our interest because it produces stability and markets. But pick our spots, in accordance with over-arching international policy priorities. Be there when humanitarian crises hit. Be clear about what Canada stands for in the world, and speak with one voice. Know what we are prepared to commit in resource terms. Engage more Canadians in refining our policies and in getting the message out.

Each of these imperatives for Canada's international role needs a developed strategy of its own, together with a proper assessment of how policy, process and perhaps machinery changes can be dove-tailed to achieve results, together with the fiscal consequences. All of these expectations can be met with a variety of options, as this paper has attested. The next step is to match those expectations with our level of ambition, as defined by the options on the table, by what is practical and what is feasible in resource terms. We need a proper understanding of which options will best position Canada to take advantage of the opportunities that await us, and why. Finally, we need a sure grasp of which options are integral to our particular way of life, to our distinctiveness as a society, in the northern half of North America.

The views expressed in this chapter are strictly those of the author and do not represent the views of the Department of Foreign Affairs.

5 Matching Ends and Means in Canadian Defence

PHILIPPE LAGASSÉ

Over the past three years, Canadians have been inundated by a series of books and reports lamenting the failure of Canadian defence policy and the coming demise of the Canadian Forces (CF). In his widely publicized study, *Canada Without Armed Forces?* Douglas Bland confidently predicts that the Canadian military is facing extinction.[1] Similarly, in *Who Killed the Canadian Military?* J.L. Granatstein presents the prevailing view that low Canadian defence spending results from a chronic misunderstanding of strategic realities by the Canadian public and their governments.[2] These assessments have been informed and bolstered by the proceedings of the Senate Committee on National Security and Defence, the House of Commons Standing Committee on National Defence and Veterans Affairs, and internal assessments conducted by the Department of National Defence (DND).

Because of their sheer volume, and the credentials of their authors, these jeremiads have dominated Canadian defence policy discourse since the events of September 11 2001. It is now 'common knowledge' that Canada spends too little on defence, that the CF is in tatters, and that Canada's contributions to international peace and security since 2001 have been paltry and haphazard.

These studies of the CF and Canadian defence policy are welcome. In the past, there has been too little public and parliamentary discussion of defence issues in Canada. There are legitimate concerns about the CF force structure. Several CF platforms, support systems, training facilities and bases are in disrepair. Paul Cellucci, the American ambassador to Canada, has repeatedly expressed Washington's dissatisfaction with

Canadian defence spending. And, most damning to Canadians' image of themselves as the world's peacekeepers, CF deployments to United Nations (UN) peace support operations are among the lowest of all contributing states. In light of these facts, it is not surprising that predictions of Canada's military demise are readily accepted.

However, warnings that Canada will soon be bereft of a military must be reassessed. This bleak picture of the CF is both overstated and unrealistic. Notwithstanding some shortfalls in CF capabilities and defence policy lapses, Canada is not, nor will it be, a disarmed nation. Despite past reductions in defence spending and unavoidable limits on current increases, the CF will be able to fulfill domestic, continental and international security roles consistent with the Canadian national interest.

Against widespread views of Canada's dismal national defence, this chapter provides an alternative account of the state of the CF and Canadian defence policy since September 2001. The argument here is threefold. First, the chapter shows that Canada's post September 11 defence policy has been fairly successful. Given the nature of the threat and Canada's middle power status, the Liberal government's initial military response to the terrorist attacks against the United States was realistic, though more needs to be done to strengthen the CF's domestic security capabilities. Next, the Canadian defence spending debate is scrutinized. Here it is held that Canadian defence expenditures are adequate and reflective of the country's place in the international system, and that the principal source of the CF's troubles is the distribution, not the size, of the defence budget. Ways to better balance the defence budget are also explored. Finally, it is argued that Canadian defence planners must follow a strict set of priorities when acquiring new platforms for the Canadian military.

CAPABILITIES AND OPERATIONS

At the time of writing, Canada's declaratory defence policy is outlined in the 1994 White Paper.[3] The White Paper ranks Canada's defence policy objectives as: 1) protecting Canada; 2) cooperating with the United States in the defence of North America; and 3) contributing to international security. Reflecting the continuing relevance of these goals, the Martin government's 2004 National Security Policy (NSP) maintains a similar hierarchy for all agencies and departments involved in national security and emergency preparedness.[4]

According to critics, however, the Canadian government has failed to provide the CF with enough resources to fulfill these objectives. In its 2002 study, *A Nation at Risk*, the Conference of Defence Associations noted that although Canada is "the second largest country in the world in area, with the largest coastline," it "is essentially incapable of defending itself against all but minimal incursions."[5] This judgment was reinforced when the Senate Committee on National Security and Defence released its October 2003 report, *Canada's Coastlines: The Longest Under-Defended Border in the World*.[6] As the title suggests, the committee found that the Canadian navy is poorly equipped to defend the nation's waters. Evidence is seen in recent foreign activities in the arctic. In 2003, a United States Coast Guard (USCG) icebreaker sailed the northwest passage, reaffirming Washington's stance that the passage is an international waterway. Similarly, in early 2004 Danish sailors planted a flag on Hans Island as part of a campaign to have the island recognized as sovereign Danish territory. In both instances, the CF proved incapable of deterring the incursion.

Critics are equally concerned about the CF's role in North American defence. According to Dwight N. Mason, former chairman of the American section of the Canada-United States Permanent Joint Board on Defence (PJBD), the continental defence partnership "is now beginning to be threatened by the decline in the resources and capabilities of the Canadian Forces."[7] If the CF cannot adequately protect Canada, then the Canadian military is also incapable of playing a meaningful role in the defence of the continent. As a result, Ottawa may be forced to cede the North American defence mandate to the United States, undermining Canadian sovereignty and Canada's reputation in Washington.

With respect to international security, critics point to the CF's limited projection and sustainment capabilities as proof of Canada's lackluster military power. To deploy forces on operations in Afghanistan, the Canadian army relied on American and rented strategic-lift aircraft because the CF lacks its own strategic airlift fleet. Were American or rental aircraft unavailable, Canada would have not been able to transport critical land force units. Furthermore, because of a high operational tempo, the Canadian army's 2002 mission in Afghanistan lasted a mere six months. Reacting to this event, Leon Benoit, then the Canadian Alliance defence critic, argued that the early return of land forces highlighted the government's mismanagement of the CF.[8]

For critics, therefore, the Liberal government's decade-long neglect of the Canadian military has crippled the CF's ability to meet the country's defence policy objectives. The CF, they maintain, is ill-equipped to defend Canada and North America, and severely limited in its contributions to overseas operations owing to a lack of basic projection and sustainment capabilities.

Worries about the CF's ability to fulfill the government's defence policy objectives deserve close scrutiny. While gaps must be filled in the CF's maritime security and consequence management capabilities, the Canadian air force is equipped to fulfill its air defence obligations. If more CF assets are redirected towards domestic tasks, moreover, Canada can fill its domestic security gaps and contribute forces to an expanded North American security concept. Globally, the record since September 11 demonstrates that the CF contributes a valued set of capabilities to the maintenance of international peace and security. Aside from the absence of a national strategic airlift fleet, the CF is equipped to fight overseas as part of multinational coalitions and to conduct peace support operations.

Canada is not directly threatened by any conventional military power. Although the oceans surrounding the country offer little protection against unconventional threats, they continue to provide Canada with a considerable barrier against conventional assaults. Hence, the CF need not be equipped to defend against a large-scale military offensive, be it at sea, on land or in the air.

Foreign activities in the arctic, however, appear to refute the idea that Canada is relieved of the obligation to mount a conventional defence of its territory. Admittedly, a greater military presence in the arctic might deter states like Denmark from sailing the northwest passage or laying claim to Canadian islands. But there is no plausible Canadian military response to the United States' conviction that the northwest passage is an international waterway. The United States is the foremost military power in the world and Canada's largest trading partner. Canada stands only to lose by confronting the United States over the northwest passage. Prudence demands that Ottawa attempt to negotiate an American right to sail the passage in exchange for US help in deterring third-party adventurism in the Canadian arctic. Put bluntly, an American security guarantee over the northwest passage would establish a far stronger deterrent than Canada could erect alone. Indeed, a "truncated but better secured" arctic sovereignty would be consistent with the evolution of the Canada-United States continental defence relationship since the Second World War.[9] Leaving aside foreign incursions in the Arctic, therefore, Canada is blessed by an absence of conventional military threats.

Terrorism is the danger confronting Canadians today. Unfortunately, while crucial, conventional military forces offer only a limited defence against this scourge. An effective domestic defence against terrorism focuses on prevention, intelligence, health services, policing and immigration, and refugee policy reform. These are primarily civilian functions. For this reason, most of the Canadian government's new national security funding is devoted to civilian departments, such as the recently established Department of Public Safety and Emergency Preparedness (DPSEP). But this is not to say that the military is uninvolved in counter-terrorism. Rather, the military's role in counter-terrorism and emergency preparedness is a supporting one.

In the event of a nuclear, biological or chemical (NBC) attack on Canadian soil, the CF is preparing units to assist civilian first-responders. A nascent consequence management team, the Joint Nuclear, Biological, Chemical Defence Company (JNBCD), will be available in 2005 to aid civilian agencies contain NBC fallout. JNBCD is based with, and will be shuttled cross-country by, the CF's C-130 tactical airlift fleet at Canadian Forces Base (CFB) Trenton, Ontario. Regrettably, two-thirds of the C-130 fleet is in disrepair, limiting JNBCD's effectiveness. If a sufficient number of functional C-130s are not kept at CFB Trenton, JNBCD will be limited to local operations. Another unit, the expeditionary Disaster Assistance Response Team (DART), is being reconfigured to better address domestic emergencies. However, DART's focus is still international. Lastly, on 8 January 2004, David Price, the former parliamentary secretary to the defence minister, announced plans to train CF reserve units to act as first responders.[10] Details of how this will affect the reserves' role on overseas operations are still obscure.

Though preliminary, these measures indicate that Ottawa is working to ensure that the CF is ready to support civilian first-responders during a national emergency. More needs to be done, however. To guarantee JNBCD's mobility, older C-130s should be replaced and a portion of the fleet reserved for domestic operations. While DART is a praiseworthy component of the CF's humanitarian assistance efforts overseas, Ottawa would be well advised to be more discriminating when deploying the unit. When DART is away, Canada's domestic disaster response capabilities are weakened. Ottawa should also consider making consequence management the reserves' primary mission. This will improve the military's disaster response time, particularly in urban centers where many reserve units are located. For this reconfiguration of the reserves to be effective, Ottawa must reduce the number of reservists sent overseas.

Maritime security presents Ottawa with similar challenges. On account of the number of containers that are unloaded everyday in North America's ports, ships are considered a likely vehicle for smuggling NBC materials onto the continent. Maritime security initiatives have therefore centered on detecting suspicious containers and hostile ships before they reach North American shores. The aim is to have a comprehensive awareness of the maritime domain. The first component of maritime domain awareness is intelligence collected and assessed by civilian agencies. Surveillance and interdiction are the second and third components. Here the lines between civilian and military responsibility are blurred, and a Canadian conundrum is exposed. In the United States, coastal surveillance and interdiction is tasked to the United States Coast Guard. The USCG sails a formidable fleet of ships and aircraft, and is commencing a re-capitalization program. The Canadian Coast Guard (CCG), on the other hand, sails a fleet of dilapidated ships whose crews lack a mandate to employ force or bear arms. Accordingly, those concerned about the defence and surveillance of Canada's coasts have turned their attention towards the Canadian military.

The CF boasts three coastal defence platforms. First are the CP-140 Aurora maritime surveillance aircraft. Originally bought to track Soviet submarines, eighteen Auroras are being upgraded with new radar systems. Yet, given their limited numbers, the modernized Auroras will provide only a limited coverage of the coasts. Second are twelve Kingston-class maritime coastal defence vehicles (MCDVs). Used to train reservists, the MCDVs have a limited maritime security role. The MCDVs are slow, minimally armed and too few to properly secure the coasts. Third are the four Victoria-class submarines purchased from the United Kingdom. When, or if, they become fully operational, the Victorias will be useful for clandestine surveys of Canada's exclusive economic zone (EEZ). But because of their small number, the submarines will provide only a marginal addition to CF's maritime security capabilities.

Including the navy's warships as coastal defence platforms improves the CF's maritime surveillance and interdiction capabilities. The Canadian navy sails sixteen warships: twelve Halifax-class frigates and four Iroquois-class destroyers.[11] The frigates are fast, decently armed, versatile ships. Current policy demands that the frigates devote twelve weeks a year to coastal defence. Dedicating the frigates to more coastal surveillance missions would enhance Canadian maritime security. A comparable case could be made for the destroyers. Though nearing the end of their life expectancy, the destroyers are also fast, well-armed ships. The navy, however, does not see the frigates and destroyers as coastal defence vessels. These ships are the core of the CF's global naval projection capabilities. Given the warships' dual roles, a debate has begun about whether the navy should curtail its global focus in favor of a coastal concentration.[12]

In the NSP, Ottawa announced the creation of marine security operations centres (MOCs). These MOCs are to be headed by CF Maritime Command (MarCom), with additional staff from the Canada Border Services Agency, Transport Canada, the Royal Canadian Mounted

Police (RCMP) and the CCG. By facilitating cooperation between Canada's maritime agencies, the MOCs aim to streamline coastal surveillance and interdiction efforts. The NSP further pledges to increase on-water patrols to better "intervene, interdict and board ships that may pose a threat to Canada."[13]

Coupled with MarCom's direction of the MOCs, this language suggests that navy ships will be tasked with more patrols. While the RCMP will likely perform some boarding and interdiction operations,[14] the absence of armaments on CCG vessels precludes their interdiction of hostile ships. Since CCG vessels are unarmed, it would be imprudent to ask the CCG to intercept ships whose crews may use force to dissuade patrol vessels from coming alongside them. Only the navy has the weapons and mandate to respond in kind to the use of force. It thus follows that the naval frigates are likely to be tasked with additional patrols. To date, however, the government has not explicitly declared that the navy will be ordered to commit the frigates and destroyers to more coastal operations. Therein lies the Canadian maritime security conundrum: the vessels that provide the navy with a global projection capability may be needed to better secure Canadian waters. Unless the CF acquires more capable coastal defence ships to complement the MCDVs, or the CCG is refurbished with armed vessels and a mandate to use force, Ottawa may decide to restrict the navy's expeditionary operations to fill maritime security gaps.

While Ottawa is faced with difficult maritime security decisions, Canada is equipped to defend its airspace. Since September 11, the North American Aerospace Defence Command (NORAD) has begun tracking internal threats in North America's skies alongside the American Federal Aviation Administration and NavCanada. NORAD aircraft have flown several thousand internal air defence sorties since the fall of 2001. Canada contributes four CF-18 fighter aircraft squadrons to NORAD. As part of NORAD's expanded mandate, CF-18 pilots may be ordered to shadow or shoot down hijacked or hostile aircraft. Despite the fact that the CF-18s are over two-decades old, their utility as an air defence platform has not diminished with age. Ottawa plans to keep the CF-18s in service until 2020.

Beyond NORAD, Canada and the United States are engaged in negotiations to expand bilateral security relations. In 2002, Ottawa and Washington formed a binational planning group (BPG) to strengthen land, maritime and military intelligence cooperation. To date, the BPG has agreed to mutual disaster assistance procedures, which would allow Canadian and American consequence management teams to perform cross-border operations in the event of a natural or NBC disaster. Talks to enhance binational maritime security collaboration are also progressing. These discussions could result in an enlargement of NORAD to include maritime and consequence management forces.

Canadian activities overseas since September 11 demonstrate the CF's expeditionary strengths. In the post-Cold War era, Canada worked closely with the United States and other allies to stabilize troubled regions and prosecute wars against hostile regimes. When the United States launched its war on terrorism in September 2001, the Chrétien government reaffirmed Canada's solidarity with the United States and commitment to collective defence and security by sending the CF to fight Al Qaeda forces and the Taliban regime in Afghanistan 'shoulder-to-shoulder' with the American military.

Canada's contribution to the Afghan war was named Operation Apollo. All three elements of the CF played a part on Apollo. Between December 2001–November 2002, the CF's special operations unit, Joint Task Force 2 (JTF2), worked with other coalition special force units to kill and apprehend senior Al Qaeda and Taliban members. Beginning in January 2002, 750 soldiers from the 3rd Battalion Princess Patricia's Light Infantry (3 PPCLI), Lord Strathcona's Horse (Royal Canadians) (LSH(RC)) and one Service Battalion deployed to Afghanistan. CF C-130s and one C-150 Polaris aircraft helped transport the 3 PPCLI battle group to the theater of operations. Once in theater, the battle group integrated into a United States Army (USA) task force founded on the 187th Brigade Combat Team (187 BCT). Together 187 BCT and 3 PPCLI undertook several missions to dislodge and eliminate Al Qaeda and Taliban forces. As part of Operation Anaconda, 3 PPCLI snipers and medical personnel helped American forces capture and kill enemy fighters in mountains near Paktia province. On Operation Harpoon, a CF and USA battalion undertook a week-long offensive which resulted in the destruction of several enemy bunkers. Two months later, in May 2002, 3 PPCLI led a three-day operation to demolish cave complexes near Tora Bora. In July 2002, the 3 PPCLI battle group returned to Canada after a single rotation.

Critics portrayed Apollo's single land force rotation as proof of Ottawa's mismanagement of the CF. In fairness to the government, it should be recognized that additional Canadian army deployments were prohibited by other operational commitments made before September 11. Like the rest of the world, Ottawa was caught off-guard by the terror attacks. While it is true that the government was overeager in committing the CF to overseas operations prior to the fall of 2001, there was no way for Ottawa to foresee that the Canadian army would be fighting a war in central Asia in 2002. Given these circumstances, DND responded with commendable speed and resoluteness to Washington's rapid decision to initiate a military campaign in Afghanistan. More importantly, those who fix their gaze on Apollo's single land force rotation tend to downplay the Canadian navy's role in the war on terror.

Canada was the first coalition partner after the United States to deploy a naval task group to the Afghan war. In the fall of 2001, the frigate HMCS Halifax sailed to the Arabian Sea and integrated into the USS Carl Vinson carrier battle group. By January 2002, the Halifax was joined by three other frigates, HMCS Toronto, Charlottetown and Vancouver, the destroyer HMCS Iroquois and the replenishment ship HMCS Preserver. Over the next twelve months, ten other ships sailed to the Arabian Sea to replace those returning to Canada. Two CP-140 Auroras were also deployed to complement the Canadian naval task groups. HMCS Calgary, the last frigate deployed on Apollo, arrived back in Canada in December 2003.

CF naval responsibilities in the Arabian Sea and Persian Gulf included force protection, fleet support and interdiction operations. Force protection operations involved CF frigates and destroyers defending other coalition vessels in theater. HMCS Preserver and Protector provided fleet support by conducting over two hundred replenishment missions. On interdiction operations, CF frigates and destroyers attempted to seize weapons, as well as Taliban and Al Qaeda members escaping Afghanistan by sea. Canadian vessels hailed more than 22,000 vessels during Apollo, and CF personnel performed over half of the boarding conducted by the coalition. Interdictions undertaken by HMCS Algonquin in July 2002 resulted in the detainment of four suspected Al Qaeda members.

The naval component of Operation Apollo refutes charges that the CF's contribution to the war on terror has been mediocre. The Canadian military hunted and battled Al Qaeda and Taliban forces in Afghanistan, the Arabian Sea and Persian Gulf for two years. Regardless of the shortfalls encountered on Apollo, this is not the performance of an irrelevant military. Indeed, the maritime interdiction, special operations and land force capabilities brought by the CF to the Afghan war were applauded by Washington. In the spring of 2002, the White House praised Canada's naval contributions to the war on terror.[15]

In the spring of 2003, while the United States was preparing to invade Iraq and the naval component of Apollo was entering its final phases, Ottawa announced a twelve-month CF contribution to the NATO International Security Assistance Force (ISAF) in Afghanistan. Having fought to remove the Taliban regime, Ottawa determined that the CF should also help in reconstructing and stabilizing the country. From August 2003–August 2004, Canada contributed the largest number of forces to ISAF. During the second rotation, a Canadian general assumed command of the multinational operation. In August 2003, nearly two thousand CF personnel arrived in the Afghan capital, Kabul. At the time, Canada's contribution was the largest in ISAF. Named Operation Athena, Canada's role in ISAF served three broad functions. First, Athena assisted the Afghan Transitional Authority (ATA) in securing Kabul. This involved CF patrols with members of the new Afghan armed forces, protecting the Kabul airport, and conducting raids of Taliban and Al Qaeda enclaves in and around the capital. Next, Athena personnel aided in the construction of several civic projects, including digging new wells and building schools. Finally, in helping to secure Kabul and protect the ATA, the CF helped the United States fight the war on terror by freeing American forces to fight Taliban and Al Qaeda near the Afghanistan-Pakistan border.

While the bulk of Canada's expeditionary forces were in Afghanistan between 2002–2004, the CF was able to participate in smaller peace support operations during the same period. On 5 March 2004, Ottawa announced that 450 CF personnel and six CH-146 Griffon tactical helicopters were deploying to Haiti to take part in the UN Multinational Interim Force. Originally slated to last ninety days, the CF deployment to Haiti was extended in May 2004. In April 2004, the CF also deployed on its fifteenth rotation to Bosnia-Herzegovina as part of the NATO Stabilization Force (SFOR).

To ensure that the CF will be equipped to participate in future overseas missions, Ottawa has invested in new army and naval platforms. Though many critics lament that the CF is not equipped to fight across the entire spectrum of conflict or deploy independently on major operations, the government has nonetheless sought to provide the Canadian army and navy with platforms suited to the types of coalition operations the CF has participated in since the early 1990s.

In the mid-1990s, DND acquired two major expeditionary land force platforms: 651 Light Armoured Vehicle III (LAV III) armoured personnel carriers and 203 Coyote armoured reconnaissance vehicles. LAV IIIs weigh under twenty tons, allowing them to be quite maneuverable and C-130J transportable. For their part, the Coyotes provide CF land forces with an impressive reconnaissance and surveillance capability. Many allied armies, including the USA, view the Coyotes as coveted assets. In the fall of 2003, Ottawa announced the procurement of sixty-six direct fire support Mobile Gun System (MGS) LAVs. The MGS complements and bolsters the capabilities of the LAV IIIs and Coyotes. Like the LAV IIIs, the MGS is C-130J transportable and highly maneuverable. Collectively, the LAV IIIs, Coyotes and MGS will provide the CF with a respectable set of land platforms on multinational deployments.

On the naval side, the Martin government has decided to procure maritime helicopters to replace the Sea Kings, and three Joint Support Ships (JSSs) to succeed HMCS Preserver and Protector. New maritime helicopters will ensure that Canada's warships are better prepared to fulfill their assigned tasks. After they are christened, the JSSs will bolster CF expeditionary capabilities in two ways. First, the addition of a third support ship will strengthen the navy's sustainability. Secondly, the planned JSSs will also serve as strategic sealift vessels. If a friendly port is accessible, CF units requiring strategic lift to be deployed may be transported on the JSSs, albeit at a slower pace than airlift. The JSSs and maritime helicopters will thus fortify the CF's expeditionary naval capabilities.

Ottawa's decision to acquire the MGS, maritime helicopters and JSSs will not fill all the CF's capability gaps. Equipment shortfalls will persist in logistical and support systems, tactical airlift, and indirect fire support. But these acquisitions do show that Ottawa is incrementally re-equipping the military for future operations overseas.

Lastly, many in the defence community believe the CF should be equipped to do more than merely contribute to multinational operations. It is held that Canada, as a trading nation, must be able to protect its global economic interests.[16] On the surface, this position has merit. Nations should have the means to defend their economic prosperity. Canadian trade, however, is primarily North American. Nearly ninety per cent of Canadian trade is with the United States. Canada's chief international economic interest, therefore, is a prosperous American economy.

Unlike Canada, the United States is a truly international trader. Washington thus equips the American armed forces to protect all major global trade routes. As Barry Posen observes, the United States maintains a "command of the commons – command of the sea, space and air."[17] No state can challenge American military dominance of the high sea, the air or outer space. Consequently, no state can block sea or air routes the United States wants open. Given this American command of the commons, investments in CF capabilities to help secure trade routes in the commons are wasteful. Canada and the United States share the same fundamental global economic interests, and the American military does not need the CF to protect those interests.

American military vulnerabilities are to be found in "contested zones," areas such as littoral waters, low air altitudes and urban centers where smaller groups can repel, deter and damage conventional military forces. It is for operations in contested zones that the United States needs allied assistance. Operations Apollo and Athena demonstrate that the CF has forces suited to these complex environments.

Rather than fretting about the CF's inability to project power in the commons, it should be appreciated that the Canadian military is structured to contribute assets where they are actually needed.

In sum, claims that the CF is unable to fulfill Canada's defence policy objectives are unduly pessimistic. While more attention should be paid to consequence management and maritime security, the CF is equipped to defend Canadian airspace and make valued contributions to multinational operations abroad. In fact, were Ottawa less eager to deploy the CF on varied multinational operations, Canada's domestic and maritime security shortfalls could be improved. Canada's military resources are not measly, but they are distributed in ways that diminish their true potential. The same is true of Canadian defence expenditures.

DISSECTING THE DEFENCE BUDGET

Canada spends approximately $13 billion CND a year on defence. This amounts to roughly 1 per cent of Canadian GDP. Compared to other Western states, spending 1 per cent of GDP on defence appears insufficient. Critics, both foreign and domestic, often accuse Canada of being a military free-rider, spending as little as possible on defence while relying on allies to protect Canadian interests.[18] A comparative analysis of NATO defence spending figures reinforces this assessment. As a percentage of GDP, Canada's military expenditures ranked 17th in NATO in 2003. This places Canada behind other middle-powers such as Spain and Poland, and ahead only of Luxembourg. Accordingly, critics shame Ottawa by tying Canada's military effort to Luxembourg's, the second smallest state in Europe with a population of only half-a-million. To raise Canada's standing in NATO, deflect free-riding accusations and ameliorate CF shortfalls, critics recommend increasing military expenditures to by at least $4 billion CND.[19]

GDP percentiles, however, offer a poor assessment of relative defence spending. Above all, defence spending as a percentage of GDP does not reflect actual expenditures. Rather, it reflects the importance of defence relative to other spending priorities, such as health and education. Secondly, defence spending as a percentage of GDP provides a weak measure of relative military capabilities. Turkey spends approximately 5 per cent of GDP on defence, while the United States spends approximately 3.5 per cent. Were GDP percentiles an accurate measure of relative capabilities, it would follow that Turkey's military capabilities are greater than those of the US. Of course, this is not the case. Since the United States' overall GDP is much larger than Turkey's, GDP percentiles mask the true spending power of their relative expenditures.

A more precise measure of relative defence spending is real dollars. Real dollars reveal a country's actual defence purchasing power relative to other states, without reference to the size of its economy or other spending priorities. Canada spent $8.2 billion USD on defence in 2002, making it the eighth highest spender in NATO and the fifteenth highest in the world. Within NATO, only the United States, the United Kingdom, France, Germany, Italy, Turkey, and Spain spend more than Canada on defence. The United States is the world's sole superpower. France, Italy, Germany and the United Kingdom are great powers.[20] Among the NATO middle powers, only Turkey and Spain spend more than Canada on defence. Turkey spends $9.2 billion USD on defence. Spain spends only marginally more than Canada, with defence expenditures of $8.7 billion USD. When measured in real dollars, Canadian defence spending appears consistent with Canada's place in the alliance.

Although Canada could match Spanish and Turkish defence expenditures, Ottawa faces no geopolitical imperative to do so. Turkey borders the Middle East, arguably the world's most volatile region. Spain is coping with Basque separatists. Canada, on the other hand, exists peaceably next to the United States. From a geopolitical perspective, it is understandable that Turkey and Spain spend more on defence. For Canada, pressures to significantly increase defence spending are few and muted.

Yet the CF is experiencing shortfalls. Naturally, this has fueled the argument that the CF is underfunded. Though a large injection of monies might permit DND to alleviate some of the CF's difficulties, an alternative explanation of Canada's military troubles is found in the distribution, rather than the size, of the defence budget.

Defence budgets are divided into three categories: personnel, operations and maintenance (O&M), and capital expenditures. Personnel expenditures cover salaries and allowances. The size of the personnel budget sets the number of military personnel. O&M expenditures pay for deployments and equipment repairs. The O&M budget determines the number and type of missions the CF can undertake. Essentially, personnel and O&M expenditures fund a military's current capabilities. The capital budget, on the other hand, is a measure of the CF's future capabilities. Capital budgets determine how much will be spent on new equipment and infrastructures. Balancing the DND defence budget, therefore, involves a trade-off between short-term expenses and long-term investments.

Personnel and O&M costs have eroded capital's share of the defence budget for two decades. Since a recommended high of 30 per cent in 1983, capital expenditures have fallen to approximately 15 per cent of the defence budget in 2003. This imbalance resulted in part from Ottawa's vigorous deployment of the CF in the post-Cold War era. Following the collapse of the Soviet Union, the Canadian government committed CF units and personnel to nearly every available UN and NATO operation. While this policy preserved Canada's reputation as a defender of international security, the costs are now being felt. Though many CF platforms should be replaced, the funds needed to do so have been held hostage by a high operational tempo. Ottawa's decision to promote Canada's internationalist image have hampered DND's ability to replace important CF platforms.

To remedy this budgetary imbalance and free more funds for capital expenditures, Ottawa must reduce the CF's operational tempo. This means fewer deployments and rotations. In the current context, this translates to choosing between a continuing Canadian role in Bosnia or Afghanistan, Haiti or the Golan Heights, and NATO's Standing Naval Force Atlantic or the Arabian Sea. It is unreasonable to expect a middle power military to take on each of these missions, and homeland security functions, simultaneously. Priorities must be set, and the international community and Canadian government should no longer expect the CF to, in the words of former Prime Minister Jean Chrétien, "always [be] there, like the Boy Scouts."[21]

In the National Security Policy, the Martin government acknowledges the need to be more circumspect when sending the CF abroad. The document states: "We must be selective and strategic when considering the deployment of our armed forces. Key questions need to be examined, including: Which efforts would be of greatest relevance to our national security interests? Do we have the capacity to meaningfully contribute to a successful outcome?."[22] In order to alleviate the CF's existing shortfalls, and for the sake of the military's future viability, Ottawa is advised to adhere to the NSP's prescription. A more selective approach to CF deployments will provide new money for capital acquisitions, and allow the services to devote additional assets to domestic security.

A selective deployment policy would also attend to the CF's training and personnel problems. As Bland notes, military capabilities are not simply a reflection of equipment and organizations. Trained personnel are as essential to defence capabilities as any platform or headquarters.[23] Over the past decade, the CF's high operational tempo has limited the amount of training Canadian soldiers have undergone. Training establishments and facilities have also suffered from a lack of funds, and critical positions are understaffed. While there is no short-term solution to the CF's personnel predicament, fewer deployments would allow soldiers to train more regularly. Furthermore, a reduced operational tempo would place less strain on soldiers' families and personal well-being, and perhaps increase recruitment and retention rates.

Canadian defence spending is a favourite target of critics.[24] Unless the distribution of the defence budget is redressed, however, an increase in defence spending may prove to be an unsatisfactory remedy for the CF's woes. Were the defence budget simply enlarged, Ottawa might be tempted to augment the military's activities abroad. In turn, this could nullify the expected gains of new defence dollars. If a bigger defence budget is merely a larger version of the current distribution, the shortfalls which result from the current distribution are likely to recur. Only a redistribution of the defence budget can guarantee that the capital funds are properly stocked. Similarly, only a commitment to a lower operational tempo will allow the CF to train and rest its personnel as needed. Absent such a commitment, the government may view the enlargement of the CF as an opportunity to deploy the military on even more operations. Instead of focusing scrutiny on the size of the defence budget, then, the defence community would better serve the CF by pressuring the government to follow the NSP's call for selective and strategic deployments.

SETTING PRIORITIES WITHIN THE CURRENT DEFENCE BUDGET

Thus far it has been argued that Canadian defence spending is consistent with the country's geopolitical context, that the CF's operational tempo should be reduced to rebalance the budget in favor of capital expenditures, that the military is being equipped to contribute valuable forces to multinational operations overseas, and that Canada's most pressing capability gaps are in maritime security and consequence management. From these observations, it follows that available capital funds should be used to strengthen the CF's coastal defence and aid of the civil power capabilities. When acquiring or modernizing platforms, DND should favour equipment that is of dual domestic/expeditionary use. This criterion must apply to all three services.

The Canadian army is saddled with many older platforms nearing the end of their life-cycles. In particular, artillery and heavy and medium logistical vehicles are obsolete. DND should not acquire new artillery in the short-term. Since artillery is primarily used overseas, it does not meet the dual use criteria. For the time being, the army must continue to rely on its older indirect fire support systems. New army support vehicles, on the other hand, are indispensable. Within Canada and overseas, soldiers, equipment and supplies are transported on land by logistical vehicles. Following the tragic death of CF soldiers riding an Iltis jeep in Afghanistan, DND ordered new Mercedes-Benz G-wagen light utility vehicles. Replacements for the army's heavy and medium support vehicles should also be bought in the next ten years.

Replacing the Canada's C-130 Hercules tactical airlift fleet should be the Canadian air force's first priority. The C-130Es, first bought in 1963, have passed their forty-year life-cycle. Many of the C-130Es are incapable of flying without significant maintenance. As a result, the CF increasingly relies on the C-130Hs. These aircraft were purchased in the mid-1970s. C-130s are necessary to transport units overseas and within Canada. These twin roles make tactical airlift a dual domestic/expeditionary capability. Buying new C-130s is consistent with a greater CF focus on domestic security. In addition, the MGS can only be transported in C-130Js.[25] DND should seek to replace the C-130E fleet with C-130Js.

When NATO forces air bombed Serbian forces during the Kosovo campaign, a significant portion of the sorties were conducted by Canadian CF-18s. In spite of this success, DND should not emphasize expeditionary air power. The projection of air power is unnecessary for Canada given the United States' command of the air, and replacing the CF-18s with a new fighter/bomber would be prohibitively expensive. However desirable, mirroring the aerospace technologies of the United States air force would unreasonably limit other equipment purchases. Hence, though it would limit the CF's expeditionary options, Canada should retain the CF-18s and restrict their role to continental air defence.

Many in the defence community are enthusiastic about providing the CF with a strategic airlift capability. This is impractical for three reasons. First, strategic airlift is expensive and far beyond the means of the current capital budget. DND has managed without a strategic airlift capability of its own for some time and should be able to do so in the future. Second, the Canadian army is becoming lighter. While a lighter force does not obviate the need for strategic airlift, it may lessen the need, at least marginally. Thirdly, the navy's coming JSSs will provide the CF with a strategic sealift. These three factors argue against the creation of a Canadian strategic airlift fleet.

Canada's destroyers are to be retired in 2010–2012. The destroyers could be replaced with similar command and control air defence ships. Given gaps in Canadian maritime security, this idea should be rejected. As Joel J. Sokolsky argues, in order to better protect Canada's coastlines, the navy's next acquisition should be a coastal defence cutter similar to those being built by the USCG. Geared specifically for homeland security and defence roles, these vessels would be interoperable with the USCG, US navy and other NATO ships.[26] Cutters could perform the patrols and maritime interdiction missions mandated by the NSP, allowing the frigates to concentrate on expeditionary operations. When possible, the delayed frigate equipment life extension project (FELEX) should also be funded. As shown on Apollo and in the Canadian EEZ, the frigates are one of the CF's most adaptable and visible platforms. Their capabilities should not be allowed to fall into disrepair.

Once the MGS and JSSs are delivered, DND should prioritize four capital equipment projects: heavy and medium logical vehicles for the army, C-130Js for the air force, and coastal defence cutters and FELEX for the navy. These acquisitions will not solve all the CF's troubles. However, alongside a lower operational tempo and more training time, these platforms would help address the more disconcerting shortfalls facing the Canadian military today.

A final consideration relates to bases and other infrastructures. As in other countries, Ottawa locates military bases in rural communities to promote economic development and employment opportunities. This practice has spread infrastructure funds too thin, leaving some bases and training facilities in disrepair. Given DND's budget constraint, a review of the military's basing needs should be initiated. Both the army and the air force require bases located across the country to ensure a proper defence and aid of the civil power. In light of other spending priorities, however, duplication and redundancy should be eliminated. A minimalist approach to military basing must be adopted to optimize defence infrastructure spending.

As a middle power of modest means and ends, Canada is limited in the number of defence spending priorities it can entertain. Assuming the defence budget remains constant, some CF capabilities must be trimmed and unneeded facilities closed. Undoubtedly, many in the defence community will decry any base's closing or abandoned capability as a sign of weakness and decline. Matching ends and means, however, does not betray weakness. Instead, it is an expression of a pragmatic and realistic defence policy.

CONCLUSION

Since September 2001, Canadian military personnel have played a valued part in the war on terrorism, by contributing to the weakening of the Taliban in Afghanistan and the long-term stabilization of that country. This was accomplished while also contributing to missions in Haiti and Bosnia. More importantly, the CF has begun efforts to better protect Canada and North America against asymmetric threats. In spite of the difficulties and high operational tempo it has experienced, the CF has executed government policy with a great deal of success. In this respect, those who claim Ottawa failed to formulate a effective defence policy over the past three years are overly critical. No other NATO middle power responded with greater decisiveness to the attacks against New York and Washington.

Predictions of the CF's demise are exaggerated. A doubling of Canadian defence spending is unnecessary to protect vital national interests. Though Canada's military resources are used inefficiently in some areas, the government has and is equipping the CF to meet the objectives of the NSP. If Ottawa adheres to a selective and strategic approach to CF deployments in the future, many capabilities gaps can be filled without a significant increase in defence spending. A lower operational tempo, moreover, will allow CF personnel to train more often and provide additional funds for capital expenditures.

Finally, even with a reduced operational tempo, DND will need to favour certain platforms and capabilities over others. To address the terrorist threat, the CF must enhance its domestic security assets. New equipment acquired by DND must have a dual domestic/expeditionary use. In addition, efforts must be made to cut the CF's infrastructure costs.

While this reassessment of Canadian defence policy since September 11 2001 has argued that the state of the CF is not nearly as worrisome as many reports suggest, it nonetheless indicates that the government faces some difficult and important choices over the coming years. By exaggerating the difficulties faced by the CF, and offering implausible solutions, recent studies distort the achievements of the Canadian military. More problematically, the current discourse diverts attention away from attainable and realistic options that will allow the CF to continue to protect Canada and North America, and contribute to international security in ways consistent with the national interest.

NOTES

1 Douglas Bland, ed, *Canada Without Armed Forces?* (Kingston: McGill-Queen's University Press, 2003).
2 J.L. Granatstein, *Who Killed the Canadian Military* (Toronto: Harper Flamingo, 2004).
3 Department of National Defence, *Defence White Paper* (Ottawa: Department of National Defence, 1994).
4 Government of Canada, *Securing an Open Society: Canada's National Security Policy* (Ottawa: Government of Canada, 2004), 5. The 2004

National Security Policy's objectives are listed as: 1) protecting Canada and the safety of Canadians at home and abroad; 2) ensuring that Canada is not a base for threats to our allies; and 3) contributing to international security. It might be argued that the second objective differs from the 1994 White Paper. However, the Canada-United States continental defence relationship is implicitly maintained by the idea that the United States helps protect Canada in order to protect itself.

5 Conference of Defence Associations (CDA), *A Nation at Risk: The Decline of the Canadian Forces* (Ottawa: CDA, 2002), 2.

6 Senate Committee on National Security and Defence (SCONSAD), *Canada's Coastlines: The Longest Under-Defended Border in the World* (Ottawa: 2003).

7 Dwight N. Mason, *Canada and the Future of Continental Defense* (Washington: Center for Strategic and International Studies, 2003), 1.

8 David Pugliese, "Romanians to Replace Canadians in Kandahar," *National Post Online*, 17 May 2002.

9 Philippe Lagassé, "Northern Command and the Evolution of Canada-US Defence Relations," *Canadian Military Journal*, 4, 1 (Spring 2003), 15–22.

10 Chris Wattie, "Reservists Touted as Terrorism Fighters," *National Post Online*, 8 January 2004.

11 One of the destroyers, HMCS Huron, has been docked due to personnel shortfalls.

12 David Pugliese, "Canada First, Defence Panel Urges," *CanWest News Service*, 1 February 2004.

13 Government of Canada, 39.

14 The RCMP has five patrol boats. They are not designed to operate far from the coasts, however.

15 United States, White House, *Campaign Against Terrorism: Coalition Update* (Washington: 2002).

16 W.D. McNamara, "The International Strategic Environment and Canadian National Security Interests," in David Rudd and David S. McDonough, eds, *The New Security Environment: Is the Canadian Military up to the Challenge* (Toronto: Canadian Institute for Strategic Studies, 2004), 38.

17 Barry Posen, "Command of the Commons: The Military Foundations of U.S. Hegemony," *International Security*, 28, 1 (Summer 2003), 7.

18 Conference of Defence Associations, 42.

19 Senate Committee on National Security and Defence (SCONSAD), *For an Extra $130 Bucks ... Update on Canada's Military Financial Crisis* (Ottawa: 2002), 15.

20 The benchmark used for a great power is a population over fifty million combined with an annual GDP over $1 trillion USD. Figures were taken

from the Central Intelligence Agency, *The World Factbook* (2003); available at http://www.cia.gov/cia/publication/factbook/.

21 Norman Hillmer, "Peacekeeping: The Inevitability of Canada's Role," in Michael A. Hennessy and B.J.C. McKercher, eds, *War in the Twentieth Century: Reflections at Century's End* (Westport, Connecticut and London: Praeger, 2003), 161.

22 Government of Canada, 50.

23 Douglas Bland, "Finding National Defence Policy in 2004," *Canadian Military Journal*, 4, 4 (Winter 2004), 5.

24 *The Economist*, "On the Cheap: Canada's Defence Policy," 13 November 2003.

25 It should be noted that there are two variants of the C-130J. Regular C-130Js are the same size as the C-130E. C-130J-30s, on the other hand, are fifteen feet longer than the C-130Js. For the sake of simplicity, both are referred to as C-130Js.

26 Joel J. Sokolsky, *Realism Canadian Style: The Chrétien Legacy in National Security Policy* (Montreal: Institute for Research on Public Policy, 2004).

6 Humanitarian Challenges and Canadian Responses

NANCY GORDON

In 2003–2004 Iraq and Afghanistan dominated both the news and Canadian government actions in the humanitarian field. In March 2004 Canada responded with troops and humanitarian relief to violence and a change in leadership in Haiti, with the prime minister announcing that the country was ready to assist in Haiti's rebuilding. The international community had left prematurely the last time around, and Canada did not want to make the same mistake again. The prime minister also announced major new funding for HIV/AIDS in May 2004, a response to the growing pandemic throughout the world, but most particularly in Africa.

The growing humanitarian crisis in western Sudan had not engendered a great deal of response from Canada up to the end of May, in spite of the UN secretary-general's warnings about ethnic cleansing. The international community could not afford to remain idle. The risk of genocide remained frighteningly real, he said in April, as the world remembered the Rwandan genocide ten years previously. By mid-June, however, Canadians and others were taking more notice, and CIDA announced an increase of $6.1 million in food and humanitarian assistance, bringing Canada's contribution to $22,000,000. There was a major earthquake in Bam, Iran in December, and food shortages in southern Africa and the Horn of Africa during 2003 and 2004. Canada responded to them with relatively small amounts of assistance.

The preocupation of policy-makers and the public was Iraq and to a lesser extent Afghanistan. Wars bring humanitarian challenges, and the Iraq war confronted the humanitarian community with major dilemmas. As the United States prepared its invasion during the winter of 2003, humanitarian agencies consulted the Geneva Conventions to see how they should react, and to see how an occupying power should act. They found that the occupying power has the responsibility to provide humanitarian relief for civilian populations, but the reality of the war and its aftermath meant that the UN and humanitarian agencies would in fact bear much of the responsibility for providing relief and reconstruction.

In hindsight, it appears that the humanitarian agencies were better prepared to deal with the aftermath of the war than the invading belligerents. The humanitarian challenges, however, were exacerbated by growing problems with security. The UN compound was destroyed in late August of 2003, killing the secretary-general's representative, Sergio Vierra de Mello, and effectively ending the UN presence for many months. Other agencies took cover, and while some of their work was continued by locally engaged staff, major humanitarian relief and reconstruction work was postponed.

The Canadian government treated Iraq as a priority in terms of resources and allocated $300,000,000 in 2003. In Afghanistan, Canada pledged $250,000,000 in aid over the next two years, bringing to more than $500,000,000 the amount of humanitarian and reconstruction assistance for Afghanistan since 1990.

Canada did not take part in the US-led coalition which invaded Iraq, a decision of the Chrétien government which resonated well with the majority of Canadian public opinion. But helping out after the war was seen initially as a means of both fulfilling a humanitarian mandate, and of joining Canada's allies in a response which suited national abilities and proclivities. It is also undoubtedly true that some policy-makers and others within Canadian society thought that a major humanitarian response by Canada in Iraq would be favourably viewed by the Bush Administration. Canadian resources were allocated to the provision of clean water and proper sanitation, food, shelter and primary health care. Spending the money was sometimes difficult for those agencies charged with these tasks; lack of security inhibited reconstruction.

The deliberate targeting of humanitarian and aid workers contradicts traditional notions of humanitarianism. Those involved have thought of themselves as impartial and/or neutral, and have further thought that such impartiality protected them from attacks by belligerents. However, in recent times they have become targets for attacks by forces within states which challenge the prevailing powers. And those attacks have succeeded in limiting the roles and functions of humanitarian workers.

In early June of 2004 five employees of Médecins sans frontières (MSF) were shot and killed in Afghanistan. MSF suspended its operations, and other humanitarian agencies "went to ground." The country's former Taliban rulers claimed responsibility for the attacks. Between January and early June 2004, thirteen aid workers were killed in the country.

These and similar actions against humanitarian aid workers have caused them to become concerned about their image or perception, not in the public relations sense, but in terms of their essential mission and how they are perceived by those they are trying to help. Hugo Slim, senior lecturer at Oxford Brookes University in the United Kingdom, spoke about these problems at a Wilton Park Montreux conference in April 2004: "There is a sense that the way humanitarians are perceived in Afghanistan and Iraq as counterparts to the War on Terror is making real problems for the wider acceptance of humanitarian action in the Islamic world and beyond. Many humanitarians feel that the company they are required to keep with Coalition forces and a new wave of opportunistic, less principled NGOs and commercial contractors in Iraq and Afghanistan is dangerously skewing their image as humane, impartial and independent protectors of the victims of war." Slim went on to say that "integrated political, military and humanitarian operations and the politicization of humanitarian assistance as an instrument of foreign policy are creating 'adverse perceptions of the humanitarian community' that are giving rise to 'threats that are now regional and global in nature.'"[1]

In Afghanistan in 2003 and 2004, the United States began to deploy what they called PRTs, or provincial reconstruction teams. Created as a means of ensuring security while reconstruction was going on, the teams were made up of armed services personnel and civilian reconstruction workers. The latter were often humanitarians from national or international non-governmental agencies. What looked good to planners in offices – teams of willing workers building a school or health clinic with the participation and protection of soldiers – was not popular with the civilians involved. There is conflict, often violent conflict, in Afghanistan, and association with one of the parties involved in the conflict leaves the population with the view that the humanitarian agency has taken sides. Such agencies, and their local employees, will be in the country long after the soldiers have left. There are well-founded fears of retribution.

The British military and its Department of Foreign International Development, along with the German government, are experimenting with similar teams in Afghanistan. The Canadian government is also planning its own version of PRTs. One can appreciate the logic of the deployment, especially in areas where security is a major problem. But most humanitarians are not in favour of this approach, and instead think that a division of responsibility in terms of expertise and function is preferable. Armies should provide security; humanitarian agencies should provide relief and reconstruction. Their work should be coordinated, but not cojoined.

Early in 2004, troubles in Haiti arose when armed opposition to President Jean-Bertrand Aristide spread through the country. Canada was quick off the mark with an allocation of $1.15 million in February to the World Food Programme and the International Committee of the Red Cross (ICRC) to provide food and medical personnel. "The effects of the lack of security, weak governance and a continuing drought have been exacerbated by the recent uprising to create an even more desperate situation for the Haitian people" said minister for international cooperation, Aileen Carroll.[2] When Aristide fled the country at the end of February, Canada said it was willing to send troops to stabilize the situation.

Following the passage of a United Nations resolution creating a UN stabilization force, Canada announced the deployment of 450 military personnel at a cost of $38 million. They joined 1,100 US marines, 500 French soldiers and 100 Chilean special-forces troops. In addition, the prime minister said that Canada would not abandon Haiti as the international community had done in 1994. He said the Canadian commitment would continue beyond a stabilization force, and could include money and personnel for policing, reconstruction and development. "What really is required in Haiti is institution-building," said Mr. Martin.[3]

In May Canada agreed to extend the deployment of its troops in Haiti, after the United Nations Security Council approved a resolution that will eventually send more than 8,000 peacekeepers and police officers. The Security Council mandate called on the UN to help Haiti in stabilizing the country, building democratic institutions and engaging in development work. Canada agreed to send police trainers and other experts to help Haiti establish the democratic institutions which will be required before a planned general election. When floods devastated the south eastern part of Haiti in May and June, Canada agreed to contribute $100,000 to the International Federation of the Red Cross and Red Crescent Societies for their relief efforts. The Canadian forces in-country provided helicopter support to rescue and relief efforts.

The Canadian government has thus taken a major interest in Haiti. There are also plans to organize a donor's conference in Montreal in the autumn. The meeting, modeled to some extent after the Berlin and Tokyo conferences on Afghanistan, would establish Canadian leadership in the overall development of Haiti, including political, economic and humanitarian issues. This will be a long-term and expensive commitment, and the government must be prepared to stay the course if positive results are to be achieved. That will mean spending money, but it will also mean sensitive leadership by knowledgeable people who know the history of the country as well as their own areas of expertise.

HIV/AIDS is perhaps the greatest humanitarian challenge facing the international community; if importance is measured in number of deaths, the scourge of that disease eclipses anything else with which we deal. At the Kananaskis meeting of the G-8 in 2002, Prime Minister Jean Chrétien made Africa his centrepiece, or at least he tried to do so. That G-8 meeting was the first after the terror attacks of September 11 2001, and the US emphasized the war on terror at the expense of other issues.

The prime minister did succeed in bringing attention to the horror of what was happening, especially in Africa, where life expectancy was falling to numbers unheard of in recent years. Stephen Lewis, the Canadian special envoy to UN Secretary-General Kofi Annan, worked tirelessly to persuade governments to increase the resources that they were allocating to the fight against HIV/AIDS.

In May 2004, Canada made two major commitments. In a major foreign policy address in Montreal, Prime Minister Paul Martin announced that Canada will contribute $100,000,000 to the World Health Organization's '3 X 5 initiative,' an ambitious program which aims to get 3,000,000 people suffering from AIDS in developing countries into treatment by the end of 2005. "Canada is a leader in the global fight against HIV/AIDS. We were the first country to introduce legislation to make low-cost high-quality drugs available to countries hard hit by AIDS and other health crises....If we don't address the AIDS pandemic urgently, other international development efforts are certain to fail."[4]

Two days later, in Ottawa, the prime minister, along with Minister Aileen Carroll and accompanied by Bono of the U2 rock group, announced an additional $70,000,000 in 2005 for the Global Fund to Fight HIV/AIDS, Tuberculosis and Malaria. The Fund was created to increase resources to fight these diseases and is a partnership between governments, civil society, the private sector and affected communities. Canada is on the Board of the Global Fund and is the Chair of the UNAIDS Program Coordination Board.

Just prior to the dissolution of the Parliament, "Bill C-9: the Jean Chrétien Pledge to Africa Act," was passed. This will allow developing countries access to lower cost generic versions of pharmaceutical products under patent in Canada.

CIDA is the major player in the Canadian government's response to humanitarian challenges. Its International Humanitarian Assistance Program (IHA) "provides financial contributions to humanitarian assistance organizations to support non-food assistance and relief programs to alleviate human suffering caused by natural disasters and conflict." CIDA sends much of its humanitarian allocation to UN agencies such as UNHCR and the World Food Programme. IHA also supports projects of the Red Cross, ICRC and international NGOs, such as CARE Canada, which specialize in emergency response throughout the world.

During 2003, the International Humanitarian Assistance division at CIDA was renamed "Humanitarian Assistance, Peace and Security." The new division has three sections: 1. International Humanitarian Assistance, which is responsible for support to international humanitarian organizations, funding to specialized humanitarian assistance programmes and responses to humanitarian appeals. It also coordinates CIDA's response to international emergencies. 2. Peace and Security, which was formerly known as the Peacebuilding Unit, manages Canada's Peacebuilding Fund and coordinates peacebuilding activities within the Agency. It is also response for selected security sector programming such as the Canadian Police Arrangement, which provides police expertise as part of Canada's contribution to international peace support operations. 3. Strategic Planning and Policy, which is responsible for strategic planning and policy functions.[5]

There is a long-standing discussion amongst those involved in humanitarian assistance that more coordination of activity would be beneficial to beneficiaries and donors alike. On 16 and 17 June 2003, representatives of government and multilateral donors, UN institutions, ICRC and other organizations involved in humanitarian actions met in Stockholm to discuss growing demand and how it is being met. The meeting's overall topic was "Good Humanitarian Donorship," and it was hosted by the Swedish government. In their search for enhanced effectiveness, efficiency and accountability, representatives endorsed twenty principles and good practices. An Implementation Group was created, chaired by Canada for the upcoming year.

In a forthcoming book, entitled *Passing the Buck: Humanitarian Action in a Calculating World*, authors Ian Smillie and Larry Minear examine the factors that motivate states to contribute to humanitarian needs. They conclude that the scope and size of an emergency plays a major role, but so do domestic policy interests and diasporas, as well as foreign policy considerations. The so-called "CNN effect" has an impact, but less than is popularly imagined.

In Canada, the attention and resources allocated to Iraq and

Afghanistan have major foreign policy implications, especially in terms of our relations with the US. The large Haitian diaspora, especially in Quebec, partly accounts for Canadian interest there. Ongoing and chronic humanitarian needs in Congo, Somalia, Colombia seem to have fewer champions or policy-related influences.

Humanitarian assistance is responsive when allocated to alleviate the effects of natural disasters. The humanitarian challenges of man-made disasters such as the wars in Iraq, Afghanistan, Sudan, Haiti, and food shortages in southern Africa are predictable and in many cases, preventable. Conflict prevention is the general term under which CIDA allocates funds to create conditions which will lead to the peaceful resolution of disputes. In "Strengthening Aid Effectiveness," the most recent CIDA strategic plan, CIDA declares that it, along with other parts of the government and the rest of the international community, must invest more in conflict prevention.

According to CIDA documents, the agency's overall goal in peacebuilding "is to support the emergence of participatory and pluralistic societies, with well-functioning and responsible government administration acting under the rule of law and respect for human rights....by promoting strong civil society, representative governance systems, economic opportunity, and the participation of women in the development process." These efforts, the reasoning continues, are aimed at building a tradition of conflict avoidance as well as effective institutions of conflict resolution in societies undergoing rapid economic and social change. The reduction of poverty and disparity, which are deep-rooted causes of conflict and instability, particularly in multi-ethnic countries with exclusionary habits of governance, also requires long-term efforts directed towards policy reform and capacity building."[6] Examples of activity in this area are support to local civil society organizations, demining, training of police, human rights monitoring and awareness training, reform of the legal system. Institution building and strengthening are stated objectives of the Martin government, and more concentration in this area is to be anticipated.

Canada allocates 57 per cent of the resources it spends on humanitarian response to the UN system through its multilateral agencies, 20 per cent to the Red Cross, 0.2 per cent to government departments, and 22 per cent through Canadian institutions and organizations.[7] The total humanitarian assistance envelope in 2001–2003 was $253.33 million out of a total CIDA budget of $2.132 billion. For millions of people, the world is neither a safer nor more secure place now than it was twenty-five years ago. The percentage of the Official Development Assistance (ODA) envelope spent on humanitarian relief should rise in response to growing needs.

Canadian NGOs, businesses and institutions are good at organizing and responding to humanitarian crises. Some of them work as sub-contractors to the UN system. When Canadian personnel are involved, Canadian expertise is developed, along with increased Canadian media attention and thus public support. The Canadian public tends to support humanitarian activity, to want to help at the time of disaster or crisis or war. The government can and should act generously on behalf of a population which recognizes its comparative good fortune.

NOTES

1 Hugo Slim, "How We Look: Hostile Perceptions of Humanitarian Action," Presentation to the Conference on Humanitarian Coordination, Wilton Park, Montreux, 21 April 2004.
2 CIDA Press Release, "Canada assists the people of Haiti," 17 February 2004.
3 Tu Thanh Ha and Paul Knox, "Canada to send 450 troops to Haiti," *Globe and Mail*, 6 May 2004, A15.
4 Office of the Prime Minister, "News," 10 May 2004.
5 CIDA website, www.acdi-cida.gc.ca/cida_ind.nsf/A11DocIds.
6 CIDA, *Canadian Peacebuilding Experience*, introduction, 2.
7 The figures are from the 2000 – 2001 fiscal year, the last for which such analysis is available.

POLICIES

7 Bubbling Up, Trickling Down, Seeping Out: The Transformation of Canadian Foreign Policy

JEAN DAUDELIN

TO SLEEP OR NOT TO SLEEP

A profound dissonance pervades current discussions of Canadian foreign policy. Everyone recognizes that the country is now more "globalized" than ever before and that its fate is extremely dependent on what happens beyond its borders. At the same time, a soft consensus has emerged according to which, over the last 25 years or so, Canada's foreign policy capabilities, broadly understood, have declined to a critical degree, with the country's weight and influence in the world shrinking accordingly, along with its ability to shape its environment in a way that suits its interests and its values.[1] Given these premises, the logical implication is that Canada's situation should also be critical: how indeed could one of the most globalized countries in the world prosper while its ability and its power to deal with that world collapses?

And yet, by almost any measure, Canada has prospered to an astonishing extent over that period: proportionately, more jobs were created than in any OECD country; more immigrants were absorbed, with minimal social tensions, than anywhere in the Western world; human development has the reached highest levels of any major economy; Canadians have suffered no major war, no significant explosion of unemployment, no major epidemics, no major environmental disaster, and so on. While the country was becoming horrendously vulnerable to the outside world, it also did better than many other nations.

Some will say it was just luck or, at last, the proof that globalization is good for you, me and everyone else. Or perhaps, something was done right, and Canada had what was needed, institutionally, to do it right. It is to the exploration of this claim that the next pages are devoted. I will argue that, as far as Canada's foreign policy is concerned, no-one has been sleeping at the switch. Not Canada, as Andrew Cohen would have it.[2] Not Cohen himself, as top bureaucrat Peter Harder recently suggested.[3] Not the many chroniclers of Canadian foreign policy decline or the small number of their contrarians.[4] My thesis is straightforward: the Canadian government has successfully managed the country's growing vulnerability to its international environment, but this management has progressively moved out of the bureaucratic apparatus formally charged with foreign policy. The champions of decline were not looking in the right place; the decay they document is undeniable, but essentially irrelevant to the ability of Canada to deal with what in the world was truly relevant to its security and to its prosperity. The defenders of "The Department," have been just as erroneous, mistaking noisy and, from Canada's standpoint, largely inconsequential activism on the global scene for real action, while the management of the country's growing internationalization was taking place behind the scenes.

What we have had is a debate about the fate of a foreign policy machinery that was indeed being starved of resources and whose central role in the management of foreign affairs was being effectively challenged. The ball was not dropped, however: Canada's foreign policy did not "decline" and was not "marginalized." The ways and means of its management just changed and, at least until September 11 2001 they changed for the better. In the background, Canada's footprint in the world has been shrinking, with the country's effective "insertion" in the world becoming increasingly regional. This, however, should not be confused with a decline in the ability of the government to deal with the challenges that effectively confront Canada, most of which are, indeed, increasingly regional. A "redeployment" of foreign policy took place that was very much in step with Canada's growing "North-Americanization."

The paper maps out this change, draws the landscape of Canada's existing foreign policy in the *fin de siècle* period (1989–2001) and identifies the main characteristics of the post September 11 situation. To get there a general analytical model is proposed in the first section. Only the model's basic assumptions will be presented here, just enough to structure a discussion that remains primarily policy-oriented.[5]

VULNERABILITY, COMPLEXITY, AND THEIR MANAGEMENT

This chapter understands Canadian foreign policy as a somewhat special case of a general problem: the management by an organization of its vulnerability to its broader environment or, more precisely, to those parts of that environment that are relevant to its functioning and, ultimately, to its maintenance. From that abstract standpoint, no fundamental difference shall be assumed to exist between foreign policy per se and those activities of a church, a criminal gang, a rock band, a chess club or a shoe company that are meant to deal with changing cultural values, tastes, technologies, neighbours' mood, energy price, rents, competition or demographics in that part of its environment that is "truly relevant" from its often narrow standpoint.

For all these social enterprises,[6] the "foreign" challenges can be understood as a combination of two dimensions: the degree of their vulnerability to their external environment, the extent to which the latter matters to them, and the complexity of that relevant environment, that is, the number of interrelated factors and issues that they need to make sense of and confront.

Increasing vulnerability to environmental factors implies that their management becomes crucial to the functioning and, ultimately, to the survival of the organization. This means that the stakes increase and that "foreign" affairs become very important for, and consequently within, the organization. The management of these vulnerabilities confers a lot of power on those responsible for it and, as a result, competition for that responsibility is likely to be strong.

Increasing complexity implies that the amount of information needed to manage those vulnerabilities also increases and, with it, the cost of that management for the organization. This has two basic implications. The first is a growing pressure for differentiation, that is, for the creation and expansion of one or even many specialized bodies to deal with "external" affairs. The second is the growing power of those who master the relevant information. At first, the required expertise might be quite general and confer coverage upon the external environment as a whole. In such cases, external affairs generalists will be sought. As the environment becomes more complex, the level of expertise and the required specialization increases further, pushing toward ever more differentiation both in terms of institutions and in terms of the degree of specialization of their staff.

A critical caveat is in order here. The pressures just identified do not determine changes. They favour them. Organizations do not necessarily

Figure 1

VULNERABILITY + COMPLEXITY –	VULNERABILITY + COMPLEXITY +
VULNERABILITY – COMPLEXITY –	VULNERABILITY – COMPLEXITY +

"adapt" to their environment. Human beings make choices in light of their own short, mid- and long-term interests, values, dispositions, and capabilities, and these choices might *or not* be consistent with successful adaptation. A "foreign policy," in other words, can be either successful, or not.

MAPPING OUT "EXTERNAL" AFFAIRS

To get an intuitive sense of the model, imagine a simple matrix with a vertical axis representing vulnerability (from low to high) and an horizontal one representing complexity (from low to high), and construct general hypotheses on the characteristics of external affairs management in each cell.

In the two upper quadrants, one finds high stakes issues, problems whose management is critical for the organization. Energy costs for an aluminium company, or US-border issues for Canada, would be in that quadrant. Because of their importance, these issues will also command a strong claim over resources, and those managing them will have significant power over the organization. At the same time, however, their field of action will also be quite heavily constrained, precisely because their decisions are so consequential. For the same reason, the management of these issues will likely be highly secretive. High stakes, strong constraints, strong claims over resources and limited public input all combine, finally, to favour policy consistency over time.

In the lower quadrants, one finds issues whose bearing on the organization is marginal, like charities' support for multinational corporations, or the Rwandan genocide for Canada and much of the Western world. Here external vulnerability is low, resources will be more difficult to mobilize, managers will have little weight in the organization but at the same time quite a lot of freedom, essentially because their decisions are inconsequential. These characteristics and the relative political weakness of external affairs managers also make these quadrants more likely to be transparent to the public, the media, or other organized interests. Managerial freedom, limited resources, strong public input and low stakes, moreover, will conspire to make policy in those fields extremely inconsistent.

Looking now at the horizontal axis, we have, in the left column, relatively simple issues, either because they involve few players, or because the information one needs to deal with them is relatively easy to acquire and to master. Relations with General Motors for a supplier of a specific suspension part would fit just there: specifications for the part are readily available, the company's survival is at stake and, no doubt, the president and CEO will be directly involved. In these situations, it is unlikely that the organization will create a specialized apparatus to manage these relations, as its authorities can easily and cheaply obtain the relevant information and take the relevant decisions. Conversely, when we move to the right of the matrix, we find issues whose complexity is such, or whose management involves so complex or so large an amount of information, that the organization will likely create or use specialized organs to deal with them. In extreme cases, the organization might even have to use a whole gamut of such specialized apparatus to do so. Going back to the car industry, one would find in these quadrants the relations of General Motors with thousands of current and potential suppliers, whose detailed management is clearly outside the reach of the company's core authorities. Combining the two, we get four typical[7] situations (see figure 2):

1 In the lower-left corner (low complexity, low vulnerability), external affairs are essentially irrelevant to the organization and extremely simple to manage. Very few resources will be devoted to their management, a specialized body is unlikely to be set up or to be heavily staffed and well financed, and very little power will accrue to those responsible for "external" issues.
2 In the lower-right corner (high complexity, low vulnerability), the pressure to get a specialized body will be strong, given the amount of information that is relevant to external affairs management. Significant investments, however, will be difficult to justify and are unlikely to be forthcoming as the issues involved have little impact on the organization. If the latter already has a specialized body, however, and if the organization is relatively wealthy, external affairs might still be a very active, if, at times, an under-financed field of activity. In situations of extreme complexity but low vulnerability, external affairs management, if done at all, will be severely

Figure 2

Complexity-/Vulnerability+	Complexity+/Vulnerability+
- High stakes; - No need for specialized body; - Constrained policy environment; - Little transparency; - Lots of resources; - Powerful managers located in the Centre; - Consistency.	- High stakes; - Strong need for specialized body; - Constrained policy environment; - Little transparency; - Lots of resources; - Powerful external affairs managers; - Consistency.
Complexity-/Vulnerability- - Low stakes; - No need for specialized body; - Freedom of action; - Potentially transparent; - Few resources; - Weak managers located in the Centre; - Fickleness.	**Complexity+/Vulnerability-** - Low stakes; - Need for specialized body; - Freedom of action; - Potentially transparent; - Few resources; - Weak external affairs managers; - Fickleness.

fragmented and poorly coordinated, as the information, coordination and control costs (both political and financial) will be prohibitive relative to the importance of the issues.

3 In the upper-right corner (high complexity, high vulnerability), pressure will be strong to have a well-financed and staffed machinery with adequate technical capabilities, as the stakes for the organization are high and as the amount of information needed to manage these complex vulnerabilities is large. Those who have the required specialized expertise will be sought after and very influential within the organization, as they have a bearing on the management of some of its most critical sources of uncertainties. Given the critical character of the issues in that quadrant, however, their managers are unlikely to have much leeway while, for the very same reason, policy is likely to be very consistent over time.

4 In the upper-left corner (low complexity, high vulnerability), by contrast, is where an "external affairs" body will be essentially superfluous. Its existence and the costs that derive from it might lessen the ability of the organization to deal with the simple but critical issues

at hand. The needed resources are made available but the options are typically few, orientations are stable and managers, while powerful within the organization, have little leeway. This is a world in which the "centre" of the organization rules and where "openness" and internationalization rhyme, paradoxically perhaps, with concentration of power and with secrecy.

To complete this brief overview of the model, I add two more propositions on the politics of external affairs *in any organization*:

a The upper-right quadrant is the one where a unified "external affairs" body will have the most power and the most prestige, and where it will command the most resources. At the same time, and for those very reasons, it is also the quadrant where the management of foreign affairs issues is the most competitive, as control over an organization's most critical source of uncertainty confers the most power over it.

b To the extent that the relative vulnerability and complexity of any given set of issues is largely a matter of perception, much competition within the organization will focus on the classification of any given issue from those standpoints. The politics of external affairs is thus about defining the extent and the location of an organization's vulnerabilities and about choosing those best able to manage them. The degree of freedom in a social and political construction process is not absolute. The environment cannot be wished away and, as a result, misperceptions can be very costly. "Reality bites," *even when it is socially constructed*. While the way in which a given context is defined and perceived can vary and is very much the result of a process of social construction, there is a limit to the ability of any organization, however powerful, to make reality what it wants it to be.

BUBBLING UP, TRICKLING DOWN, SEEPING OUT

This section maps out the evolution of Canadian foreign policy over the last forty years, using the model just outlined. These pages should not be construed as a "test" of the general hypotheses just outlined. They only propose a narrative that is structured around them. Rigorous testing of the model, on which I am working, goes well beyond the scope of this paper.

The context of Canadian foreign policy is examined first, and then foreign policy per se, that is, the management of the country's perceived vulnerabilities. A third sub-section then looks at the fate of the Department of Foreign Affairs, and therefore at the consequences of

Figure 3

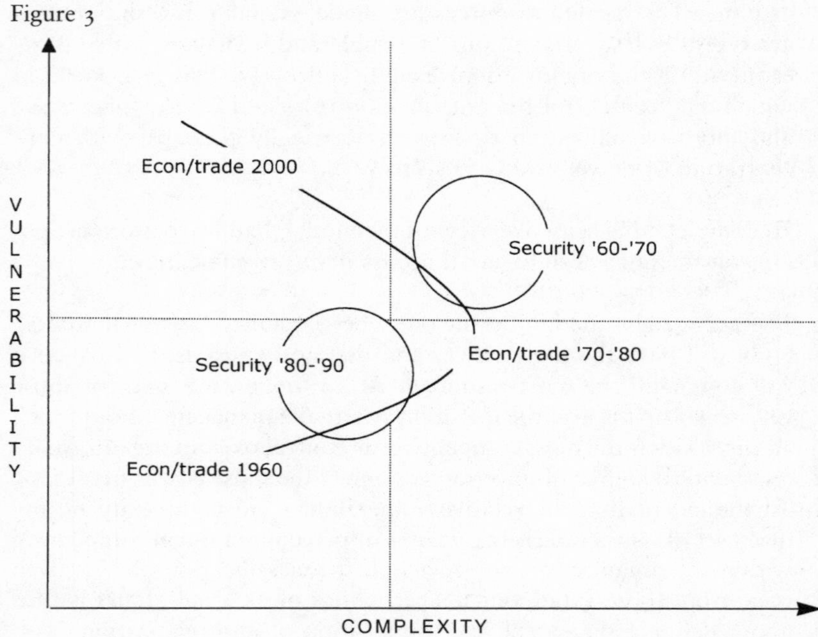

the changes in Canada's perceived vulnerabilities for the bureaucratic apparatus that is formerly charged with their management.

Changing Context

The evolution of Canada's foreign context between 1960 and September 11 2001, is roughly outlined in figure 3. Three main tendencies are emphasized with security issues being progressively displaced, economic factors gaining prominence, and the United States becoming the main focus of these economic vulnerabilities.

a) *Displacement of Security Issues* Security issues progressively faded as perceived sources of vulnerability for Canada. The Cold War lost its threatening edge and the country's disengagement from the European front met with little domestic resistance. With the fall of the Berlin Wall, the floor collapsed; defence became a strange concept and investment in military capabilities unjustifiable in the face of budgetary constraints. What is left is primarily concentrated in the North-American theatre.

Traditional security in the 1960s was located in the upper-right quadrant, where it held a degree of importance and involved the management, primarily within the North Atlantic Treaty Organization (NATO) but also at the United Nations (UN), of a sometimes complex game of alliances. Issues and players were many and their management often complicated. Significant resources were made available to the diplomats responsible for it and Canada held its own as a major mid-size military power.

By the year 2000, defence had moved to the lower-left quadrant. Perceptions of vulnerability were too low to justify significant investments. The redeployment toward North America intensified this disinvestment. Canadians placed their security eggs in the US basket and, as a result of their neighbour's willingness to foot the bill, they also perceived free riding as a legitimate option. This mood was well understood by politicians, who saw only benefits in "killing the military." Jack Granatstein is thus perfectly right to emphasize how much the Canadian public played a role in that killing,[8] a diagnosis consistent, if no doubt unwittingly, with Norman Spector's deadpan assertion that "[i]t's rational for us to 'free ride' on U.S. defence expenditures."[9]

b) *The Rise of Trade and International Economic Issues* Beginning in the 1970s, Canada's vulnerabilities were increasingly believed to lie in the field of trade and international economic relations.[10] The oil crises of the 1970s played a critical role in the perception that the biggest threats might come less from traditional weapons than from the increasing dependence of the country's economy on foreign suppliers and markets. The quickly growing importance of trade in Canada's economy completed a picture in which the country's security came be defined primarily in economic terms.

Economic issues thus became internationalized and moved, at first, from the lower-left corner to the upper-right one: vulnerability was increasing but also the complexity of the issues involved and the number of relevant partners. More resources were devoted to the file, and the trade's growing importance was reflected, partly, in the integration of the trade commissioners into the foreign affairs department.

Relatively quickly, however, and as the importance of economic issues continued to increase, the picture also grew simpler as Canada's economic vulnerability became increasingly focused on the United States, a process that was heavily encouraged by the Auto Pact and then both institutionalized and deepened by the Canada–US Free Trade Agreement (CUSFTA), and later, albeit to a much lesser extent, by the North American Free Trade Agreement (NAFTA).

Figure 3 maps this evolution by using trade dependence as a proxy for vulnerability[11] and an index of trade dispersion[12] as a measure of complexity. The curve moves from the lower-left (relatively low vulnerability and low complexity) to the upper-right (as both vulnerability and complexity increase) before veering back to the upper-left (extreme vulnerability with a degree of simplification).

c) *Increasing Focus on the United States* The growing importance of the United States can only partly be described as a reduction in complexity. The extent to which the two countries have integrated over the last forty years is difficult to overestimate and, as a result, Canada's economic vulnerability, although essentially bilateral, has become extremely complex. This has two main consequences in terms of the constraints imposed on the management of external affairs, broadly understood.

On one side, environmental pressures push towards reverse differentiation, that is towards the centralization of the management of economic issues, as the latter become critical for the country and as most of them regard the relationship with a single partner, the United States. At the same time, and to the extent that Canada's high and concentrated economic vulnerability is broadly recognized, it becomes easy to justify significant investment in the management of that relationship and to cut down on the resources and capabilities devoted to other files.

On the other hand, however, there is a pressure for *extreme* differentiation, as the amount of information needed to manage the relationship increases exponentially: not only does the number of issues that have a Canada–US dimension explode, but the technical knowledge required to deal with them and the sheer number of people involved all contribute to an enormous increase in the requirements and in the cost of their management. Although extremely important, and for reasons to be made clear below, this hyper-differentiation of Canada's vulnerabilities is not represented in Figure 3.

Changing Foreign Policy

Confronted by the displacement of security issues, by the rise of trade and finance preoccupations and by the growing importance of the US for Canada, the government evolved in a way that proved to be, at least until September 11, extremely functional, successfully adapting to the changing context. The first move, already discussed, was to disinvest from traditional security. Adaptation to changing economic vulnerability was more complex, however, and involved three distinct processes, which I think are best described as "bubbling up," "trickling down," and "seeping out."

a) *Bubbling Up* As John Kirton has shown for the first Chrétien mandate, critical issues, almost invariably related to the bilateral relationship with the United States, were increasingly managed "from the Centre,"[13] with power over them shifting, to paraphrase Donald Savoie, "away from the ministers [of Foreign Affairs and their department] towards the centre, and also, within the centre itself, (...) to the prime minister and his senior advisers at both the political and public service levels and away from Cabinet and Cabinet committees."[14]

Their management is perfectly described by the general characteristics of the upper-left quadrant as presented in Figure 2: high stakes; little need for a specialized body; a heavily constrained policy environment; little transparency in the process, even from the standpoint of Cabinet members; resources provided as needed; and quite remarkable consistency over time – as in the case of the Liberals' conversion to the idea that NAFTA was not so bad after all. Two more characteristics can be added here. With little department input, ministers themselves are pushed aside and power lies with high-level civil servants and policy advisors with direct access to the prime minister. When ministers have a say, moreover, it is less as political heads of departments than as advisors with access. Canada's "decision" process in the case of Iraq and on border issues following September 11 are cases in point. The creation, within the PCO, of a special unit devoted to Canada-US relations is probably the most explicit institutional expression of that movement. The fact that this unit is headed by a civil servant, Jonathan Fried, who also happens to be the prime minister's advisor on foreign policy, is a further demonstration of the degree of centralization of the process, of its opacity, and of the overwhelming weight of a few critically placed civil servants, to the detriment of elected officials who have to answer to Parliament.

b) *Trickling Down* The simplification of external affairs into essentially bilateral affairs has a flip side in the growing complexity of the latter. This, as noted, generates enormous pressure for institutional differentiation. Once again, the government has adapted quite well to this pressure, essentially through the emergence, in almost every single line department, of specialized shops dealing with external affairs. The management of the growing number of issues that result from the deepening interdependence with the US has thus trickled down to the sectoral departments who have the needed expertise. That expertise, in turn, is jealously guarded and is the basis of claims, often successful, of autonomy from the Department of Foreign Affairs in the management of those files, making coordination extremely difficult.[15] This is the primary area of so-called intermestic affairs, a field that should rather be called, were it not so awkward, the "US-mestic" agenda.

In terms of the matrix, the intermestic agenda is clearly on the right side, given its complexity. On the vulnerability axis some issues, such as sanitary standards or electric power management norms, rank quite high, while others, like drug certification or the regulation of web-based casinos, rank lower. What is important is that, as in the previous case, control over the file has moved away from external affairs specialists. This dynamic explains the multiple tugs of war between line departments and Foreign Affairs,[16] the increasing inability of the latter to get a grip on those files in the name of coordination, and finally its calls, increasingly strident, for support from the centre in doing so.[17]

c) *Seeping Out* The increasing complexity of many bilateral files, however, feeds another process: a large number of issues simply escape from government control as the information required to manage them is too complex and fragmented to be gathered and processed economically. In many instances, in fact, this escape process is institutionalized and organized by the government itself and is part and parcel of the management of external vulnerabilities. Free trade agreements are a case in point, but regulatory convergence has similar effects and formerly "external" affairs become intra-firm transactions or whole industrial sectors' standards and protocols. In such cases, it is the border itself that disappears.

The rationale for deeper integration with the United States lies precisely there:[18] it makes little sense, politically or economically, to even try to control and regulate many formerly "international" transactions. Much has been done in this area through CUSFTA and NAFTA, as well as in the area of border control and migration. The 2003 blackout and the more recent mad cow and SARS crises suggest that, in quite a few areas, significant incentives exist to get rid of the boundary.

As for security, big bilateral files and NAFTA, the adaptation process appears to have been quite functional. While the ultimate economic benefits of NAFTA can be disputed, it is clear that the regime has made a massive increase in interdependence possible at low cost and without generating major tensions either between Canada and the US or within Canada.

In sum, through such bubbling up, tricking down and seeping out processes, the management of Canada's changing external vulnerabilities appears to have been competent and effective. This conclusion is consistent with the enviable situation in which the country's increasingly vulnerable economy finds itself.

Meanwhile, Back at Fort Pearson...

These three processes share one important implication. The management of Canada's external vulnerability has progressively escaped from the reach of the institution that is formally charged with that responsibility. The bureaucratic salience of "The Department," as insiders call it, has declined. Its power, its prestige and, as a result, its ability to recruit and keep first-rate employees and to enforce a degree of coordination among the various government sectors involved in "external affairs" have also declined. In the context of budgetary restrictions that have prevailed for more than a decade now, the political marginalization of Foreign Affairs has been matched by a declining ability to access financial resources.

This decline and relative marginalization is the topic around which much recent public and scholarly discussion revolves. As the previous section suggested, however, this should not be confused with a decline in the ability of the Canadian government to manage external affairs adequately. Moreover, the decline of Foreign Affairs should not be exaggerated. In many ways, as we will now see, the department has also adapted to the new context and priorities, with the management of trade issues and of US relations becoming increasingly important and autonomous within the organization, and with the maintenance of significant capabilities and activities in newly marginal areas.

a) *Internal Differentiation* The 1982 amalgamation of the Trade Commissioner Service, into what later became the "Department of Foreign Affairs and International Trade," did not result in a full integration of trade and foreign policy. The trade "side" of the department thrived on the growing prominence of multilateral and bilateral negotiations and regimes, leaving the rest of the department behind and often in the dark. Canada's very active involvement in the Uruguay Round[19] and especially in the North American trade negotiations[20] was managed and driven by a small group of extremely committed civil servants who were in many ways sheltered from the rest of the department. The divorce between the two sides, fed on the initial reluctance of the department's diplomatic establishment to exchange what used to be called "high politics," the war and peace issues, for the economic nuts and bolts of "low politics."[21]

This informal divorce was most clearly played out at the beginning of Jean Chrétien's regime, in the confrontation of two prominent members of the Liberal team, Roy MacLaren and Lloyd Axworthy, and especially in the drastically different directions in which they took, respectively, the trade and foreign affairs components of the supposedly joint ministry. It began around NAFTA, on which free-trade fan MacLaren won the day over Axworthy. The government left Axworthy in the cold, at the Department of Human Resources, while MacLaren, who was given the international trade portfolio, pushed an agenda that was very much at odds with the way in which Canada's diplomacy had traditionally seen itself: "Foreign policy is trade policy," as he famously declared in a speech delivered at the conclusion of the national consultation that preceded the preparation of the 1995 "Canada in the World" policy statement. MacLaren, moreover, had lots of space as André Ouellet, at Foreign Affairs, spent much more time on Quebec and its then-forthcoming referendum, than on any "external" file. By the time Axworthy finally got to Fort Pearson, in January 1996, his fondness for "human security" and his disregard for trade files only deepened the internal rift.

A similar, if less openly political, differentiation developed in the management of the US file. Here, the "Centre" was calling the shots and the Embassy in Washington increasingly became an extension of the Privy Council Office (PCO) and the Prime Minister's Office (PMO), rather than a "normal" outpost of Foreign Affairs. Nowhere was this more obvious than in the individuals chosen as ambassador to the US over the last fifteen years: perhaps with the exception of John DeChastelain, who only stayed for a year, and their individual qualities notwithstanding, all had remarkably direct access to the Centre, from Allan Gotlieb, Derek Burney and Raymond Chrétien, who had a close personal relationship with the prime minister himself, to Michael Kirgin, who served for two years in the PMO as special advisor on foreign policy.

Given the rising importance of both trade issues and relations with the US, these twin processes of differentiation, once again, make perfect sense and one could say that they reflect the Department of Foreign Affairs' ability to adapt to the new context. There are limits to internal differentiations, however, and they appear to have been reached in the very files that were just examined, as a special unit was created within PCO charged explicitly with coordinating Canada-US relations, and with the announcement, in the spring of 2004, of a formal separation of the trade "side" from the rest of the ministry of foreign affairs.

b) *Significant Capabilities Maintained* The second caveat to the marginalization thesis is that whatever "decline" one can document must be put in perspective. Canada's foreign service, while slightly smaller than its 1990 peak of 4419 employees, has remained essentially stable, at about 3900, since 1994. Canada has embassies in all significant countries of the planet, missions in almost every international organization in existence, and it sends delegations to almost every international conference. Its diplomatic corps continues to be staffed by competent and sometimes exceptional individuals. The salary gap that had developed over the years between foreign service officers and other public service categories, was largely filled in recent years.

Diplomats, moreover, have never stayed idle. In fact, especially under the guidance of an energetic Lloyd Axworthy, the department has in recent years been exceedingly pro-active. That activism, which the next section briefly reviews, has been heavily determined by the tendencies that we examined: most of the department's initiatives appear to be confined to the lower-right corner of the matrix, and its workings conform quite well with the "ideal" characteristics of the management of marginal but relatively complex issues. For the most part, and keeping in mind the two caveats that we just examined, the department now deals primarily with low stakes issues, and the diplomats involved have significant leeway but at the same time relatively few resources and a limited ability to muster support in the broader bureaucracy. Perhaps most significantly, the process, precisely because of its low stakes, can be quite transparent with consultations and, more broadly, with a very real if essentially irrelevant democratization of foreign policy.[22] Finally, as shown by the quick, if partial, burying of human security by John Manley (briefly foreign affairs minister before and after September 11), foreign policy in that field can be remade and redefined by fiat without major consequences.

Canadian Foreign Policy between the Centuries (1989–2001)

A simple way to visualize the changes that took place is to map out the key issues, themes, and actors that dominated the period that separates the end of the Cold War from the attack on the World Trade Centre. To this basic picture, drawn in figure 4, I have also added a few more issues and players who have emerged since. Note that this exercise is inescapably impressionistic and that only the roughest tendencies are identified here. Still, the portrait drawn gives a good idea of Canada's *relevant* international context and of the way in which it has been and, to a large extent, continues to be managed.

The figure points to a concentration of foreign affairs issues in two quadrants. The upper-left corner (high vulnerability/low complexity) is the field of what could be called "core politics." It is an area where

Figure 4

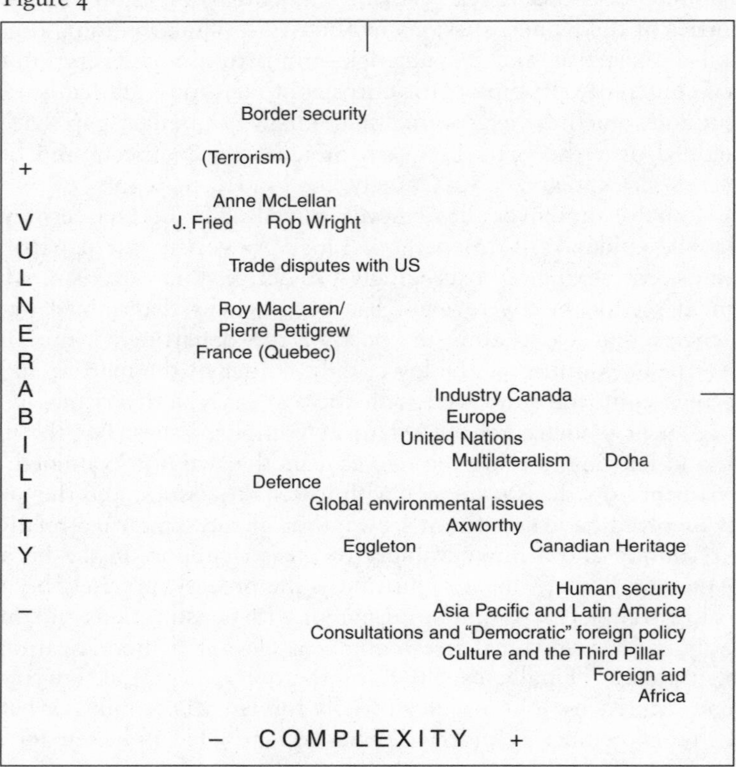

highly consequential decisions are taken, where the Centre and a very small group of ministers and public servants take decisions, and where they do so in a very closed environment. Almost all the issues in that quadrant have to do with Canada's relationship with the United States. The lone exception is the relationship with France which, periodically, and exclusively because of national unity concerns, rises to the fore. When it does, the Centre takes charge and, as with all the other issues in that quadrant, resources are quite easily mobilized.

The lower-right quadrant (low vulnerability/high complexity) is the most crowded. This is where most activism takes place, where most speeches are delivered, and where most consultations are held. Most issues in that quadrant, moreover, are concentrated in the extreme corner. They can generally be considered "fringe" issues. Resources to manage them are scarce and much action takes place, in the term of Hampson and Oliver, at the "pulpit."[23] Most of these issues are extremely complex and their management extremely delicate. At the same time, these are also the issues about which Manley said that Canada had to leave for the restaurant washroom when the time came to discuss personnel and financial payment of the bill. In this corner, one finds human security, all "Third World" policies, including Latin America,[24] international cultural policy and other "third pillar," or "fifth wheel,"[25] issues.

There is also a third grouping of issues, where Europe, the UN and more generally multilateralism are located. These files are "stuck in limbo." Very clearly, their relative importance, that is, the level of vulnerability that should be associated with them, will be hotly debated in the forthcoming policy review. At this point, however, a compelling case does not appear to have been made, either from a security or economic standpoint, for giving them a higher priority.

Then there is the issue of terrorism. At this point, the problem has effectively been framed though the lens of Canada's bilateral relation with the United States (upper-left quadrant). Given the global, including intra-US, disagreement on the ways in which the issue is to be tackled, and given also the extremely high stakes involved, both economic and security-related, that definition could very much evolve to something whose management calls for a much more multilateral approach, which could imply a transformation of Canadian foreign policy.

CONCLUSION: THE NEW CENTURY AND ITS CHALLENGES

Let's go back to figure 4 and note how empty the upper-right quadrant is. Remember that the issues that should appear there, especially those that involve high vulnerability and a significant degree of complexity, are the ones where a specialized and strong foreign affairs apparatus is required. This is where foreign ministries have golden ages, an abundance of resources and where foreign affairs departments draw on the best and the brightest. This is where Canada was between the mid-1950s and the mid-1970s.

The disappearance of issues with these basic characteristics is the main reason why the Department of Foreign Affairs has lost so much political clout in recent years. It is the main reason why the government could cut so much, in terms of formal foreign policy capabilities, and get away with it. It is also why it made perfect sense to manage the country's external vulnerabilities in a different way, centralizing on the one hand, hyper-decentralizing, on the other. Finally, this is also why, having done so, Canada did so well in recent years, in spite of the astonishing increase in its external vulnerabilities.

An interesting question now is to see how different the emerging context will be and how many issues will pop up or move back into that "ideal" quadrant. Very clearly, security is clawing back prominence from trade and economics. The way in which security issues will be framed globally, and the extent to which, for Canada, it will be possible to define them independently of the profound, and radically asymmetric, interdependence that has developed with the United States, will likely determine the extent to which the country's foreign policy apparatus will be marginal or not in the management of Canada's external vulnerabilities.

The important issue, however, lies elsewhere. It regards the ability of the government to manage effectively the country's *relevant* international environment, something it has done, all in all, remarkably well in recent years. It helps neither the world nor Canada itself to confuse these two issues, as happened in much recent public and academic debate about Canada's global presence, about how much above or below its weight the country has been "punching," or about how shameful free riding or washroom going really was. To keep thinking that good intentions or manners can effectively drive a foreign policy is delusional. The last four decades have shown that, in the end, successful choices were made because they were consistent with the management of the constraints that were imposed on the country.

NOTES

This paper is part of a broader research program on the foreign policy of Brazil and Canada since 1945. That program is supported by a grant from the Social Science and Humanities Research Council of Canada. My thanks to Nelly Kim Desrosiers and Chigusa Tanzawa for research assistance, to Françoise Roberge for critical references and pointed questions, to Dane Rowlands for his help with the theoretical model, and to the editors and the participants in the 2004 *Canada Among Nations* workshop, for comments.

1 Andrew Cohen, *While Canada Slept: How We Lost Our Place in the World* (Toronto: McClelland & Stewart, 2003); Jack Granatstein, *Who Killed the Canadian Military?* (Toronto: Harper Collins, 2004); Fen Hampson and Dean Oliver, "Pulpit Diplomacy," *International Journal* 52, 3 (Summer 1998); Jean-Francois Rioux and Robin Hay, "Canadian Foreign Policy: From Internationalism to Isolationism?" *International Journal* 54, 1 (Winter 1998–1999), 57–75; Norman Hillmer and

Maureen Appel Molot, eds, *A Fading Power: Canada Among Nations, 2002* (Toronto: Oxford University Press, 2002); Kim Richard Nossal, *The Politics of Canadian Foreign Policy* (Scarborough, Ont.: Prentice Hall Canada, 1998).

2 Cohen.

3 Peter Harder, "While Cohen Was Sleeping," Speech delivered before the Retired Heads of Mission Association, Ottawa: March 2004.

4 Lloyd Axworthy, *Navigating a New World: Canada's Global Future* (Toronto: Knopf, 2003); Paul Heinbecker, "Canada Got it Right on Iraq," *Globe and Mail*, 19 March 2004, A17.

5 The framework builds primarily on non-functionalist organization theory (Crozier and Friedberg, 1977) and on institutionalist sociology (Max Weber, *Economy and Society* (Berkeley: University of California Press, 1978)) and economics (Coase, 1987).

6 Weber.

7 Or, to speak like Max Weber, four "ideal-typical" ones.

8 Granatstein.

9 Norman Spector, "Nix the Toys for the Boys," *Globe and Mail*, 10 October 2002, A23.

10 Andrew Cooper, Richard A. Higgott and Kim Richard Nossal, *Relocating Middle Powers: Australia and Canada in a Changing World Order* (Vancouver: UBC Press, 1993); David Malone, *Canadian Foreign Policy Post-9/11: Institutional and Other Challenges* (Calgary: Canadian Defence and Foreign Affairs Institute, May 2003).

11 Economic vulnerability could also be assessed in other ways – for example, dependence on critical primary imports, or on foreign direct investment – with perhaps different results. At this point, however, it is assumed, I think reasonably, that extreme trade concentration, which is what we have here, is indeed a marker of vulnerability.

12 This index of dispersion was developed by my colleague, Dane Rowlands. It is similar to the Gini coefficient that is used to assess the level of concentration of wealth in any given economy. In this case, what is measured is the level of concentration of trade.

13 John Kirton, "Foreign Policy Under the Liberals: Prime Ministerial Leadership in the Chrétien Government's Foreign Policy-making Process," in Fen Osler Hampson, Maureen Appel Molot and Martin Rudner, eds, *Asia Pacific Face-Off: Canada Among Nations 1997* (Ottawa: Carleton University Press, 1997).

14 Donald Savoie, *Governing from the Centre* (Toronto: University of Toronto Press, 1999), 7.

15 Malone.

16 Ibid.

17 Privy Council Office, *Canadian Foreign Policy in the New Century* (Ottawa: Privy Council Office, 2003); Harder, "While Cohen Was Sleeping."

18 William Diamond and Michael Hart, "Canada and the Global Challenge: Finding a Place to Stand," *Commentary* (Toronto: C.D. Howe Institute, 2003).

19 Michael Hart, *Fifty Years of Canadian Tradecraft; Canada at the GATT, 1947–1997* (Ottawa: Centre for Trade Policy and Law, 2001).

20 Bruce Doern and Brian Tomlin, *Faith & Fear: The Free Trade Story* (Toronto: Stoddart, 1991); Hart; Max Cameron and Brian Tomlin, *The Making of NAFTA: How the Deal was Done* (Ithaca, N.Y.: Cornell University Press, 2000).

21 Cooper, Higgott and Nossal.

22 Cameron and Tomlin; Denis Stairs, "The Changing Office and the Changing Environment of the Minister of Foreign Affairs in the Axworthy Era," in Fen Osler Hampson, Norman Hillmer and Maureen Appel Molot, eds, *The Axworthy Legacy. Canada Among Nations 2001* (Toronto: Oxford University Press, 2001).

23 Hampson and Oliver.

24 Jean Daudelin, "Foreign Policy at the Fringe," *International Journal* 58, 4 (Autumn 2003).

25 John Graham, "Third Pillar or Fifth Wheel," in Fen Osler Hampson, Michael Hart and Martin Rudner, eds, *A Big League Player? Canada Among Nations 1999* (Toronto: Oxford University Press, 1999).

8 Managing Through Networks: The State of Canada–US Relations

JOHN HIGGINBOTHAM
and JEFF HEYNEN

In a major foreign policy speech while campaigning to become leader of the Liberal Party, Paul Martin enunciated his vision of the management of Canada-US relations:

"We must," he said in April 2003, "engage Americans face-to-face at important levels of our respective political systems – prime minister and president; premiers and governors; members of parliament and members of Congress; mayors, business and union leaders, and civil society".[1]

If it is carried through, the "Martin doctrine" reflects an important evolution in Canada's approach to the United States. Paul Martin's desire for a more "sophisticated" approach to the bilateral relationship, later enshrined in the government's December 2003 machinery changes and its February 2004 Speech from the Throne, is telling for three reasons. First, it reflects new Canadian continental vulnerabilities and risks that need to be managed collectively, stemming from a string of shocks from south of the border during the last few years (for example, September 11, SARS, Mad Cow, the August 2003 blackout). Second, it recognizes the increasing density and salience of cross-border contacts involving multiple actors, exemplified by the proliferation of bilateral players within the Canadian federal and provincial governments. Third, the choice of Paul Martin, before and after becoming prime minister, to focus on mechanisms of the relationship, stems from the absence of consensus within Canada and the government on dramatic new policy initiatives. Given political distractions and blockages both in Canada and the US, incremental process has so far trumped policy or institutional breakthroughs.

Whatever the hopes of the immediate post September 11 period, it is clear that the planets are no longer aligned for achieving Canada-US or North American "mega-deals." Pulled domestically between nationalists and continentalists, chastened with diminished stature in the House of Commons, and facing a United States besieged in Iraq and riven internally, the Martin government will be constrained in charting bold directions in Canada-US relations. Instead, the Canadian government is well-advised to focus on what makes the relationship work; namely, pursuing long-term Canadian interests incrementally, in part though mobilizing the extensive transgovernmental networks of collaboration. However, much work needs to be done to educate Canadian decision-makers about the micro-politics of the US and to educate US policy elites about Canada. To that end, one idea worth exploring is the establishment of a Canadian-based and government-sponsored Foundation for North American Co-operation.

CANADA AND THE US: THE CANADIAN PERSPECTIVE

The post September 11 period has spawned a frenzy of analysis in Canada regarding the future direction of bilateral relations. A survey in the fall of 2003 by the C.D. Howe Institute identified fifteen proposals put forward mostly by academics and policy institutes over the previous two years.[2] These studies attempt to address a number of key questions. What mechanisms can be put in place that will secure the physical border while facilitating trade? Should Canada pursue a "grand bargain" or "comprehensive deal" with the US, wherein numerous sectoral interests would be addressed within a more robust security arrangement, or instead pursue a step-by-step approach to strengthening the relationship? Should any new bilateral arrangement between Canada and the US include Mexico? Should the North American Free Trade Agreement (NAFTA) evolve from a free trade agreement to a customs union, whereby a common external tariff would eliminate the need for rules of origin? Should both Canada and the US recognize each other's standards or enhance regulatory co-operation? How can Canada and the US better resolve lingering trade disputes, given the resilience of US trade remedy actions? Should restrictions to labour mobility be lessened between Canada and the US? How can bi- or trilateral institutions be strengthened?

Despite the range of issues addressed in these proposals, there is much commonality in their conclusions. According to most, Canada should purse a bilateral initiative building on the smart-border approach which would remain open to Mexico. It should also remove unnecessary and expensive barriers to the free flow of goods, services and people while moving towards a common external tariff and enhanced regulatory co-operation or harmonization. Any discussion of monetary union or the building of robust supranational institutions, however attractive in theory, should be avoided for the moment. Some low-key contingency planning work along these lines has been carried out by the federal government.

Even these proposals presently remain well ahead of public opinion. While the various ideas have been vigorously debated among Canadian academics and think tanks, they have yet to incite much broader public or political interest. Opinion polling does show that Canadians are quite open-minded and practical about enhancing co-operation with the US, but the unpopularity of the Bush Administration in Canada and the conflict in Iraq leads Canadian politicians to proceed gingerly towards any initiatives that appear to tighten links with the current US government. The vein of pragmatism among Canadians regarding enhanced co-operation with the US will need to be carefully tapped in coming months should any Canadian government wish to overcome innate suspicions about overly close relations with the US, embedded in three of Canada's four main political parties.

A minority government will of course face extra challenges in handling controversial Canada-US issues. The leitmotif of the thirty-eighth Parliament will be unpredictability, marked by variable majorities on votes, revitalized standing committees (no longer with Liberal majorities), pressures on resources towards social policies, and the inherent tension between pursuing bold new policies and error-free governance. While government initiatives viewed as co-operative with the US (for example, new forms of security co-operation, Ballistic Missile Defence and increased defence spending) would likely receive Conservative support, they risk inflaming the passions of the revitalized NDP, Bloc Québécois and possibly US-sceptics in the Liberal party. The politics of Canada-US relations could well become more polarized in this political environment, further complicated by the uncertainties of the 2004 US election.

THE US AND CANADA: THE AMERICAN PERSPECTIVE

More ominous for bullish supporters of permanent fixes or great leaps forward in the bilateral relationship is the current embattled and self-absorbed mindset of the US administration. Strong "bilateralists" ignore the US geo-strategic mindset at their peril. As a nation at war against terrorism, Americans are above all concerned about securing their homeland. Lingering subterranean uncertainty over the security of the Canada-US land border and Canadian security and immigration policies continues to trouble US legislators, senior officials and the media. Whether any real concern is warranted or not, Canadian co-operation will ultimately be measured in terms of Canada's perceived support in securing "fortress North America" both from within and without in the event of another major terrorist attack on US territory.

Given the overwhelming security preoccupations of the US and the deep involvement of the US in Iraq, Canada has, not surprisingly, failed to register on the priority list of US foreign policy post September 11 2001. There have been real successes, particularly the Smart Border Declaration of December 2001, although much of the federal government's approach to the US during this period has been reactive. Concerted efforts have been undertaken to mend bridges with the US, partly through peacekeeping support in Afghanistan, aid to Iraq, the creation of the Department of Public Safety and Emergency Preparedness (as a partner to the US Department of Homeland Security) and a new national security policy. However, these initiatives have garnered little attention among US policy-makers and "influencers" outside of a few specialists. Should Canada support US Ballistic Missile Defence, years of sitting on the fence have significantly lessened what little American goodwill Canada might have received. Ballistic Missile Defence remains a "no win" decision politically for the Canadian government at home, and budget realities will prevent spending increases of a magnitude that would register significantly on the US radar.

In addition, a highly divided US electorate, mirrored in a polarized Congress, will likely limit the resolve of any administration to pursue major trade or border initiatives with its northern or southern neighbours. As it stands, neither the Republican nor Democratic parties possess much zeal to extend NAFTA. Moreover, the cumulative effects of electoral redistricting over the past three decades, among other pressures, decreases the likelihood of historic electoral gains by either US political party in the 2004 election. Regardless of who occupies the White House, the US electorate, steeped in the politics of security and anti-terrorism in the post September 11 era, will remain polarized for the foreseeable few elections. Meanwhile, the US "insecurity" mindset has indirectly fuelled protectionist pressures in areas of vital export interests to Canada, from lumber to wheat to cattle. Trade liberalization is presently not a winning strategy in the US. This portends limited interest in focusing on non-security related initiatives with Canada.

Finally, should Canada attempt to advance efforts on any major trade or border initiatives with the US, it is likely that this will need to be done in a more complicated trilateral context. Approximately 29 per cent of immigrants to the US come from Mexico; 12.5 per cent of all Americans are now of Hispanic origin, the largest visible minority group in the US. Members of the US administration and Congress are now less disposed to leave out Mexico when addressing border or trade issues, particularly given the sizable Hispanic factor in US domestic politics. Both the State Department and the National Security Council now view Canada to a growing degree through a trilateral or hemispheric rather than trans-Atlantic lens.

IMPORTANCE OF NETWORK MANAGEMENT

This current period of general stress and uncertainty in Canada-US relations can be expected to continue. Given that Canada remains divided over the meta-direction of the bilateral relationship and the US government remains highly distracted, the most feasible scenario for Canada is to focus on enhancing the non-contentious and co-operative elements of the relationship that work best. This makes it all the more important that Canadian analysts better understand the vast range of linkages between both nations and determine how these can best be shaped and exploited. Building on these sectoral strategies, Canada can refine its broader conceptual and implementation planning with a view to possible major "deals" in the future.

Canada-US relations have long been driven by a complex set of systems and coalitions that crisscross boundaries. Accelerating interdependence among advanced industrial societies has created an intricate spider's web of linkages touching all spheres, be it transactions among businesses, cross-border coalitions of environmental activists, or contact between families. Interaction between governments is equally complex, given the federal government's historic role in setting Canada's foreign policy and its wide responsibilities for economic policy, provincial and territorial governments' growing participation in international activities, and even municipalities' efforts in promoting trade and investment.

While these linkages have always been a defining element of the Canada-US relationship, what has changed over the past two or three decades is the range and scope of actors that define cross-border contact. This has had critical implications for transgovernmental linkages; that is, international networks of government officials.[3] While the "state" has far from disappeared in an era of globalization, the role and function of states have altered. New players have emerged, each with different allegiances, expertise and international reach. Scholars have attributed these shifts in part to a change in the structure of organizations: from hierarchies to networks, from centralized compulsion to voluntary association.[4] An underlying driver of the changes has been the globalization of trade and investment flows and the information technology revolution, which has significantly expanded communication capacity while diminishing traditional authority. While not disappearing, governments are disaggregating more and more into separate and functionally distinct parts. According to one noted scholar, "these parts – courts, regulatory agencies, executives, and even legislatures – are networking with their counterparts abroad, creating a dense web of relations that constitutes a new, transgovernmental order."[5]

Canada is in the forefront of this global trend, particularly in its relations with the giant neighbour to the south. Federal government sectoral departments (also called "line" or "functional" departments) have long been active in foreign affairs.[6] For decades, international developments have had an increasing impact on national policy issues, requiring domestic departments to take into account the international dimensions of their issue areas in policy formulation and program delivery, in part because of continual trade and investment liberalization. In recent years, this internationalization of domestic policy issues has intensified. Studies in Canada and elsewhere have examined how governments are adjusting internally to address this challenge of "intermesticity," the overlap and integration of domestic and international issues.[7]

From these studies, some key trends can be identified: First of all, international policy has become somewhat more decentralized within governments (from foreign and trade ministries to sectoral departments) and between governments (from the national to sub-national governments), thereby widening the circle of international affairs participants. This has made foreign policy making more complex and less susceptible to central coordination or priority-setting. Secondly, technical expertise has become more critical in the conduct of foreign relations, which cannot reside within a single ministry. Many domestic departments participate intensively in international institutions and in the development and negotiation of bilateral or multilateral rules. These departments have also frequently grown in-house trade policy and trade development expertise. Third, most domestic departments have established international bureaux or divisions to manage or coordinate a growing portfolio of international activities. Specialists dealing with detailed international issues are scattered across scores of departments and agencies.

Notwithstanding these trends, Foreign Affairs Canada (FAC) and our embassies and consulates in the US continue to play a critical role on some dimensions of the bilateral relationship, particularly in containing crises, facilitating access to senior contacts in the US government and in keeping an ear to the broader US policy and political landscape. Equally important is the quality of relations between the prime minister and president and between Canadian ministers and US Cabinet secretaries. There can be no substitute to mutual trust and political will in advancing the bilateral relationship. While much of the border innovation (for example, pre-clearance arrangements, harmonized overseas operations, intelligence co-operation) were conceived and developed at the official level during the period following the 1995 Shared Border Accord between Canada and the US, it took the events of September 11 and subsequent joint pressure of John Manley, the key minister on the Canadian side, and Tom Ridge, heading homeland security in the US, and their two leaders to achieve implementation.

But during political "down-cycles" in the relationship, co-operation on specific and often technical issues between working-level officials typically provides vital ballast in maintaining the effectiveness of the relationship and offers avenues to explore new collaborative ventures in a low-key way. Since very few issues, and often the most contentious ones, reach the pinnacle of the relationship, the bulk of cross-border contact takes place by public servants through cooperative channels, whether it be scientists sharing information on food safety, officers co-located at ports of entry, or senior managers on joint working groups examining energy matters.

Recent research conducted by the Canada School of Public Service has explored the extraordinary range of functional linkages at all levels (federal, provincial, territorial) in the conduct of Canada-US relations.[8] The linkages can generally be organized into two categories: bilateral processes and bilateral agreements. (See tables 1 and 2.) Processes and agreements are not mutually exclusive and in fact are often linked. The following two tables provides some examples, both organized roughly in descending order of formality. They exclude, however, the most informal channels of interaction, such as professional conferences or workshops, from which substantive collaboration often arises.

In addition to bilateral processes and agreements, multilateral channels serve as a third crucial area of interaction between the Canadian and US governments. Joint bilateral problem-solving with the US frequently occurs within and on the margins of multilateral fora. Indeed, collaboration with the US through multilateral fora has often been conceived as an optimal way of managing key bilateral issues for Canadians. The World Trade Organization (WTO) and NAFTA are perhaps the most important multilateral channels for Canada, where considerable bilateral contact and conflict resolution occurs across a range of economic sectors. A number of institutions under NAFTA were established that have extended cross-border cooperation beyond trade

Table 1 Select Bilateral Processes

Type	*Explanation*	*Examples*
Prime minister and presidential visits and summits	High-level meetings serve as important events to move issues forward on the bilateral agenda. They typically constitute the only time the US government fully concentrates its attention on Canada.	Meetings are typically held in either Ottawa or Washington or on the margins of multilateral meetings, such as the G-8 or NATO.
Premier-governor meetings	Important drivers of the bilateral sub-national relationship. Meetings often take place through regional forums.	Annual meetings of the Conference of New England Governors and Eastern Canadian Premiers; Western Governors Association and Western Premiers Conference
Ministerial-secretary meetings	Key mechanisms to drive progress on sectoral issues.	Quarterly meetings between the US secretary of state and the Canadian secretary of state for external affairs took place during the 1980s (now defunct).
Commissions	Institutionalized bodies usually of an indefinite duration to investigate or adjudicate specific issues.	International Joint Commission, Pacific Salmon Commission, Great Lakes Fishery Commission, International Boundary Commission
Joint boards or panels	Less formal than commissions, bilateral boards often provide a forum to review progress on issues and to facilitate further contact.	The Permanent Joint Board on Defence (PJBD) was set up by Canada and the US under the Ogdensburg Agreement (1940). It includes working-level military and diplomatic representatives from both nations.
Joint operations	A general term to describe actions conducted by joint civilian or military staffs under arrangements or agreements.	The North American Aerospace Defence Command, established in 1958, is one of the most prominent bi-national institutions. It facilitates the joint monitoring and defence of North American airspace.
Joint programs	Joint programs are established by both countries under specific formal or informal agreements to foster bilateral cooperation in various areas of interest.	The Nova Scotia-New England Exchange Program (1988) promotes the exchange of university students between Nova Scotia and New England institutions.
Working groups	Scientific committee, panel of experts, specialists or government representatives, established to address a specific issue.	The Canada-US Transportation Working Group, established in 2002, works to enhance binational and interagency coordination on border infrastructure matters.

Table 1 *(continued)*

Type	*Explanation*	*Examples*
Task force	A temporary group or organization established to carry out a specific task or tasks, or to address a specific issue and make recommendations to policymakers.	Co-chaired by the minister of natural resources and the US secretary of energy, the Canada-US Power System Outage Task Force 2003 was created to investigate the 14 August 2003 power blackout.
Panels	Group of experts/specialists set up to address a specific scientific, technical or socio-economic issue. A panel can also be formed by two parties to settle a dispute.	The Great Lakes Panel on Aquatic Invasive Species is a federal/provincial/state initiative created in 1991 to deal with the introduction of aquatic invasive species to the Great Lakes Basin
Advisory groups	Advisory bodies are created to advise policymakers on the implementation of formal agreements by way of recommendations and reports.	The Provinces/States Advisory Group on Agriculture Issues brings together provincial departments, US states departments of agriculture and federal officials. It advises the federal Canada-US Consultative Committee on Agriculture.
Exchange of personnel	Exchange of personnel for training and also for operational purposes.	There are approximately 600 Canadian Forces personnel currently serving in the US, mostly in NORAD-related assignments.
Joint training	Participation by assigned personnel in joint formal or informal exercises (including learning activities, workshops, military exercises, drilling, fire and rescue training, etc.)	Several departments and agencies (e.g. RCMP, Canadian Customs and Revenue Agency) conduct joint training of Canadian and US officials.
Meetings of legislators	Meetings of elected officials (generally non-ministerial rank), often of an informal nature to discuss a broad range of issues.	The Canada-US Interparliamentary Group was founded in 1959 and has generally met on an annual basis. A number of provincial and state legislatures have twinning or exchange arrangements (e.g. Saskatchewan and North Dakota legislatures).
Fora	Meeting, cooperative initiative or bilateral/multilateral consultation group formed for general discussion of an issue.	The Cross Border Crime Forum is a consultative forum established in 1997 bringing together police and security officials from Canada and the US at both the federal and sub-national levels.

Table 2 Select Bilateral Agreements

Type	*Explanation*	*Examples*
Treaties	Legally binding agreement between two or more states. Usually reserved for matters of some gravity that require solemn agreements. Their signatures are usually sealed and they normally require ratification. Treaties are pursued less frequently due to the difficulties of obtaining US Senate ratification.	Boundary Waters Treaty (1909); Boundary Demarcation Treaty (1925)
Protocols	Agreements less formal than treaties or conventions. They often address particular clauses of the treaty, those formal clauses not inserted in the treaty, or the regulation of technical matters.	Federal Trade Commission-Competition Bureau Information Sharing Protocol
Memorandum of Understanding (MOU)	In international negotiations, a MOU is considered to be a preliminary document, not a comprehensive agreement, on which there has been accord. Most MOUs imply that something more is eventually expected.	MOU between US Department of Defense and Solicitor General Canada on Counter-Terrorism Research and Development (1995)
Exchanges of letters/notes	Record of a routine agreement that consists of the exchange of two documents, each of the parties being in the possession of the one signed by the representative of the other. The technique of exchange of notes is frequently resorted to, either because of its speedy procedure, or, sometimes, to avoid the process of legislative approval.	Exchange of Notes recording an agreement between Canada and the US relating to the Issuance of Certificates of Competency or Licences for the Piloting of Civil Aircraft (1938)
Mutual Recognition Agreements (MRA)	Formal agreement between two countries that provides for a reciprocal reliance upon facets of each other's regulatory systems, to the degree specified in the agreement.	MRA between the accounting bodies in Canada, the US and Mexico under the terms of NAFTA (2002).

issues, such as the Commission for Environmental Cooperation and Commission for Labor Cooperation. Other important multilateral organizations include the United Nations, the Organization of American States (OAS), the North Atlantic Treaty Organization (NATO), the Organization for Economic Co-operation and Development (OECD), the G-8 and the Asia-Pacific Economic Co-operation (APEC). Canada and the US often have similar or parallel goals within these settings. These bodies can be an important asset for Canada in leveraging US support for Canadian positions by building coalitions with others. In addition, they can create diplomatic "capital" with the US and soften the edges of American positions by helping the US communicate their perspectives to the world where views are not in conflict.

Research undertaken by the Canada School of Public Service also suggests that one important explanation for the remarkable strength of Canada-US relations resides in the person-to-person linkages between officials, including ministers and legislators. Practitioners commonly state that there is a high degree of informality to these relationships, which are focused on information sharing, joint-problem solving and joint operations. Bilateral contacts are said to be richer and more immediately productive than with officials from almost all other governments. Indeed, practitioners commonly noted that there is often an indirect relationship between formality and the effectiveness of international co-operation, especially at the multilateral level. Trust is an essential component of the "social capital" embedded in the Canada-US relationship, which diminishes the requirements for formalized meetings or complicated rules guiding co-operation or the sharing of information. Probably no other bilateral relationship is as deep, comprehensive and subtle as Canada's with the US, run as it is by this unusual blend of rules and customary practice.

In summary, the bulk of governmental interaction between Canada and the US occurs through highly specialized and functional channels that have evolved over decades. For the most part, these channels operate "under the radar," supporting the work of ministers but receiving limited public visibility. Working through these channels, be they on regulatory co-operation or joint scientific assessments, can help defuse conflictive issues before they reach policy or political levels. When properly employed, they also do the spadework for higher level initiatives.

STRENGTHENING THESE NETWORKS

Trustful person-to-person linkages below the ministerial level are vital to establishing a culture of trust between Canadian and US governments. Since these channels constitute the bedrock of the relationship, coordinators of the relationship need to ensure they are energized. Given the complexity of the relationship, it is impossible to control the bilateral agenda. Rather, Canadian governments should strive to activate these networks in as coherent a fashion as possible. As a first step, governments need to recognize some of the weaknesses inherent in these diffuse channels, which are addressed below.

Horizontal Collaboration

Despite the extensive nature of these transgovernmental networks occurring at the federal and provincial levels, there is a general lack of understanding of what they do, largely a result of their specialized nature and lack of serious media attention. The bulk of this functional interaction occurs without the intermediation of Foreign Affairs Canada (FAC) or the Privy Council Office (PCO). Accordingly, horizontal collaboration (between departments within a government) and vertical collaboration (between orders of government) can often be more difficult than with US governments, where strong bilateral relationships can develop over time among well-defined professional groups (for example, regulators, police forces, military personnel).

Intergovernmental Collaboration

It is common knowledge that provincial and, to a lesser extent, territorial governments have long been actively engaged in "foreign affairs," through efforts aimed at economic development, such as trade missions, or sectoral collaboration with US state governments in areas like transport routes. It is not surprising, then, that intergovernmental collaboration on bilateral issues is extensive. This stems largely from areas of concurrent jurisdiction (agriculture and immigration) as well as overlapping responsibilities (such as the environment, natural resources, policing, and transportation). Intergovernmental coordinating channels include specialist units in the line departments (especially within federal departments), quarterly conferences organized by International Trade Canada on border and trade issues, and period briefings of provincial officials by the Canadian Embassy in Washington, DC.

There is a strong sense among provincial officials that intergovernmental collaboration can be enhanced. Canadian governments as a whole have considerable knowledge of the regional variances of the US, given the network of Canadian consulates, extensive provincial-state government contact, and informal regional networks. But the flow of information and process of consultation remain less than optimal. It is critical that Canadian officials at all levels of government share this expertise on a regional and sectoral basis. It is also important that, wherever possible, Canadian governments speak with one voice in their interaction with US governments on specific priority issues. Division among Canadian actors can often be easily exploited by US counterparts, particularly on contentious trade issues, such as intergovernmental divisions over handling of softwood lumber.

Political Attention

There are also a number of important bilateral institutions that have suffered given lack of political attention. The Permanent Joint Board on Defence, established in 1940, is composed of military and diplomatic representatives from both nations to serve as a window on Canada-US defence relations. While the PJBD has long since lost most of its planning capability, it arguably remains effective for Canada in gaining access to US defence officials and encouraging discussion of and action on current issues. Canadian chairs, however, have not generally been well versed in military affairs. Similarly, the Canada-US Interparliamentary Group, established in 1959, provides Canadian parliamentarians an important opportunity to interact with critical policy-makers in the US system. Evidence suggests, however, that Canadian membership in this Group has not always included MPs or Senators with strong interest in bilateral issues. The federal Parliament may be able to learn from some of the experimentation going on at the provincial and territorial level, such as various legislative twinning and exchange arrangements with state governments (for example, Saskatchewan and North Dakota, Yukon and Alaska). In general, the synergies between legislators on both sides of the border have not been fully exploited.

Guidance and Resources

Many sectoral officials engaged in bilateral relations are calling for more guidance, support and resources from the top, both within departments and by coordinating agencies. This includes, for example, better horizontal information exchange, formal coordinating mechanisms, policy tool kits and frameworks that are relevant to the specialized level. The federal government has typically resisted radical changes to the machinery of government or attempts to exert firm central control over the international activities of all departments. In December 2003, the federal government established a new Cabinet Committee on Canada-US Relations, chaired by the prime minister to ensure an integrated, government-wide approach. While it remains too early to assess the effectiveness of this committee as well as its dedicated secretariat, this is a positive step in providing greater coherence on cross-sectoral issues. It is also too early to judge the success of splitting the Department of Foreign Affairs and International Trade into two components. Viewing it optimistically, it may produce a more integrated approach to managing bilateral commercial and economic networks by the trade ministry, in parallel with an enhanced coordinating role for the Privy Council Office and Foreign Affairs.

Finally, there is a general sense that enhancing our sophistication in interacting with the US will require additional resources, or perhaps a reshuffling of resources within government. Canada's historic penchant for multilateralism and diversification in foreign affairs has sometimes come at the expense of sophisticated representation and lobbying in the US, even though 87 per cent of Canada's trade goes to the US. Participating in a United Nations conference in Geneva may hold greater allure to the average official or his deputy than building contacts at a highly specialized gathering in Cleveland or Milwaukee. There are signals that Foreign Affairs is addressing this gap, as evidenced by the Enhanced Representation Initiative, leading to the creation of new or upgrading of established consulates throughout the US by the fall of 2004, and the creation of a secretariat at the Canadian Embassy to support linkages among legislators, set up in part to address Alberta's decision to establish dedicated representation in Washington. It remains to be seen, however, if this represents a significant increase in FAC's resources in the US or a reallocation of existing resources already earmarked for US representation.

Among sectoral department officials, enhanced bilateral sophistication will require access to timely and carefully tailored information on US political and trade developments in their areas of interest. It will also necessitate learning opportunities on the wider US political system and its dynamics. Considerable expertise already exists within Canadian governments, often at the working level, regarding the conduct of bilateral relations, yet the churn of officials and organizations, impending public service retirements, and the highly dynamic nature of the US policy environment render person-to-person and intergenerational training an indispensable tool.

LOOKING AHEAD

Given the current political realities in Canada and the US, there is no tidy solution to improving bilateral relations. In the absence of a significant or catastrophic shock to the relationship, it would be naïve to assume that a change in the US Administration or Canadian government will result in large changes to the fundamentals. It is telling that the number of bilateral irritants, while small relative to the size of the relationship, remains quite consistent throughout the Chrétien-Clinton and Chrétien/Martin-Bush periods. These include both trade (lumber, wheat) and non-trade (Kyoto, landmines, Ballistic Missile Defence) issues. Many of these disputes are linked to deeper factors in the relationship, particularly the power of Congress and the influence of the private sector in US politics. To quote Derek Burney, Canada's former ambassador to US, "there will never be a dispute-free nirvana of the relationship."[9]

During this period of uncertainty and risk in the bilateral relationship, Canada should work to strengthen the fundamentals of the relationship; namely, understanding and exploiting the vast array of formal and informal sectoral linkages that mediate transboundary relations. This approach allows for maximum flexibility in the direction of the relationship and is not contingent solely upon the quality of the relationship at the highest levels. It also allows considerable scope for collaboration on issues that are non-ideological (for example, joint programs aimed at improving "North American" productivity, implementation of smart technologies and policies at the border, information-sharing and gradual convergence among regulators, enhancing interoperability among defence forces). Progress can thus be sustained through a low-key and bottom-up fashion.

For Canadian governments, this requires focusing on a few fundamentals. First, senior officials need to better understand the extent of sectoral collaboration occurring between the Canadian and US federal governments and between provincial and state governments. The Canada School of Public Service has recently published a compendium of these linkages, but much additional analysis needs to be undertaken. Bilateral channels and issue networks should be systematically evaluated in order to determine where they might be enhanced, streamlined, or eliminated. This process would also help determine which sectors may require additional resources or institutionalization or if cross-sectoral institutions might be required. Equally important, government practitioners must gain a clearer sense of when, and under what circumstances, particular bilateral strategies, institutions, or agreements should be pursued with US counterparts.

Second, sustained attention must be given to maximizing federal-provincial collaboration on bilateral issues. Intergovernmental collaboration on international trade issues has generally been the most advanced given that provincial governments are often called upon to implement agreements. There is room for enhanced collaboration on a variety of other sectoral issues like energy, food safety, policing and security. Linked to this is the importance of resolving issues at the regional level before they escalate nationally. Identifying and resolving conflicts regionally are far more effective than letting them escalate to the national level, where the diffusion of interests marginalizes Canada's voice in the US.

Third, Canadian policy-makers must really understand the details of the US policy-making process and how Canada can most effectively assert its interests. This requires showing Americans, both members of Congress and the Administration, how working with Canada on a common issue will help them. It necessitates activating US domestic constituencies where possible. The private sector, interests groups, and think tanks have enormous influence in the US political system, especially through well-organized lobbying efforts, their involvement in electoral campaigns, and their specialized knowledge. Canadian governments and private sector players must seek alliances with these bodies that share common interests while carefully avoiding the perception of foreign interference in US domestic politics. In addition, Canadian officials need to know when to engage higher levels in order to move an issue forward. The most vital bilateral links, particularly when responding to crises or contentious issues, occur between the prime minister and president and between ministers and Cabinet secretaries. Canadian officials must know when to engage these levels in order advance policies that may be held up by bureaucratic inertia, inter-agency turf battles, or divisions within Congress.

Lastly, efforts need to be given to bolstering US officials' understanding of Canadian realities and points of views. At the same time, Canadian officials need to educate themselves and Canadians more broadly to the benefits of bilateral collaboration. Anti-Americanism will always be a counterweight, either visible or latent, to integrationist zeal in Canadian politics. But naysayers of bilateral collaboration must be reminded that engagement with US officials is the principal means by which Canadian actors can assert their sovereignty in a proactive fashion. An independent Canada is entirely consistent with being perhaps the world's most interdependent and multilateral nation.

A CONCLUDING PROPOSAL

There are a variety of means to strengthen the multiple networks Canada has at its disposal and ultimately to better understand and influence the US. One way would be to establish a dedicated and independent Canadian-led "Foundation for North American Co-operation" as an arms-length foundation or institute from the federal government. Financial considerations aside, the time to establish such an organization is auspicious. During a period when bold bi- or trilateral initiatives are unlikely to emerge, serious reflection on the present and future shape of continental relations must be encouraged. Whatever the details of its organization and mandate, it should embody a network-based approach to shaping the relationship. There is presently no significant real or virtual centre in Canada where research is systematically conducted on US domestic and international policy making and on emerging issues of potential impact on Canada. Some strong expertise on the US and Mexico presently exists within Canadian universities and think thanks, but it remains scattered. A major responsibility of the Foundation could be to foster a deeper understanding of US and Mexican perspectives in Canada while working towards a longer-term vision of North America.

The functions of such a Foundation would be fourfold. First, it would undertake and support policy-focused research by universities and think-tanks on Canada-US issues, as well as Canadian perspectives on US domestic and international issues. Second, it would strengthen intergovernmental communities of practice (federal, provincial and municipal) within Canada and across the border on bilateral issues and enhance understanding of how Canadian concerns can best be articulated and defended in the US environment. Third, it would build familiarity with Canada and Canadian interests among US decision-makers (Congress, Administration, state government) and influencers (universities, think tanks) through organized conferences, study-tours, and visiting fellowships on both sides of the border. Fourth, it would help nurture a future generation of scholars on Canada-US and North American issues through undergraduate scholarships and reciprocal internship programs. While the activities of such an organization would evolve in line with its expansion, few would contest that Canadian policy makers will require an increasingly sophisticated understanding of Mexican as well as US policy domains over the long run.

In a period of uncertainty and stress in the bilateral relationship, governments need to inject a high degree of realism into what can be accomplished. Given the political constraints in both countries, there is much merit in advancing progress on sectoral issues in a sustained and low-key manner through better use of existing transgovernmental channels. This quiet and unobtrusive nature of collaboration is arguably a measure of its success. At the same time, political and senior management leadership will be required to ensure that these networks are vitalized, coordinated and can sustain the higher voltages of crisis management or institutionalization as circumstances determine. At best, this approach will prepare the way for important policy or program initiatives leading to a major new bi- or trilateral arrangement as the political biorhythms on both sides of the border settle down. At least, they will help further strengthen bilateral co-operation in advance of unforeseen shocks to the relationship.

NOTES

The views expressed in this chapter are those of the authors and do not reflect the views of the Government of Canada.

1 Address by Prime Minister Paul Martin, "Canada's Role in Complex World," Toronto, 30 April 2003.
2 Danielle Goldfarb, "Beyond Labels: Comparing Proposals for Closer Canada-US Economic Relations," *C.D. Howe Institute Backgrounder* 76 (Toronto: CD Howe Institute, October 2003).
3 This is distinct from transnationalism, which refers to international activities of non-state actors. For a useful discussion of these concepts, see Anne-Marie Slaughter, "The Real New World Order," *Foreign Affairs* 76, 5 (September-October 1997), 183–97.
4 Jessica T. Mathews, "Power Shift," *Foreign Affairs* 76, 1(January/February 1997).
5 Slaughter, 184.
6 An early academic study of these relationships is Annette Baker Fox, Alfred O. Hero, Jr., and Joseph S. Nye, Jr., eds., *Canada and the United States: Transnational and Transgovernmental Relations* (New York: Columbia University Press, 1976).
7 Government of Canada, Privy Council Office, *Towards an International Policy Framework for the 21st Century* (2003).
8 This research was undertaken by the CSPS Action-Research Roundtable on Managing Canada-US Relations.
9 Derek H. Burney, "The Risk of Complacency – The Need for Engagement," *Speech delivered to the Canadian Chamber of Commerce Business Summit*, (Toronto: 30 October 2003).

9 Canadian–American Relations: Old Fire, New Ice?

ROBERT BOTHWELL

Canadian-American relations are, to put it kindly, an old preoccupation for Canadians. They have been defined as a syndrome, a phobia, a good marriage, a bad marriage, cousinhood, and so on. Canadian views of the United States were once described as "the narcissism of small differences."[1] When looking at Canadian-American relations, there is a lot of detail, but sometimes nothing much to be said. "I hope you haven't come to talk to me about the sex-life of the salmon," US Secretary of State Henry Kissinger once said to the Canadian ambassador. But that was exactly what he had come to discuss.

That is a historian's perspective, but it is probably the most useful thing a historian can bring to a contemplation of Canadian-American relations and the discussion of Canada's place in the world. "Been there, done that," may not be the most inspiring words a policy analyst may hear, especially someone whose living may depend on purporting to break new ground, but it is a little reassuring, nevertheless. I hasten to add that it is not all good news. The most recent book on the subject, by the pollster Michael Adams, calls the relationship "fire and ice," and argues that Canada and the United States are diverging culturally, with Canada heading toward secular Europe, and the United States adopting Christian fundamentalism as one of its defining characteristics for the twenty-first century.[2]

The patterns of Canadian-American relations are very old and very strong. In some respects they date back to the colonial wars, the time when Canada was most on the American consciousness. It is always useful to remember that the two countries had a common origin in a civil war in the 1770s. Canada remained on American minds until roughly the 1820s or the 1830s, when the revolutionary generation died off in both countries, and when thoughts of revenge gradually simmered down into a residue of envy on the Canadian side, and oblivion on the American.

Transborder relations were never absent, even in time of our one subsequent war with the Americans. During the War of 1812 Americans were happy to buy, and Canadians to sell, goods that helped sustain the American armies on the northern frontier, or British troops in Montreal. Or vice-versa. This was hostility with a difference.

It is true that later in the nineteenth century there was the period of Manifest Destiny, much stressed by Canadian nationalists of an earlier generation and awaiting rediscovery by the nationalists of this one. Manifest Destiny of course means that the United States was intended by God to rule over all of North America from palm to tundra. Canadians, hearing the phrase, usually thrilled with horror, not unmixed with pride and satisfaction. "They noticed." Put another way, Canada was worth acquiring.

For the most part *they* didn't think so, nor did they notice, except in the sense that that *they* regarded Canadians as just like Americans. Canadians pretended to be insulted. Perhaps some actually were, but it was handy to have Americans think that way, when buying gas or negotiating with the local traffic cop, en route to Florida.

But can it be true? Are Canadians just like Americans? And am I indulging in the usual English-Canadian obliviousness about French Canada? What, after all, about the French Canadians? Well, plainly they speak a different language. Nevertheless one of the more amusing phenomena of the past couple of decades has been the discovery by Quebec separatists of their "*américanité.*" The word is self-explanatory, and it served a purpose in the lead-up to the Quebec referendum of 1995. It describes a real phenomenon, the attraction between, and the resemblance among, French-Canadians and Americans. Its political purpose apart, it closely parallels the English-Canada to United States relationship, and so it serves to suggest that we are all, after all, in the same boat.

The American political scientist Louis Hartz once described Canada – he really meant English Canada – as a "fragment," certainly as compared to the United States and Great Britain.[3] It was not self-sufficient, incomplete by itself, needing and seeking linkages elsewhere. English-Canadians found these across the Atlantic, or south of the border. For French-Canadians, the linkages were as often as not to Rome, to the headquarters of Roman Catholicism, or, less frequently, in France. Hartz had a point, especially when he situated Canada not merely in a

North American context, but in a wider trans-Atlantic world, stretching to the shores of the mother country, Great Britain. It is well to remember that linkage, especially because the patterns of Canadian relations with the United States have their roots in an earlier era, in Canadian relations with Great Britain.

Canada and its much larger twin, the United States, had enjoyed the luxury of geographical and political isolation, and for over a century – from 1815 to 1914 – could concentrate their energies on internal development. It was easy but not entirely accurate to attribute the isolation to sheer distance, and as a result it was easy to exaggerate the fact of isolation, especially in the United States, which had cast off their European political ties in 1776. Nevertheless, the United States remained protected by the British Empire, whether it officially liked it or not.[4] Canada was different, politically and emotionally, though not strategically; and it remained until the 1940s a generally happy and co-operative member of the British Empire.

Americans were usually content to see it that way. Britain and the British Empire had a mixed reputation in the United States. Big Bill Thompson, the mayor of Chicago, used to boast that he would bust King George on the snoot should the British monarch ever sail up Lake Michigan to the Windy City. This was popular with Irish voters in Chicago. Even blue-blooded New Englanders liked to recall the Revolutionary War and its heroic struggles. The United States, from George Washington on, periodically vindicated its sovereignty, refusing, in John Quincy Adams's phrase, to be pulled like a cockboat in the wake of the British man-of-war. But the fact remained that the British Empire and the United States spoke the same language and made generally the same assumptions about foreign policy and, indeed, many other matters. And when the Empire was threatened, as it was twice in the twentieth century, the United States rightly or wrongly, took it as a sign that its interests were threatened too. Canada, therefore, was inoffensive in its attachment to the British Empire, and familiar by geography and population. It should have been, because so many Canadians moved to the United States that the Canadian-born were, for many years, one of the two or three largest batches of foreigners counted in the American census.

There were, of course, two kinds of Canadians. There was the invisible kind who spoke English and were indistinguishable from Americans, Saul Bellow and Wallace Stegner, to name only two. Stegner maintained some memories of his Canadian childhood, while Bellow did not. These Canadians settled across the country from Boston to Los Angeles. Americans were generally surprised to learn that Mary Pickford or Glenn Ford had been born in Canada, but if they were, what did it matter? They were just like Americans, as their successful careers acting American parts proved.

Then there were the French-Canadians, who settled mostly in New England, close to home in Quebec. The only thing for them, Franklin Roosevelt advised Mackenzie King, was assimilation. It was working in New England, the American president advised the Canadian prime minister. King should try it too. The result would be an English-speaking and Anglo-Saxon norm across the continent, with a political distinction to give it a unique North American flavour of happy coexistence and international cooperation.

Economic connections were already large. Canada surpassed Great Britain as the United States' principal trading partner in the 1920s. American investment flowed north, sometimes naturalizing itself (as in the cases of Alcan or Canadian General Electric) and sometimes not. Tourism was an accepted part of the mix, as Americans motored north to enjoy cooler breezes in the summer and listen to the call of the loon. In an age without air conditioning, that was better than the ninety-five degrees and urban racket. The song "Canadian Sunset" appealed because many Americans, often people with modest incomes, had been able to see one. If there was familiarity, it was because Canada and Canadians were familiar.

Time passed. The British Empire declined and fell, though Americans, and Canadians too, did everything they could to prop it up. Or almost everything: both the American and the Canadian governments favoured the devolution of the Empire as its various components became too sophisticated or unruly to accept imperial tutelage. To win the world wars, Canadians and Americans evolved a system of mutual sacrifice, external and internal, producing class harmony and widespread affluence at home and multilateral harmony abroad. They borrowed weapons, troops and ideas from each other in the common cause. The Cold War came, threatening shared liberal and democratic values, but the Cold War was won, eventually, in part because of the harmonization of domestic politics in both countries.[5]

The Cold War had not been without friction or cost on the allied or western side. Each confrontation, whether Korea or the Taiwan Straits or Berlin, had produced dissonance among the allies. If there was a characteristically Canadian approach, it was that of Lester Pearson, external affairs minister and then prime minister in mid-century. Pearson had no doubts of the general beneficence, good effects and good intentions, of the United States and its foreign policies. But he had a long memory, stretching back to an era before the Cold War, before the world wars, before American energies were mobilized and channelled into the cause of anti-communism. Perhaps it would all go away. Perhaps the Americans, like the British, would overreach, and their policies would outrun either the political will or the economic resources to support them. Large and admirable the United States certainly was, but it was not infinitely so. The United States needed a better sense of limits, even of limitation, and Pearson did his best to bring that about.[6] Pearson's counterpart and sometime friend, Dean Acheson, found Canadian vocalizations on diplomacy tiresome. Acheson reminded Pearson that he had problems too, more and bigger. The implication was that Canadian concerns would have to wait.

Canadian behaviour during the Cold War sometimes struck Americans as confusing or worse. On the one hand, Canadians generally supported the western alliance. When the United States faced the Cuban missile crisis in 1962, Canadian opinion, if not the Canadian government, rallied to the cause. The government was soon gone, greatly to the pleasure of the electorate, and the American president, John F. Kennedy. On the other hand, there was Canadian nationalism, which sometimes expressed itself as anti-Americanism. This was a staple of US Embassy reports from Ottawa back to Washington in the 1950s and 1960s. American diplomats, perhaps remembering John Quincy Adams and his metaphorical cockboat, advised patience and restrained the enthusiasms of their colleagues, who saw no reason why Canada and the United States should not seize the moment and forge a deeper unity.[7]

The moment was in any case ill chosen. The Vietnam War drove a wedge into the western alliance. Canada declined to participate, not that the US government made a very forceful effort to secure Canadian participation. Instead Canada sat beyond if not above the fray, as a member of an international truce supervisory commission in Vietnam from 1954 to 1972. The war was increasingly unpopular with Canadian opinion, a fact that is often remembered. What is less remembered is that Canadian opinion mirrored American opinion, and that Canadian opponents of the war took some of their most rabid views directly from their counterparts in the United States.

Nevertheless, the Canadian role in Vietnam and in Indochina generally did cause some Americans to wonder where, exactly, Canada stood. As an American diplomat told a Canadian diplomat in 1961, "I remarked that it had come rather as a surprise to our people when the Canadian Delegation advanced what seemed to be the view that Canada did not regard itself as a Western power but rather in the role of neutral."[8]

The Canadian answer on this and other occasions was that Canada served the western cause best when it acted impartially, according to the facts of the case. Often enough, such a posture served American interests as well, or the Canadian action was held to be of insufficient importance to merit reproach or retaliation. Canada was after all a sovereign country, and some Americans understood that it had to put that sovereignty to use. In any case, exceptions had to be balanced against general cooperation and overall mutual sympathy.

That would not have been the complete answer, as the Americans suspected. Many Canadians, like many Americans, were weary of the Cold War and its tensions, as well as its real dangers. Many, again like many Americans, objected to the fervent and sometimes unscrupulous anti-communism of the McCarthy period in the United States. The minister at the American Embassy in Ottawa, Rufus Smith, commented reasonably and fairly on the phenomenon in 1969. "The reasons [for anti-Americanism in the Canadian media] are many," he wrote, "and in some measure similar to those which account for the abundance of adverse content in domestic broadcasting in the US. Added to that are elements of Canadian nationalism, genuine anti-US sentiment, and the all-too-human penchant for kicking the big guy when it can be done safely. It is not a new phenomenon, but has been true, with ups and downs, of Canadian news media for as long as they have existed."[9]

There were usually limits to Canadian anti-Americanism. The Cold War served as a kind of control. As long as Canada was on the western side, what many Americans regarded as tiresome Canadian moralizing could be accepted, if not appreciated. President Ronald Reagan remained polite with Prime Minister Pierre Trudeau, though he and his entourage liked Conservative leader Brian Mulroney better. Trudeau for his part could barely contain his scorn for Reagan, but he never pushed it to the point where, on a great issue of foreign policy, he distanced himself from the Americans. Generalities were one thing, specifics, such as cruise missile testing, on which Trudeau obliged Reagan, quite another.

It helped that Canada was by far the Americans' largest trade partner, the seat of billions in US investment, and crucial to the comfort and prosperity of some northern border areas. These facts helped keep Canadian-American relations steady. When it was suggested, under President Richard Nixon and again under Ronald Reagan, that it might be useful to chastise Canada over automobiles or Vietnam over the National Energy Program, the idea was sidelined, and eventually forgotten.[10]

During the 1980s, things changed. For specialists in international affairs, the memorable event was the end of the Cold War. This was undeniably important, but as important was the transformation of the domestic political scene in western countries. Two factors were especially salient. Ideologically, the liberal consensus that had guided the political economy of North America, western Europe and Japan since the Second World War began to come apart. This began to produce changes in the way states behaved, at home and then abroad. The British had Thatcherism, the Americans Reaganism, and the Canadians an amalgam of the two.[11] "The lady's not for turning," Margaret Thatcher told her cheering supporters, and she was true to her word. Compromise was out, "wets" were out of fashion and out of government, and individual initiative and responsibility were in.

Individual initiative was already at work in demography, the other changing component of national life. Canada had during the 1970s and 1980s a liberal immigration policy, which by the 1990s had certainly changed the complexion of Canada's cities and the sound of its politics. The United States had an unofficial immigration reality, attracting millions of Spanish-speakers, mostly Mexicans, to its borders. Those who did not stop in the maquiladora zone in northern Mexico came on to populate much of the southwestern United States. Even in Washington, far from the border, bilingual signs sprouted as business came to terms with new customers.

At the same time, the southern states benefited from the maturation of air conditioning systems, which made life and work not just possible but pleasant. Americans no longer had to come to Canada in search of respite from the heat. Canadians, who were enjoying their own air conditioning boom, did not notice, or if they did, moved to Arizona.

The effect was much more than recreational. Mexico became an important item on the American political agenda far beyond the border. Naturalized immigrants and their children became an important and distinctive political phenomenon, and American legislators paid attention. The Canadian population of the United States shrank (in part because of Canadian prosperity in the late twentieth century as well as more restrictive American immigration laws), and as it shrank it aged. At the same time, the northern tier of states became less important, as wealth and people moved to the air-conditioned south. That, as we shall see, was also very important in Canadian-American relations.

Geography is not always a predictor of individual attitudes, or political behaviour. The south and west came to dominate American politics in the 1970s and 1980s, it is true, but two of the southern presidents, the liberal Jimmy Carter and the centrist Bill Clinton proved to be friendly, even helpful, to Canada. George H.W. Bush, a Connecticut Yankee by birth and upbringing and a Texan by adoption, was friendly to the Canadian prime minister, Brian Mulroney. Ronald Reagan was a throwback to the years of Canadian immigration: he may not have known Canada, but he knew and liked Canadians, such as the aforementioned Glenn Ford and Mary Pickford. That fact made Trudeau go down more easily.

There was not always Canadian-American agreement during the 1990s. Bilateral disputes like the perennial softwood lumber question marred the Reagan-Mulroney accomplishment of free trade, but in the best of times Canada and the United States had sparred over trade. Generally, however, trade if not investment gladdened the hearts of Canadian business during the decade, and the trade figures, pointing ever up, confirmed a happy trend. Neither Canada nor the United States was covered in glory as a result of some of the international issues of the 1990s, such as Somalia or Bosnia, but Canada was a strong supporter of and contributor to the NATO intervention in Kosovo in 1999.

Economically the 1990s went better for the United States than for Canada. A recession in 1990 had afflicted both countries and for a time had seemed to underline the gloomy predictions of academic seers that the United States had entered a period of "decline." The notion was known by the awful name "declinism," one of the silliest bits of jargon ever to enter the language. Unemployment rose and government revenues shrank in both countries.

Governments (Bill Clinton's in the US and Jean Chrétien's in Canada) responded with savage budget cuts which, in Canada, severely handicapped the military. Clinton sooner than Chrétien benefited from a strong revival of the US economy that produced high tech jobs, a soaring stock market and an investment boom. The high tech spilled over into the defence field, making the American military so far advanced, technologically, that it dwarfed its counterparts in other countries, a fact that became very clear during the Kosovo campaign.

The "lessons" of the foreign policy adventures of the 1990s were not universally agreed, or shared. Most American allies, including Canada, assumed that with the end of the Cold War the United States would be true to one of its historical traditions and accept that it was again a country like others, just bigger and richer, and of course more important. The allies forgot that some, indeed many, Americans had never believed that the United States was a country like other countries. Such Americans now believed that the end of the Cold War meant that the United States must never again accept to be threatened by a powerful military rival like the defunct Soviet Union, and that it must use its power, economic, political and ultimately military, to defend and perpetuate its pre-eminence.

That view found its way into a defence planning document produced in the Pentagon in 1992. In the words of a later historian, the United

States "should work actively to block any possible competitor to American power."[12] The document was swiftly repudiated: it was too blunt, it offended too many people, and it complicated the United States' relations with its allies. President George H.W. Bush did not agree with it. The world in 1992 seemed to be profoundly at peace, and disturbances were distant and almost irrelevant. The notions the Pentagon document embodied, however, did not go away.

The 1990s may have been a time of missed opportunities, especially because of the flawed presidency of Bill Clinton, who spent so much time battling scandals that he had little opportunity or political capital left for diplomacy. Nevertheless, Clinton got through a World Trade Organization to replace the constipated General Agreement on Tariffs and Trade. The focus of the world's diplomacy would be economic co-operation, free trade and free investment, led by the United States to be sure, but nevertheless a rule-based system of international interchange. But it was beyond Clinton to secure passage of an International Criminal Court, or the Kyoto Protocol. Even had Clinton been able to make a better fight of it, it is probable that he would not have succeeded.

And beyond Clinton, there lurked Osama bin Laden and the spectre of Islamist terror. Bin Laden reached out and touched Canada through a terrorist cell in Montreal that in the fall of 1999 dispatched one of its members, Ahmed Ressam, to drive from Victoria to Los Angeles, there to detonate a huge bomb at the international airport on the occasion of the 2000 millennium celebrations. Ressam was detected and arrested at an American border station, but the ramifications of his narrowly averted adventure helped focus American attention on Canada. Was Canada truly a good or at least reliable neighbour and friend if it allowed people like Ressam to contrive their plots?[13]

All this is to say that there were trends in the United States and in the world that did not promise well for Canadian-American relations in the new century, and especially after its defining event, the terrorist attacks on New York and Washington on September 11 2001. The immediate consequence of the 2001 atrocity was the closure, for the first time since the War of 1812, of the Canadian-American border.[14] Air and sea frontiers were sealed as well, and Canadians received 33,000 aerial refugees from Whitehorse to Gander.[15]

The border was eventually reopened, but not before delivering a severe shock to the assumptions that had informed Canadian-American relations. Before 2001 the border, even in wartime, was a revenue-collecting membrane, with some minor prophylactic qualities. After, it was a potentially lethal impediment to Canadian trade, 87 per cent of which or more went south to the United States.

The Canadian government did its best. It poured money into security, it tried to improve border controls, and it negotiated a "Smart Border Declaration" with the United States. It had to. Another Ressam, or worse, a successful Ressam, would present Canada with the most drastic consequences. Already, in September 2001, it was automatic for American politicians to speculate that the terrorists had got to the United States through Canada. That was not the case, but the danger remained.

Bilateral relations with the United States were difficult enough, but multilateral relations proved to be another magnitude of difficulty. The United States in its response to the terrorist attack relied on its allies only in direst necessity, for land or air or sea access to Afghanistan. NATO's invocation of Article 5 of the 1949 North Atlantic treaty – an attack on one was an attack on all – was treated as a harmless irrelevance at best.

Canada supported and contributed to the war in Afghanistan and its aftermath, which at the time of writing shows no sign of ending. Canada did not support or contribute to the war in Iraq, or at any rate the military part of the war (Canada did promise $300 million toward Iraqi reconstruction). From Prime Minister Chrétien's point of view, the American rush to war in Iraq was too much too soon. It took little account of the niceties of international behaviour. It ignored the United Nations, which for all its defects was the only international body with even the semblance of authority over international war-making.

"Many Europeans were painfully shocked," writes Walter Russell Mead, " ... to discover just how little the United States government at times can care about public opinion among people who do not vote in American elections." In fact, Mead notes, many people outside the United States concluded that "300 million people who live in the United States are getting more say [than] the 6.3 billion people who live in the rest of the world."[16] The rest of the world, in Mead's view, had better adjust to this reality. That specifically includes the "earnest Canadians," whose exhortations to virtue, a rhetorical style inherited from the Pearson era, drive more realistic diplomats headlong towards the exit of whatever salon they might happen to be in.[17]

Canadians do not vote in American elections, or, perhaps better, not as many as used to vote in those elections. The shrinking Canadian content in the American electoral mix is dwarfed by the Mexican content. When President George W. Bush came into office, he identified Mexico as the United States' most important foreign relationship, and, he might have added, a more important domestic fact too.

There was a hiatus after September 2001, for Mexico also has a long and insecure land frontier with the United States, though one that is much more heavily patrolled and, in places, fortified. Mexicans and Canadians even discovered, briefly, that they had something in common, for Mexico like Canada refused to participate in Bush's war in Iraq, and both countries received appropriately stern lectures from their respective American ambassadors. On political issues, as long as they remain strictly political, Canadians and Mexicans may indeed discover a common cause.

The fear that politics may slop over into economics does worry some Canadians. It is especially important to those Canadians, many already strongly pro-Bush, who believe that Canadian behaviour, good or bad, is likely to have direct economic repercussions from an irritated American government. It is certainly not impossible to imagine an American government responding to another Ressam case, for example. When the Canadian government refused to join in the Iraq War, three provincial premiers immediately voiced their indignation, and let it be known that as far as they were concerned, Bush not Chrétien had the right side of the issue.[18]

The best solution from the point of view of some sectors of the business community, and presumably their friends among the provincial premiers or opposition politicians in Ottawa, was enhanced integration with the United States, establishing a perimeter around North America and applying common standards (and perhaps a common administration) to imports of goods and people into the continent. It is a naïve solution, colliding directly with the anxious and active Mexican lobby in Congress and elsewhere. What might have been possible in 1948 or even 1968 is possible no longer. It is doubtful whether the idea is politically saleable within Canada, entailing as it does a rapprochement with the toxic Bush administration in Washington.

It is in Canada's interest to avoid giving needless offence to the United States, but as American commentators have noted, it is in the United States' interest to avoid giving further offence abroad. That the United States will seek help as the Iraqi quagmire deepens is certain. Canada has never stopped giving aid on the security front, and in Afghanistan, where Osama bin Laden and his gang once resided and may still dwell. There may well be other incidents of terror, to which Canadians are not immune, and from which they are not exempt.

Not everything has changed. Though Canada may be unpopular with the American right wing, most Americans still have friendly feelings. A Gallup Poll in February 2004 showed nearly 88 per cent of Americans thought well of Canada, and only just over 10 per cent reported negative feelings.[19] This is not to suggest that Canada stands out strongly in the minds of many Americans. A young American tourist vacationing in Europe was asked whether by chance she was not American. "We were hoping you were Canadian," one European told her. "Canadian?" the American replied. "Since when was it cooler to be Canadian?"[20]

The American's quip returns us to the question of *Fire and Ice*. "Cool" does not mean ice, or if it does it is very, very dry ice. Fashionable ice. If Canadians are cool, then so is the sex life of the salmon, in Kissinger's phrase. Are Canada and the United States diverging, as Michael Adams argues? He presents lots of evidence from his own expert polls and as we have seen, the demography of the United States (and Canada too) does point to a divergence of interest as the United States re-sorts itself in a south-westerly direction. Polls from the highly respected Pew Research Center in the United States seem to support this view. In Walter Russell Mead's view, the old American elites, with which Canadian elites were so comfortable, are being displaced by new and culturally dissimilar groups, as part of the ongoing miracle of the market.

These are serious contentions, likely to be much debated, but they are not the whole story. The chief Pew pollster, Andrew Kohut, has noted that, while the United States does seem to be diverging from the western norm, the north-eastern states have not disappeared from the picture or changed all that much. "When we look deeper into the data, we find the gap between Americans and Canadians is not a national gap, it's a regional one," Kohut told the Canadian Society of New York. Northern Americans are likely to think along the same lines as adjacent Canadians, though as Kohut also notes, some parts of Canada, like southern Alberta, are likely to think like adjacent Americans. There are lots of Albertan-Americans, as there are lots of New-England Canadians.

Change there may be, but it may be less fundamental, and less apocalyptic than some observers predict. Geography and cultural heritage, along with shared interests and values, will continue to link Canadians and Americans. But, following Kohut, it will be *some* Canadians, and *some* Americans.

NOTES

1 S.F. Wise, "The Annexation Movement and its Effect on Canadian Opinion, 1837–67," in S.F. Wise and Robert Craig Brown, eds, *Canada Views the United States: Nineteenth Century Political Attitudes* (Toronto: Macmillan, 1967).

2 Michael Adams, *Fire and Ice: The United States, Canada and the Myth of Converging Values* (Toronto: Penguin Canada, 2003).

3 Louis Hartz, *The Founding of New Societies: Studies in the History of the United States, Latin America, South Africa, Canada and Australia* (New York: Harcourt, Brace & World, 1964).
4 Walter Russell Mead, *Power, Terror, Peace and War: America's Grand Strategy in a World at Risk* (New York: Knopf, 2004), 22.
5 Ibid., 44–5.
6 Pearson's best efforts were not spectacularly effective, when it came to the United States. Both over Korea and Vietnam, his hesitations and compromises did little more than irritate the United States government, though they did appeal to many Americans. See Denis Stairs, *The Diplomacy of Constraint* (Toronto: University of Toronto Press, 1972).
7 Clarence B. Randall, a high official under Eisenhower, promoted economic union. George Ball, similarly-placed during the Kennedy and Johnson administrations, promoted freer trade and wrote that Canada's destiny was ultimately to be absorbed in the United States.
8 US National Archives, RG 59, State Department Papers, 611.42/5–2661, MEMCON, R.E. Usher, deputy director, SEA and E.R. Rettie, Counsellor of the Canadian Embassy, 28 May 1961.
9 Ibid., RG 59, 67–69 Series, file POL CAN-US, Ambassador Adolph Schmidt [but drafted by Rufus Smith] to State, 17 December 1969.
10 J.L. Granatstein and Robert Bothwell, *Pirouette: Pierre Trudeau and Canadian Foreign Policy* (Toronto: University of Toronto Press, 1990), chs 3 and 9.
11 Canadian national politics did not immediately see the effects, but provincially they appeared as the "Common Sense Revolution" of the late 1990s in Ontario.
12 James Mann, *Rise of the Vulcans: The History of Bush's War Cabinet* (New York: Viking, 2004), 210. The document was called "Defense Planning Guidance." Revised, it was issued under the name of then-defense secretary Richard Cheney.
13 Canada's porous refugee claims system, and the admission of Ressam to Canada, are documented in Stewart Bell, *Cold Terror: How Canada Nurtures and Exports Terrorism Around the World* (Toronto: Wiley, 2004).
14 Even in 1812, the fact of war was no barrier to trade, since Vermont farmers kept the British army in Montreal plentifully supplied.
15 The Canadian hospitality was gratefully received by the stranded air passengers, but omitted from President George W. Bush's list of countries to be thanked when he addressed Congress some days later.
16 Mead, 63.
17 Ibid., 65. Unusually, Mead betrays some sympathy for Europeans, "who are likely to roll their eyes and sidle toward the exit" to escape from their Canadian interlocutors.
18 The three were Premiers Gordon Campbell of British Columbia, Ernie

Eves of Ontario, and Ralph Klein of Alberta. In the summer of 2003, Premier Klein did the rounds in Washington trying to get a beef ban relating to Mad Cow disease lifted. His presence in the American capital indicated his view that Canadian diplomacy by itself was insufficient.

19 Gallup Poll Social Series: World Affairs. The poll was taken between 9 and 12 February 2004.

20 Marco Della Cava, "Ugly Sentiments Sting American Tourists," *USA Today*, 3 March 2003.

10 The Road from September 11: Canada–US Defence Relations in the Terrorist Era

ELINOR SLOAN

The nature of the threat to North America today is forcing significant changes in the way in which the Canadian Forces (CF) works with the US military both at home and abroad. On the one hand, the new threats are demanding an increased integration of Canadian and American defence and security capabilities at home. On the other hand, these threats, along with the onward march of technology, are raising the requirement for increased interoperability with the US military and a focus on defence "transformation" for missions abroad. Points of contention could arise in either of these areas.

Some of the current continental defence issues go well beyond those that formed the framework of Canada-US defence cooperation during the Cold War, and have the potential to infringe on Canada's sovereignty or its interpretation of international law. Canada will have to stake out its position on several issues, while taking the necessary measures to ensure it has the credibility and influence to support its position. Overseas defence issues center on niche roles in the "American Empire" and the costs and requirements of maintaining interoperability with US military forces. Commitments the Canadian government has made to buy equipment for the CF will have to be seen through, and the size of the CF will have to increase, if Canada is to be able to operate effectively abroad to guarantee the security of Canadians at home.

DEFENCE AT HOME

The most significant Canada-US institutional structure for the joint defence of North America is NORAD, the North American Aerospace

Defence Agreement that was signed in 1957–58 and led to the establishment of a bi-national Canada-US command in Colorado Springs. Over the years, NORAD's mission has evolved in step with the changing threat environment, first encompassing air defence against bombers, then taking on aerospace warning and control with respect to ballistic missiles, and finally adding the surveillance and monitoring of aircraft suspected of illegal drug trafficking. Throughout this period, and even with the advent of new types of missions in the post-Cold War era, one consistent feature of NORAD remained in place: NORAD always looked outward to address threats that were approaching the continent.

In the post September 11 era NORAD has broadened its focus from looking exclusively outward, to looking both outward *and* inward at potential domestic airborne threats.[1] NORAD is still responsible for detecting, identifying and, if necessary, intercepting potentially threatening air traffic entering North American air space. But, after more than forty years of looking outward from the continent, NORAD has had to adjust itself to threats that arise from within. A good example of the changes in the Command's operating procedures is that, today, the NORAD operations center listens to conversations on the Federal Aviation Administration network on a full time basis and would know instantly of a suspected hijacking.[2] In addition, as part of Operation Noble Eagle, a joint US-Canadian operation launched after September 11, Canadian and US forces are monitoring and intercepting all flights of interest within continental North America.

NORAD's command and control system is structured to protect Canadian sovereignty and give Canadian personnel a visible role in NORAD operations. By tradition, NORAD's commander is an American and the deputy commander is a Canadian general. Canadian officers are posted in various positions at NORAD headquarters. NORAD is assigned permanent air defence forces but American military personnel cannot *command* those Canadian forces assigned to NORAD. The NORAD command structure operates under the principle of operational *control*.

Clearly, grasping the distinction between operational control and operational command is essential to our understanding of sovereignty in a NORAD context, and thus of sovereignty in any possible future NORAD-like arrangement involving land or maritime forces. *Operational command* is the authority granted to a commander to assign missions or tasks to subordinate commanders, to deploy units, or to reassign forces. *Operational control* is much more limited, in that authority is granted to a commander only to direct forces to accomplish specific missions or tasks which are usually limited by function, time or location. Canada, for example, has agreed to have a certain number of aircraft on daily alert within NORAD. But the Canadian government has specified in advance how these aircraft may be used in the event of a crisis.

In this way Canada has retained the right to employ its NORAD forces as it sees appropriate. Not only has Canada retained operational command of its forces, but also, in the event of a crisis, Canadians are intimately involved in operational control decisions. Aircraft and personnel respond through NORAD's integrated chain of command. Ultimately, NORAD answers equally to the president of the United States and the prime minister of Canada.

New Threats

The nature of the threat to North America in the decades following the Second World War was such that it demanded increased cooperation between the United States and Canada to address airborne and ballistic missile threats to North America. Even after the Cold War, continuing concerns in these areas were strong enough to maintain the aerospace warning and control mission of NORAD. Growing worries about rogue state ballistic missiles also fed into this assessment.

But in the years leading up to September 11, US and Canadian intelligence agencies, academia, government agencies, and bi-partisan commissions were most concerned with the prospect of the terrorist use of weapons of mass destruction (WMD), nuclear, biological, chemical or radiological weapons, on North American soil. The fact that the September 11 attacks were conventional did nothing to dampen concerns about WMD. This was because the sheer magnitude of the attacks demonstrated a change in the nature of terrorism, traced since the mid-1990s, from politically motivated attacks with limited casualties, to attacks with ill-defined objectives seeking mass casualties. As a result, since September 11 concerns about the terrorist use of weapons of mass destruction have only grown stronger.

New Responses

The threat to North America today is such that it is driving increased US-Canadian cooperation to address land and maritime threats to North America. Specific scenarios might include a terrorist attack along the Canada-US land border and bridges using a weapon of mass destruction, or terrorists placing a nuclear device on a container ship docked at a major port or using an offshore trawler to launch a biochemical attack. Responding to the threat is particularly challenging because it demands not only increased Canada-US military cooperation, but also increased cooperation between each of the two militaries and their respective domestic agencies responsible for homeland security missions. Canada's navy, for example, is exploring increased maritime cooperation bi-nationally with the US Navy and US Coast Guard, and nationally with Transport Canada and the RCMP.[3] Similarly, Canada's army is undertaking to increase its cooperation both with the American army, as well as the Canadian Department of Public Safety and Emergency Preparedness.

In the United States, increased civil-military cooperation, and any possible changes in roles and responsibilities, are mostly being worked out between Northern Command and the Department of Homeland Security. Northern Command is one of nine commands in America's unified command structure, which assigns elements of the air force, navy, army, and marine corps to a particular geographic region or functional issue.[4] Created in 2002, Northern Command's geographical area of responsibility covers the continental United States, Canada, Mexico, and parts of the Caribbean. Its specific responsibilities include the defence of America's land approaches, and the defence of America's sea approaches out to 500 miles. The Commander of Northern Command is doubled-hatted as the commander of NORAD, thus ensuring that overall responsibility for the homeland defence of the United States in the air, land and sea dimensions resides in one agency. To provide military assistance in support of civil authorities, including the "consequence management" of terrorist WMD strikes, Northern Command has been assigned the Joint Task Force-Civil Support units that were previously assigned to Joint Forces Command.

In some cases, the complexity grows further, with military and civilian agencies on both sides of the border all involved in a particular cooperative effort. An example is the Great Lakes-Saint Lawrence Seaway Cross Border Task Force, which involves the US navy, the Canadian navy, and civilian US and Canadian agencies.[5] Another is TOPOFF 2 (for Top Officials), a five-day, full-scale exercise held in May 2003 that simulated how Canada and the United States would respond to a WMD disaster. The exercise involved a whole range of US and Canadian agencies, as well as officials from both militaries.[6] All of these issues generally fall under the category of military support to civilian-led "homeland security" missions and are largely beyond the scope of this chapter.

Canada and the United States have been discussing increased military cooperation for the defence of North America since the September 11 attacks. In the early months there were numerous reports that Canada and the United States were discussing the creation of a command that would oversee not only air forces, as currently captured by NORAD, but also the land and maritime forces guarding North America.[7] But this prospect created an outcry in Canada, especially among members of the Liberal Cabinet.[8] Over the next several months, the government stressed that Canada was not being asked to join America's new Northern Command, nor was it actively considering any new NORAD-like command to include land and maritime forces.

High-level bilateral negotiations ensued, and in December 2002 Canada and the United States announced an agreement to establish a Canada-US Planning Group to examine increased Canada-US land and maritime military cooperation for the defence of North America. Created in spring 2003, the group is co-located with NORAD headquarters in Colorado Springs, and is headed by the Deputy Commander of NORAD. It includes about 50 officers, half American and half Canadian, and is charged with: preparing contingency plans for jointly deploying military forces within North America in the event of a crisis, including potential terrorist attacks and natural disasters; coordinating maritime surveillance and intelligence sharing to give leaders in both countries a comprehensive threat assessment; coordinating and stepping up joint military exercises between the Canadian and American armies and navies to help them deter threats and respond to crises; and improving the military's links and standard operating procedures with police and other emergency services in the civilian world.[9]

Although the stated objective of establishing the planning group was to work out the details of a coordinated response in advance of a potential crisis, in fact many of the important decisions were hammered out in the months before the group was created. Rather than having a set of standing operating procedures, as NORAD would have in dealing with an aerospace threat, the planning group would evaluate each emergency on a case-by-case basis. Unlike NORAD, there would be no standing forces assigned to the planning group. It would be a headquarters organization that is permanently in place and could call on forces from the different services as required.[10] In the event of a crisis, any Canada-US military force called up by the planning group would operate under the operational control of the "home" country; that is, under Canadian operational control if within Canada, and under American operational control if within the United States. This could be contrasted with NORAD, where the operational control of a fighter aircraft does not change when the aircraft crosses the border. Overall, the planning group was presented as an alternative to a formal joining of the US military's Northern Command or to the creation of some sort of a "super–NORAD" military structure.

Since that time it has become clear that these decisions are not set in stone and continue to evolve. The planning group is not so much an established entity but rather, as its name would suggest, a planning team working on the details of some future established entity. One idea under discussion is the creation of a Canada-US maritime command, modeled after NORAD and including an integrated command structure, to protect against coastal terror attacks.[11] Another idea, voiced by the (American) Deputy Commander of Northern Command, is a "North American version of NATO," that would see NORAD adapted into an integrated military command that would include maritime and ground force operations.[12]

Increased Canada-US institutional cooperation is logical and is governed both by response times and geography. For the first it is important to ask, how much time do we need to respond effectively to a land or maritime threat to North America? NORAD was established because Canadian and US security demanded a near-instantaneous response to potential air and, later, aerospace threats to the continent. Forces and command arrangements had to be in place in advance because the time between when an aircraft or missile was detected, and when a response was needed to defend against them, was (and is) literally only minutes. Land and maritime threats to North America do not travel so quickly. But they are unique in that they come from terrorists who are difficult to detect. Moreover, they could involve rapidly spreading and highly lethal weapons of mass destruction. There may be very little time to assess the nature of the threat and decide on an appropriate response, particularly when it comes to land based threats or maritime threats close in to shore.

Because most of Canada's population lives close to the Canada-US border, any threat to it is likely to take place within a few hundred miles of the frontier. This consideration, combined with the fact that the threat knows no borders, means that US interests would likely be directly involved in the event of a crisis. And, even if the threat was confined to Canada, geography dictates that back up support could more quickly arrive from south of the border than from other areas of Canada.

Future Considerations: Land and Maritime Cooperation

As the Canadian government moves forward, it should insist that any expanded Canada-US military institutional arrangement to cover land and sea based threats to North America be centred on an expanded NORAD. Its command and control arrangements protect Canadian sovereignty and give Canada a much greater voice in continental defence affairs than would otherwise be the case. If the North American Aerospace Defence Command were transformed into a North American Defence Command, the requirement established under the planning group that each situation be assessed on case-by-case basis may not be necessary once possible scenarios and contingency plans are fully developed by the planning group. Every situation is different and will inevitably require crisis-specific solutions, but having a set of standard operating procedures for various contingencies can only enhance the prospect of an effective military response. For similar reasons, an integrated military command with limited standing forces in place for responding to land and maritime threats would also be a sensible approach. Both would also enhance the military's ability to provide support to civilian-led homeland security missions.

Most importantly, the Canadian government must continue to insist that land or maritime forces be deployed under the operational control of the home country. In the current NORAD framework, American fighters could cross the border into Canada and still be under the operational control of an American officer. This framework is not sufficient, in terms of Canadian sovereignty, when it comes to maritime and especially land force responses to threats to North America. If a land force unit is sent to respond to a WMD disaster in Windsor, a Canadian officer must be in charge. If a ship suspected of transporting a nuclear device enters Canadian waters off Vancouver, then a Canadian vessel should be in operational control. Both these scenarios would directly affect US security, and it can be assumed that the United States would undertake to carry out the operation if Canada were militarily unable to do so. Clearly the old adage that "if we don't secure our territory, the Americans will do it for us" would be highly operative in these situations. It is imperative, in sovereignty no less so than security terms, for Canada to maintain sufficient military forces so that it is capable of taking control of these sorts of operations.

Ballistic Missile Defence

Decisions surrounding the final institutional mechanism to encompass increased Canada-US military cooperation for the land and maritime defence of North America are likely to be taken in the period leading up to the 2006 NORAD renewal. In the meantime, a much more pressing issue must be decided: whether or not Canada should participate in America's ballistic missile defence program. Based on a perceived threat from rogue state ballistic missiles, notably North Korea and Iran, as well as lingering concerns about an accidental ballistic missile launch from China or Russia, the Bush Administration took the decision in December 2002 to proceed with the deployment of a global ballistic missile defence system. The Pentagon is to field twenty ground-based interceptors at sites in Alaska and California in 2004 and 2005, and another twenty interceptors on board Navy Aegis cruisers by 2005. Because of the deployment schedule, Canada is faced with an almost immediate decision on whether or not to participate.

Since the early 1960s, and as codified in the 1996 renewal agreement, NORAD's primary mission has been aerospace warning and control: warning and detection of aircraft and ballistic missiles, and interception of aircraft. In NORAD parlance, the detection mission is stated as Integrated Tactical Warning and Attack Assessment. To provide ITWAA, NORAD relies on information from Strategic Command[13] about ballistic missile launches and trajectories and events in space, and on information from the Canadian and US air defence systems about aircraft movement.[14] If Canada decided not to take part in ballistic missile defence, it would still be involved in the air defence warning and interception mission. NORAD would not disappear. In fact, the air defence mission has been revitalised in the post September 11 era. The potential "air breathing threat" posed by civilian airliners, and future concerns about cruise missile threats to North America, have ensured a continued relevance of the air defence mission. NORAD remains the logical agency to carry out this mission.[15] Moreover, NORAD would have an increased role in continental security if it were to be expanded to include responsibility for the maritime and land defence of North America.

If Canada decided not to take part in ballistic missile defence, then NORAD, and Canada, would lose the ballistic missile warning and detection mission. This is because it is not possible to divide the warning of and response to ballistic missiles; physically it would all take place in the same room.[16] The warning and detection mission would be transferred to NORTHCOM, which would also be assigned responsibility for missile defence. Canadians would leave the room and, although NORAD would not disappear, it would decline in stature because it would have lost one of its biggest missions.

For Canada, there would be two important implications. First, the lack of information about ballistic missiles approaching Canada, and our non-participation in any response, would represent a decline in Canadian security. Although the ballistic missile threat to North America is considered low, it is not zero and it may be rising. In the coming years, the range and accuracy of ballistic missiles available to proliferators will likely improve, and access to the weapons of mass destruction that make these delivery vehicles so dangerous will continue to spread. How could Canada guarantee its security if it had no means of knowing if a ballistic missile was approaching its territory? The United States would not be obliged to tell us and probably would not have the opportunity to do so until after the fact. How could Canada say it is secure if it had no means for defending against ballistic missiles, no role in any decision surrounding a response, and no way of ensuring a US system afforded Canadian territory the same degree of protection as that of America? Critics may recommend a "wait and see" approach, but the option of waiting until the threat more fully presents itself is problematic because of the time and investment needed to build an effective defence.

The second important implication of a Canadian decision not to participate in ballistic missile defence would be the loss of access to strategic level information in the realm of space.[17] Part of the ballistic missile warning information comes from America's land-based ballistic missile early warning system, first deployed in the late 1950s with sites in Alaska, Greenland, and England, and designed to detect ballistic missiles coming over the polar ice cap. But much of the information comes from America's Defense Support Program system of satellites.[18] First deployed in the 1970s, the system detects heat generated by a missile or booster exhaust trail for strategic and tactical missile launch detection. The satellites are earmarked for replacement by a Space-Based Infrared High System beginning in 2007, which will use infrared surveillance for missile warning.

Although these systems provide operational or theatre level information about the North American continent, they also go far beyond the tactical and operational level to provide a strategic picture of developments around the globe. By virtue of Canada's role in ballistic missile warning, Canada has enjoyed access unparalleled by any other nation to America's space based assets and strategic level considerations. Significantly, this "window into the global picture" would be closed should Canada decide not to participate in ballistic missile defence.[19]

Historically, Canada has resisted invitations to participate in America's ballistic missile defence programs in part out of concern that a BMD system might set off a new arms race. It was felt that Russia and possibly China would respond to a missile defence shield by building more missiles, in the hopes that at least some would get through. This concern was largely removed when America withdrew from the Anti-Ballistic Missile Treaty in 2002 and this elicited only muted criticism from Russia and China. That said, questions remain in this area.[20]

Canada has also resisted participation in ballistic missile defence because it is against the weaponization of space. The crux of the issue is the differing US and Canadian interpretations of the 1967 Outer Space Treaty, to which both countries are signatory. The only activity the Outer Space Treaty explicitly forbids is "the orbiting of nuclear weapons or other weapons of mass destruction, their installation on celestial bodies, or the stationing of such weapons in outer space in any other manner." Beyond this, the Outer Space Treaty permits the "peaceful use" of outer space in accordance with "international law, including the Charter of the United Nations." Canada has focused on the "peaceful use" component and interpreted this to mean that outer space can only be used for non-aggressive purposes, such as surveillance and communications. The United States, by contrast, has focused on the reference to the UN Charter. Because article 51 of the Charter recognizes the inherent right of self-defence, the Outer Space Treaty is interpreted as permitting those outer space missions necessary for national security, including not only surveillance and communications but also the possible application of military force from space-based weapons.

The goal of America's Missile Defense Agency is to develop, test, and prepare for fielding a "layered" ballistic missile defense system that can engage missiles in all three phases of flight. These include the boost phase from launch to the completion of propulsion fuel burn; the mid-course segment outside the atmosphere; and the terminal phase when the missile re-enters the atmosphere. Although the primary emphasis is on land and sea-based interceptors, and to a certain extent airborne interceptors, the Missile Defence Agency is also pursuing technology for space-based interceptors, which would be particularly useful for destroying a ballistic missile in its boost phase. Budget documents indicate the Pentagon would like the Missile Defense Agency to have a test version of a space-based interceptor ready by 2012.[21]

The fact that the present administration has made ballistic missile defence a priority does not mean that some new technological situation in this area has suddenly presented itself. Indeed, lost in the contemporary debate about ballistic missile defence is how technologically difficult it remains to "hit a bullet with a bullet," and how doubly difficult it is to hit a bullet with a space-based interceptor. The United States pursued BMD in the 1960s and abandoned it because of technological unfeasibility and a change in the security environment. In 1983 US President Ronald Reagan announced a grand design for ballistic missile defence but this too was dramatically scaled back within a few years. In 1999 US President Bill Clinton signed into law the National Missile Defense Act, requiring the United States to implement a system to protect against limited attacks "as soon as technologically possible," but technology did not make it possible. Clinton deferred a deployment decision to the next administration.

It is conceivable that over the next decade or two it will not prove technologically possible to field space-based interceptors for ballistic missile defence, or that there will be a change in the international security environment such that the United States will decide its resources are better spent elsewhere. In the meantime, Canada should agree to participate in the early land and sea-based elements that are currently being deployed. Moreover, it should press for NORAD to be the command and control center for the system. Quite apart from considerations of security, sovereignty, and access to strategic information noted above, only as a participant in ballistic missile defence would Canada have the opportunity to further its views on the non-weaponization of space. Should the United States proceed to weaponize space in the next decade, Canada would have to reevaluate its position.

DEFENCE ABROAD

Canadian security and defence is not only decided at home. The nature of the threats to North America is such that their origins are most often overseas, and are best tackled abroad, before they reach our shores. In the future, two broad types of military capability will be needed to address the threat abroad: "robust" peacebuilding or stabilization forces, such as the International Security Assistance Force in Afghanistan, and warfighting forces that have undergone a process of modernization or defence "transformation." These forces are not mutually exclusive and there are many overlapping military characteristics.[22]

One of the key military attributes for missions abroad is rapidly deployable forces that are highly mobile on the battlefield and yet remain very lethal and continue to provide force protection. In this context, Canada's decision to purchase the Mobile Gun System, known as the *Stryker* in the United States, is a sensible one. The Mobile Gun System is flexible and agile on the battlefield and, weighing in at about 20 tons, much lighter than a tank and therefore more rapidly deployable. The United States is in the process of dramatically restructuring its ground forces into three types of brigades: heavy brigades, armed with *Abrams* tanks and *Bradley* fighting vehicles; light mechanized brigades, armed with the *Stryker* Mobile Gun System; and airborne brigades, armed with paratroopers and the *Apache* attack helicopter.[23]

The *Stryker* mobile gun system has been the subject of considerable criticism, both in the United States and Canada, for being vulnerable to rocket-propelled grenades and not offering sufficient protection to the soldiers that operate them. But the *Stryker* was never intended for front line combat; this is reserved for units equipped with the *Abrams* tank. Despite the reduced protection they offer combat troops, *Stryker's* substantial firepower coupled with high mobility fits well with many of the situations in which military forces will be asked to operate. *Stryker* brigades have been deployed successfully in Iraq since December 2003, and they would play the core security role in any future US stabilization and reconstruction divisions, an idea now under consideration in the United States. *Stryker* brigades are also expected to be well suited for city engagements and urban warfare.[24]

Canada's acquisition of the Mobile Gun System, combined with the fact that the United States is making the brigade its central ground force unit and Canada's army is already organised around brigades, will make the Canadian army structurally highly interoperable with America's light brigades. But technological challenges will continue to present themselves. It is imperative the Canadian government fully fund the army's intelligence, surveillance, target acquisition and reconnaissance (ISTAR) project, which is developing technology to link battlefield sensors from a variety of Canadian ground force platforms, as well as, potentially, air and naval platforms. ISTAR was announced in 2003 and its $650 million price tag is to be paid for over ten years. Moreover, ISTAR technology must take into account interoperability requirements and the need for Canadian platforms to be able to receive information from, and transmit information to, American platforms. This may require an additional investment.

For missions abroad Canada should also look closely at US thinking surrounding the creation of stabilization and reconstruction divisions.[25] A Canadian adaptation in this area would involve arming our brigades with the Mobile Gun System and significantly increasing the size of our brigade groups to include many more units of combat support and combat service support forces. These include logistics, military police, construction engineers, civil affairs, medical, psychological operations, and communications personnel. Canada should aim for bringing the traditional 3:1 ratio of combat to combat/combat service support units up to an even ratio of 3:3 (1:1); that is, an increase of about 1,500 personnel for each of our brigade groups, or a total increase of 4,500 troops in the army alone. Requirements in response to today's security environment are such that the Canadian Forces simply is not large enough. People, as much as new equipment, will need to be the focus of Canada's future defence investments.

The contemporary security environment also demands naval forces that can interdict ships carrying terrorists and their weapons. Currently the naval platform best suited to the "global coast guard role" of interdiction operations is frigates.[26] Not surprisingly, with its fleet of

Halifax Class Multi-Role Patrol Frigates, Canada made a major contribution to the war on terrorism in 2001–2003 with naval interdiction operations in the Arabian Sea. The ability to carry out such operations represents a valuable niche role for the Canadian Forces in the "American Empire." They make a tangible contribution to increasing international security, and they are flexible enough that Canada can pick and choose its area of operations in accordance with domestic political imperatives. Moreover, our frigates and destroyers are highly interoperable with US naval platforms and can fit "seamlessly" into a carrier battle group. The navy's task groups cannot operate independently without its supply ships, the Auxiliary Oil Replenishers, which are aging and close to the end of their operational life. The recent decision to fund the new Joint Supply Ship is therefore an important if Canada is to be able to provide an effective contribution to future operations abroad.

Precision force has been used in a wide range of conflicts since the end of the Cold War, from the first Gulf War, to Bosnia, Kosovo, Afghanistan, and the second Gulf War. Canada's CF-18s played a major role in the Kosovo air campaign because its aircraft had recently been upgraded with laser-guided munitions, and because they were able to operate from a nearby NATO base in Italy. These aircraft are currently undergoing upgrades on their command and control systems, and could potentially be outfitted with satellite-guided munitions, which would rectify the interoperability problems and deployment limitations experienced in the Kosovo campaign. Yet, in terms of speed and agility, Canada's CF-18s are simply not in the league of the US Air Force's new stealth F-22, now under production, nor the Joint Strike Fighter, scheduled to appear around the end of the decade.

Canada is currently an informed partner in the Joint Strike Fighter program. An important factor to consider in any future acquisition decision is the utility of these aircraft in responding to military threats abroad. Although the United States has recently begun a process of establishing small bases in an increased number of places around the world,[27] it is still a difficult challenge in the post-Cold War era to find a location close to the scene of a conflict from which to deploy a land based aircraft. For this reason, the United States is concentrating its power projection resources in its carrier battle groups, purchasing a next generation carrier and scaling back the land-based variant of the Joint Strike Fighter in favor of the carrier-based version (it is also scaling back its number of F-22s buys). For Canada, acquiring the (land-based) Joint Strike Fighter would be exceedingly costly and may result in a niche role that is not relevant to future contingencies abroad. Given competing priorities and limited resources, Canada should place its emphasis on upgrading its CF-18 for the renewed air defence role at home.

CONCLUSION

The post September 11 security environment is driving a Canada-US defence relationship that is arguably more closely integrated than at any time in history. No longer confined to the aerospace dimension, Canada-US cooperation for the defence of North America is necessarily expanding to the land and maritime dimensions. Canada will have to establish firm positions in certain areas, most notably the requirement that maritime and land forces operate under national control on Canadian territory and in Canadian territorial waters, and it will have to ensure it has the forces and capabilities to back these up. It will also have to work within, not outside, the US ballistic missile defence system to further its views on the non-weaponization of space.

For operations abroad, Canada has made some important equipment and technology decisions that must be seen through if Canada is to make an effective contribution to coalition operations. But this is only half the story. In the future global environment, guaranteeing the security of Canadians at home will require stabilization missions abroad, and for this niche role in the "American Empire," there is no substitute for increasing the size of the Canadian Forces.

NOTES

1 Lieutenant-General George MacDonald, "Canada–US Defence Relations: Asymmetric Threats and the US Unified Command Plan," *Testimony before the Standing Senate Committee on National Security and Defence*, 6 May 2002; General Ralph Eberhart, *Testimony Before the Senate Armed Services Committee*, 20 March 2002.

2 By contrast, on September 11, FAA flight controllers took fifteen minutes to notify NORAD that they thought a flight out of Boston had been hijacked, leaving NORAD only six minutes to respond before the plane hit the World Trade Center.

3 In the United States, the Coast Guard conducts maritime security and interdiction missions within 200 miles of US shores, while the navy does so in areas beyond 200 miles. In Canada, Transport Canada is the lead department for marine security, while the RCMP conducts police functions along the coasts related to issues like drug smuggling, assisted if necessary by the navy. The general coastal protection role remains with the navy. The Coast Guard does not have a security role.

4 The nine commands are Joint Forces Command, Special Operations Command, Transportation Command, Strategic Command, European Command, Pacific Command, Southern Command, Central Command, and Northern Command.

5 Agencies involved include the Pentagon, the Canadian navy, the US Departments of State and Justice, the Canadian Department of Foreign Affairs and the RCMP, among others.

6 For a full list of agencies involved and the scope of the exercise, see Department of Homeland Security, *Top Officials Exercises Series: TOPOFF 2: After Action Summary Report*, 19 December 2003, http://www.dhs.gov/interweb/assetlibrary/T2 Report Final Public.doc.

7 Tim Naumetz, "Canada Begins Talks With US Over Joint Defence," *National Post*, 9 February 2002.

8 David Pugliese, "Unified Command Upsets Ottawa Politicians," *Defense News*, 11–17 February 2002.

9 Department of National Defence, "Enhanced Canada-US Security Cooperation," *Backgrounder* (20 March 2002).

10 Lieutenant-General George MacDonald, *Testimony before the Standing Senate Committee on National Security and Defence*, 14 August 2002.

11 Sheldon Alberts, "Canada, US Study Response to Attacks on Parliament Hill," *Ottawa Citizen*, 15 November 2003.

12 Lieutenant-General Edward Anderson, Deputy Commander of Northern Command, "Remarks to a Conference on Homeland Defence and Land Force Reserves" (Calgary, Alberta: University of Calgary, 26 March 2004).

13 This information formerly came from Space Command, the commander of which was double-hatted as the commander of NORAD. On 1 October 2002, Strategic Command absorbed Space Command, Northern Command was created, and the NORAD commander was double-hatted as the NORTHCOM commander.

14 Joseph T. Jockel, *Four US Military Commands: NORTHCOM, NORAD, SPACECOM, STRATCOM – The Canadian Opportunity*, IRPP Working Paper Series no. 2003–03 (Montreal: Institute for Research on Public Policy, 2003).

15 George Lindsey, "Potential Contributions by the Canadian Armed Forces to the Defence of North America Against Terrorism," *International Journal* 58, 3 (Summer 2003), 317.

16 Joseph T. Jockel, "A Strong Friend is a Good Defence," *Globe and Mail*, 14 January 2004.

17 James Fergusson, "Canadian Defence and the Canada-US Strategic Partnership: The Aerospace Dimension," in *Conference Publication: Canadian Defence and the Canada-US Strategic Partnership* (Canada: Canadian Defence & Foreign Affairs Institute, Fall 2002), 24.

18 The Defense Support Program satellite system operates in geo-synchronous orbit, or "high earth orbit," some 37,000 kilometers above the earth's surface and consists of 8 to 10 satellites.
19 Fergusson, 22.
20 Philippe Lagassé, *The SORT Debate: Implications for Canada*, IRPP Working Paper Series no. 2003–01 (Montreal: Institute for Research on Public Policy, 2003).
21 Pugliese.
22 Warfighting requirements for addressing terrorism include: precision force; advanced intelligence, surveillance, and reconnaissance capabilities; advanced command and control capabilities; special operations forces; flexibility and speed on the battlefield; smaller, more mobile and modular units/ground forces; rapid deployability to the theatre; jointness among services; support to forces ashore; and naval interdiction operations. Peacebuilding requirements for addressing terrorism include: advanced intelligence, surveillance and reconnaissance capabilities; advanced command and control capabilities; special operations forces in some situations; rapid deployability to the theatre; critical mass/larger size of force; increased combat support and combat service support capabilities; and technologies unique to peacebuilding like non-lethal weapons.
23 Vernon Loeb, "Army Expansion Could Last 5 Years," *Washington Post*, 30 January 2004, A19.
24 Kim Burger, "Fighting in the Streets," *Jane's Defence Weekly*, 20 November 2002.
25 Hans Binnendijk and Stuart Johnson, eds., *Transforming for Stabilization and Reconstruction Operations* (Washington, D.C.: National Defence University, November 2003).
26 Melena Zyla Vickers, "LCS Could Bolster Defense Against Terror," *Defense News*, 14 July 2003.
27 David Rennie, "America's Growing Network of Bases," *Telegraph*, 9 November 2003.

11 Liberal Continuities: Jean Chrétien's Foreign Policy, 1993–2003

GRAHAM FRASER

During his decade in office, Jean Chrétien moved from being a prime minister with a limited foreign policy agenda to a leader whose foreign policy drove his agenda. This is, in fact, the pattern for modern prime ministers. Early in their term, they name strong ministers of foreign affairs and give them some room; at the end of their careers, they name newcomers as they take charge of many of the files. Pierre Trudeau began deeply skeptical of the Department of External Affairs, and named Mitchell Sharp as his first secretary of state for external affairs. He ended with a world-wide peace tour, and Mark MacGuigan and Allan McEachen as minister. Brian Mulroney named Joe Clark at the beginning and Barbara McDougall at the end, getting deeply involved in the anti-apartheid fight, Haiti and Canada-US relations.

Although he was once, very briefly, secretary of state for external affairs himself, Jean Chrétien seemed potentially so domestic a prime minister that the Conservatives initially ran an attack ad questioning how Canadians would feel having him represent them abroad. His early appointments were strong ministers, whose foreign policy priorities could be expressed on a bumper sticker. André Ouellet's would read "Trade trumps aid — and Quebec trumps both." Lloyd Axworthy's would be "Soft Power." John Manley's would say "The Americans are our best friends." Bill Graham, a rookie in cabinet, would have had an all-embracing – but unfocussed – "We are the World."

In his last year as prime minister, Chrétien became deeply absorbed in international affairs, driving the Africa agenda at the G-8 meeting in Kananaskis and making the decision that would, in some ways, define the latter part of his prime ministership: keeping Canada out of the war in Iraq. During that period, he named a committee chairman, Bill Graham, to his first position in cabinet, a sign that he, like his predecessors, would dominate foreign policy in his last months in office.

In the trajectory of his decade in office, Chréten's foreign policy was, in large part, shaped by two imperatives: trade and national unity. Then, as he became more senior and more confident, he was more outward-looking in his approach. However, overshadowing the decade of Chrétien's prime ministership was a quiet crisis of morale in the foreign service.

THE TRADE IMPERATIVE

When Jean Chrétien fought the election campaign of 1993, one of his major themes was that he was not Brian Mulroney. What he implied by that, in foreign policy terms, was that he would change both Canada's relationship with the United States, and alter the terms of the North American Free Trade Agreement (NAFTA). Partly as a result of what Chrétien said during the election campaign, there was a widespread belief in Washington among the small group of those who follow Canadian politics that, as prime minister, he would name Lloyd Axworthy as his foreign minister, something that was foreseen with considerable pessimism by the community of Canada-watchers.[1]

But Chrétien took a number of cautious steps in his first months. During the election campaign, the United States sent a quiet warning to Chrétien not to use the word "renegotiate" when he talked about NAFTA. US President Bill Clinton's ambassador, James Blanchard, traveled to Quebec City to deliver the message to Jean Pelletier, who had been Chrétien's chief of staff as opposition leader, and would become the prime minister's chief of staff after the election. "Your new government will have the life-and-death power to kill NAFTA in an instant. And you can kill it without anyone ever knowing you killed it," Blanchard told Pelletier. "You can kill NAFTA if, the day after the election, Jean Chrétien says that he's hoping to renegotiate it. If he says that, it's dead, because Congress will say they are not going to vote on it until they see the new deal and they'll walk away from it."[2]

Pelletier assured Blanchard that Chrétien was a free-trader and that he did not want to kill NAFTA. But there was substantial unease in Clinton's White House when Chrétien was elected, as many White House advisors were convinced that the new government was determined to insist on renegotiating NAFTA. Clinton's special trade representative, Mickey Kantor, got on the phone to negotiate with

Chrétien's trusted advisor, Eddie Goldenberg. A series of late-night discussions ensued. What emerged was a compromise: there was a side note confirming that water was not part of the original Canada-US Free Trade Agreement (FTA), Canada retained the cultural exemption negotiated in the FTA, and the US retained its right to retaliate.[3] With those agreements, at best defensive and primarily symbolic, Chrétien ratified the NAFTA, reinforcing Brian Mulroney's most significant achievement that had been fought every inch of the way by the Liberal Party only five years before.

It was a significant indicator of Chrétien's foreign policy priorities. These had been illustrated during his first meeting with Clinton at the Asia-Pacific Economic Co-operation Summit in Seattle in mid-November, just two weeks after Chrétien's government was sworn in on 4 November. "After the opening formalities, someone mentioned trade, and Chrétien took off like a hyped-up boxer at the sound of the bell," Blanchard wrote. "Animated, hyper-nervous, talking a mile a minute in his convoluted English, he went on and on about energy policy and water rights and trade matters while Clinton looked dazed."[4] When Clinton asked Chrétien about Bosnia and Haiti, both files in which Mulroney had been deeply engaged, Chrétien was equally nonplussed. That snapshot set the tone for the beginning of Chrétien's mandate: trade would trump diplomacy.

Chrétien's first act had been to name André Ouellet to External Affairs and to change the name to Foreign Affairs and International Trade. This was followed by an innovation that Chrétien was particularly proud of: Team Canada missions that put all of Canada's premiers and as many business leaders as wanted to go on a trade mission. "To an unprecedented degree, Chrétien put his personal enterprise into helping Canadian firms sell their goods and services abroad," observed trade negotiator Gordon Ritchie, who called the Team Canada program "the centrepiece . . . which he personally led with impressive success."[5]

While Ouellet's appointment was a recognition of his seniority, it also served a particular political imperative. The Bloc Québécois chief, Lucien Bouchard, was the leader of the opposition and, as a former ambassador to Paris and a sovereignist eager to show his expertise on international affairs, he could be expected to target the lead-off question on foreign policy in the daily House of Commons Question Periods. Ouellet could respond in French with political skill and nuance; Axworthy could not.

Other than an abiding interest in the 1994 crisis in Haiti – there were thousands of Haitians in Montreal, many of them living in his riding – Ouellet made little impact on Canadian foreign policy, although he presided over a number of significant decisions. The first was the decision to marry trade and foreign affairs, a change which reflected the new emphasis on trade over diplomacy. The second was the 1994 foreign policy review which, after a series of public hearings, produced a three-pillar model for Canadian diplomacy: "the promotion of prosperity and employment," "the protection of our security, within a global environment," and "the projection of Canadian values and culture." It was, in Stephen Clarkson's words, "a process more significant than its product ... genuflecting before the familiar trinity of peace, prosperity and national unity."[6]

THE UNITY IMPERATIVE

Since 1967, a significant aspect of Canada's foreign policy has been driven by the desire to limit the impact of the Quebec independence movement in foreign capitals, and to counter what Ottawa saw as hostile intentions by France towards Canada in its flirtation with the Quebec government and the independence movement.[7]

Relations with France got off on the wrong foot. During a visit by Quebec Premier Jacques Parizeau to Paris in 1995, Canada's ambassador to France, former Conservative cabinet minister Benoît Bouchard, set off a minor diplomatic row when he called the president of the French National Assembly, Philippe Séguin, who was sympathetic to the cause of Quebec independence, "a loose cannon." Chrétien himself did not improve relations when he tossed aside the pro-independentist comments of the Paris mayor and presidential candidate, Jacques Chirac, suggesting that he had as much chance of becoming president as Parizeau did of winning the referendum.[8] While Canada had an amateur diplomat as its ambassador in Paris, Quebec had a professional, veteran Claude Roquet, who had left External Affairs in Ottawa years before because he felt he had little future there as a francophone, joining Quebec's fledgling para-diplomatic service. Roquet proved very effective in mobilizing French political support for Quebec. Chirac had suggested clearly that France would recognize Quebec's independence following a successful referendum, provoking Chrétien's annoyance. To make things worse, Chirac proved Chrétien wrong by winning the presidential election in May 1995, only a few months later.[9]

However, once Chirac became president, Chrétien did not have the luxury of a lingering quarrel. His chief of staff, Jean Pelletier, had become a close friend of Chirac when the two men were mayors, and he set to work reconciling the two men.[10] It was sufficiently successful that, two years after the referendum, Chirac responded to Chrétien's request that he delay the issuing of a stamp commemorating the thirtieth anniversary of President Charles de Gaulle's "Vive le Québec libre" speech. Chirac also called Quebec independence "totally buried in Quebec."[11] In 2002, when Chrétien flew to Paris to meet Chirac to discuss the G-8 Summit in Kananaskis, eight days after the French president's re-election, he was able to deflect questions about Quebec with a joke. "Did we talk about Quebec? Certainly, because we talked about Canada and Quebec is part of it," he quipped.[12] The sense of crisis was a thing of the past.

THE AMERICAN TIGHTROPE

There was a similar adjustment in Chrétien's relationship with Washington. After the awkward beginning, Chrétien responded by appointing his nephew, Raymond Chrétien, as Canada's ambassador to Washington. An experienced career diplomat who had previously been ambassador to Zaire, Mexico and Belgium, he had the advantage of an intimate relationship with the prime minister, which was immediately understood and appreciated in Washington.

Chrétien had campaigned on the theme that he would keep his distance from Washington, which resulted in an odd paradox. He and Clinton hit it off sufficiently that Chrétien would fly to Washington to play golf with Clinton. But, ever mindful of his criticisms of Mulroney's friendship with President George H. W. Bush, the prime minister would sneak into town without letting anyone know of the trip. Perhaps to compensate, Chrétien would periodically take opportunities to underline how different Canada was from the United States. On a visit to Washington, he talked about "our cherished health care system" and his introduction of "one of the toughest gun-control laws in the Western World."[13]

The relationship was a productive one. During the 1995 Quebec referendum, Clinton gave a clear indication that the US, while remaining uninvolved, preferred a united Canada. In 1999, he made a powerful speech at Mont Tremblant in favour of federalism.[14] Chrétien responded, after Clinton's second term was complete, with warm praise for Clinton as "a friend and a statesman of the first rank."[15] That firm president-prime minister relationship ended, first with the election of George W. Bush, and then with September 11 and the war in Iraq.

SOFT POWER

Joseph Nye of Harvard University coined the term "soft power" in 1990,[16] defining it first as "the complex machinery of interdependence" and later as "co-opting people rather than coercing them." It became one of his themes,[17] and was adopted by Lloyd Axworthy as a shorthand for what became the defining theme of his tenure in foreign affairs: human security.

When he succeeded Ouellet in January 1996, Lloyd Axworthy became actively involved in making this the focal point of his foreign policy. Human security is defined in contrast with national security, concentrating on threats to human and communal safety rather than the defence of borders. It was embraced by Axworthy as an overarching concept that included the ban on anti-personnel mines, the establishment of the International Criminal Court, the protection of refugees, women and children in conflict, small arms control, and efforts to stop human trafficking. One of his last acts as foreign minister was to host a conference on children in conflict.

In a number of ways, he was successful, launching the treaty process which resulted in the signing of the landmine treaty, and lobbying effectively for the creation of the International Criminal Court. But his use of soft power had its limitations. Despite his misgivings, he was at the centre of the decision-making that led Canada to participate in the military intervention in Kosovo. Axworthy describes how he and Chrétien reached a compromise on China, "The Prime Minister took a special interest in establishing good ties with the Chinese regime, for he saw China as a major opportunity to advance our trade interests. I, on the other hand, wanted to push on human rights issues," he wrote. "Eventually, we agreed on a policy of direct bilateral engagement. I was given the go-ahead to travel to China, initiate a human rights dialogue and provide legal assistance and training."[18]

It was a deal that held. Chrétien functioned as the political realist, but gave Axworthy the space to operate as an idealist. While there was some awkwardness in the arrangement, it seemed to work effectively for both men. Nevertheless, after almost five years as foreign minister, Axworthy decided to leave politics and he was replaced by someone with a very different set of priorities.

AMERICANS ARE OUR BEST FRIENDS

John Manley, Axworthy's successor, made it clear from the outset that his major priority was to manage the Canada-US relationship. As he put it, soon after he was named to the job, "It's sort of self-evident that the United States is our key bilateral relationship, not by a small margin but by an enormous margin. Managing that relationship has to be at the top of the list."[19]

That relationship was altered with the election of George W. Bush, only two weeks after Manley was sworn in on 17 October 2000. One of the problems, at least on the surface, came from the fact that Ambassador Raymond Chrétien was widely believed to have said that Democratic presidential candidate Al Gore would be better for Canada as president than the Republican Bush. While this might well have been the case, it is not what he said. In an address in Ottawa in May 2000, Chrétien observed that then-Governor Bush was a Texan, instinctively looked towards the south and Mexico, and did not know Canada well. As a result, he said, the Embassy would have more work in making the new White House aware of Canada if Bush won, while Gore was already familiar with Canada. This was interpreted by one reporter (and by Progressive Conservative leader Joe Clark) as an endorsement, by Jean Chrétien's nephew and Canada's ambassador to Washington, of Al Gore. (Others saw it as a sufficiently self-evident observation about the two presidential candidates that they did not report the comment.) However, apocryphal or not, the suggestion that Chrétien had endorsed Gore became a central building block in the argument, developed and reiterated by the *National Post*, that the Chrétiens had offended the Bush Administration even before it was elected.

The strength of Manley's belief in a strong relationship with the United States emerged most vividly after September 11 2001, and the speed and forthrightness with which he responded was striking. "If we weren't committed to our best friend and ally, just what would we be committed to?" he asked.[20] And in a memorable interview with Paul Wells, then with the *National Post*, Manley said that Canada faced "glaring inadequacy" in intelligence gathering, defence and foreign aid capability, and blamed successive federal governments for failing to convince Canadians that spending in those areas was essential. "You can't just sit at the G-8 table, and then, when the bill comes, go to the washroom," Manley said. "If you want to play a role in the world, even as a small member of the G-8, there's a cost to doing that."[21] Manley was given responsibility for security, a responsibility he kept after his brief stint in Foreign Affairs, and succeeded in getting $7 billion for internal security, the equivalent of half of Canada's defence budget.

In fact, Canada moved remarkably quickly to legislate on security matters following the terrorist attacks of September 11. On 15 October 2001, a 170-page anti-terrorism bill was introduced in the the House of Commons, proposing amendments to sixteen pieces of legislation.[22] However, as Joel Sokolsky of the Royal Military College pointed out recently, this has not given Canada much respite from US complaints that we do not spend enough on defence. "Since 9/11, we have spent a greater proportion on domestic security as compared to Defence than the United States has," he said. "We don't get any credit for spending at home. You only get credit for what you do overseas."[23] On Manley's watch, Canada developed a Smart Border Declaration, and sent troops to Afghanistan. However, he did not remain at Foreign Affairs long enough to make a permanent mark.

WE ARE THE WORLD

Bill Graham became minister of foreign affairs with a number of disadvantages. He was a newcomer at a time when the prime minister was most active on foreign policy. Major elements of Canada's relations with the United States had been left with Manley, significantly undermining his authority. His desire for a full foreign policy review had been squelched by the prime minister. And his experience, first as a professor of international law, and then, for seven years, as chair of the Standing Committee on Foreign Affairs and International Trade, militated against his having a limited series of priorities. As a result, during the last period of Chrétien's term in office, he was overshadowed by the prime minister, and it was difficult for him to establish his own identity as foreign minister. Throughout his tenure as minister, Graham tried to express Canada's traditional attempt to support a balanced position on the question of Israel and the Palestinians, but his refusal to express unequivocal support for Israel's right to defend itself infuriated many in the Jewish community, and made Graham a target for bitter criticism.

11 SEPTEMBER AND AFTER

Chrétien was always reluctant to seek attention in the United States, and the terrorist attacks on September 11 did not affect that instinct. Unlike Britain's Tony Blair, whom Chrétien privately referred to as "Tory Blair," Chrétien did not respond well in situations where the public expression of emotion was required. He attended a massive public ceremony of sympathy and solidarity with the US on Parliament Hill in the days after September 11, but delayed traveling to Ground Zero; when he did go, he was accompanied by the other party leaders, as if to insulate himself from any accusation that he was taking political advantage of the tragedy. However, perhaps insensitively, he used an interview to be broadcast on the first anniversary of the attacks to say that the West was arrogant in its dealings with the rest of the world, offending some who interpreted this as another slap at the Americans and the Bush Administration.

Canada responded quickly to the request to send troops to

Afghanistan, but as the United States increased the pressure for military action against Iraq in the fall of 2002, Chrétien held back, insisting on waiting for the report of United Nations weapons inspectors, and proof of the presence of weapons of mass destruction. "A proof is a proof," he said as he emerged from Cabinet in March 2003. "What kind of a proof? It's a proof. A proof is a proof. And when you have a good proof, it's because it's proven."[24] His skepticism proved to be prescient. The prime minister sent out contradictory signals on what Canada would do if there were an invasion of Iraq, and then refused to discipline ministers or MPs who criticized George Bush and the American government, thereby making Graham's attempts to smooth over relations with the Americans, through his warm relationship with US Secretary of State Colin Powell, much more difficult.

In August 2002, Chrétien had announced that he would step down in February 2004. It was widely assumed that his last eighteen months would be a lame duck period in which he would achieve little. But he seemed determined to end his term in office as a more progressive leader than he had been when he began, particularly in the area of foreign policy. Chrétien took even his own officials by surprise when he announced that Canada would double its aid contribution, increasing the aid budget by eight per cent annually, and when he announced that Canada would ratify the Kyoto Accord.

Another area where Chrétien seemed determined to leave a mark was in Africa. His interest first became clear as early as November 1996. During a weekend at the prime ministerial country retreat at Harrington Lake, his attempt to re-read the classic Quebec novel, *Menaud Maître-Draveur*, was continually interrupted as he was drawn, horrified, to the shocking images on television of refugees fleeing violence in Zaire.[25] Chrétien's nephew, Raymond, had been the United Nations' special envoy to the Great Lakes' region in Africa and had attempted to achieve a ceasefire. The novel was abandoned for the telephone; the prime minister's conversations with his nephew soon became a series of discussions with leaders around the world, beginning with South Africa's Nelson Mandela and continuing with calls to Germany, France, Britain, Senegal, Argentina, Chile, and Brazil. The result was that Canada led a short-lived force to Africa, short-lived because the ensuing cease-fire led to thousands of refugees returning home on their own.

Chrétien's action, while laudable, was also a reminder that Canada had a reputation to mend from a previous operation in Africa. In March 1993, soldiers from the Canadian Airborne tortured and killed a Somali teenager, Shidane Arone. The incident, its initial cover-up and the public shock at its ugly reality resulted not only in the disbanding of the Airborne, an elite paratroop batallion, but a Commission of Inquiry which had a traumatic effect on the leadership of the Canadian Forces. It ended careers, and caused sweeping changes in the way the military operates. As the *Irish Times* pointed out, "The abysmal behaviour of Canadian troops over the past three years has left a cloud over [the] armed forces and resulted in the resignation last month of Canada's top commander, Gen. Jean Boyle."[26] The Chrétien intervention was an attempt at redemption.

Chrétien subsequently used his chairmanship of the G-8 in Kananaskis to put Africa on the agenda, and became a strong supporter of the New Partnership for Africa's Development (NEPAD). He used his last year in office to pursue a more activist international agenda, particularly in the area of aid and development. This agenda came as a surprise to many; it was part of the unpredictable quality in a prime minister who presided over a party, a government, and a series of foreign ministers, who included left-wing liberals and conservatives, nationalists and continentalists. The result was an unusual volatility in Canada's relationship with the United States, as Chrétien moved from a position of private intimacy with Clinton to public dissent with Bush, against a background of ever-deepening trade dependence.

The Cost of Cutbacks

When diplomat James Bartleman returned to Ottawa from a foreign posting in the spring of 1994, he found Foreign Affairs to be deeply demoralized and depressed. He cited several reasons: an overloaded foreign policy agenda, an understaffed and underpaid department, political appointments as heads of mission, a crowded and decaying Pearson Building, a salary freeze, and an exodus from the department. "Foreign Affairs remained mired in decades-old jurisdictional disputes with other government departments," he wrote. "No-one knew who was in charge at the top. Leadership at the political level was exercised by a confusing triumvirate of ministers responsible for general affairs, trade and aid, backed up by another layer of ministers. And the real power and often the day-to-day management of foreign-policy issues was shifting from the ministers at Foreign Affairs to the prime minister, increasing an already crushing workload for the officers who had to serve the Privy Council Office as well as their own departments."[27]

In addition, foreign activities were becoming increasingly popular for other departments. As Evan Potter has written: "In an environment where a premium is put on the quick formulation and articulation of policies, it is not altogether surprising that embassies are increasingly bypassed in the communications loop. As one senior External Affairs official has confided, 'foreign offices have become post offices where only the form, rather than the function, of foreign policy survives.'"[28] That was written just over ten years ago, and little has happened to alter Potter's observation.

In the early 1990s, a number of events occurred which had an impact on the management of Foreign Affairs. Demographically speaking, the department suffered an amputation of its most experienced people. Foreign Service personnel were told that they would not serve abroad if they reached the thirty-five-year mark in the department. As a result, a whole generation of people who had joined the department in their early or mid-twenties and were then in their late fifties were brought home, or told they were no longer wanted abroad. At the same time, two complementary trends began to accelerate. First of all, the integration of trade as the central mission of the department began to have an ever greater impact. Secondly, the traditional diplomatic function of reporting on political trends in foreign countries began to be downgraded, transferred to intelligence assessment, and then, finally, transformed into an exclusively intelligence assessment function which was shifted to the Privy Council Office.

All this occurred in a context of cutbacks. As Stephen Clarkson pointed out, the department's budget was cut ten times in the decade following 1988–89, and the cumulative cuts totaled $292 million.[29] When Axworthy became minister of foreign affairs in January 1996, one of his first obligations was to cut the department's budget by 15 per cent, without closing embassies.[30] As Joe Clark pointed out, these fiscal constraints came at a time when the international pressures (and opportunities) facing Canada were increasing, not diminishing.[31] These factors had an impact on management, morale, human resources – and the effectiveness of embassies. All of those elements of the Canadian Foreign Service became significantly worse.

Just how bad only became clear in 2001. The Department of Foreign Affairs and International Trade commissioned the consulting firm, William Mercer, to do a survey of attitudes in the department. It was conducted between June 15 and July 4.[32] Remarkably, 837 of 1,047 foreign service officers replied to the poll, an 80 per cent response rate. The survey's findings are stunning, a grim study in disillusionment. As Mercer summarized it: "While 77 per cent of respondents answered that when they entered the foreign service they viewed it as a lifetime career, only 28 per cent responded that they intend to spend their entire career with the foreign service." Not only were 23 per cent thinking of leaving within a year or at the end of their current posting, another 25 per cent were undecided about their future.

The questionnaire revealed a department that is highly educated (45 per cent have MAs, 15 per cent have professional degrees in law or medicine), multilingual and originally drawn to diplomacy out of a sense of idealism. They had become embittered, deeply demoralized, and suspicious of their superiors. Part of the grievance was money. Foreign Service officers start at $38,000, and promotions are slow. When I wrote about this, I got an e-mail from a Canadian diplomat abroad confirming that, as a lawyer, he had left a practice where he was earning $120,000 a year, to become a Foreign Service officer at $38,000 a year.

The problem was, and remains, deeper than simply money. Spouses have their careers interrupted and disrupted, and diplomats feel they are treated with less respect than their friends in the private sector working abroad, or their public service colleagues in Ottawa. Fewer than 25 per cent of those surveyed felt that promotions or assignments are based on a clear, transparent and defensible process; only 21 per cent are optimistic they can meet their career objectives if they stay with the foreign service.

This was the cream of the crop, traditionally, the best and brightest of Canadian universities, drawn to the elite of the public service and inspired by the pioneers of Canadian diplomacy. They were the best. Six thousand took the foreign service exam, 400 were interviewed, and only sixty were offered jobs each year. Now, they felt overworked, underpaid, neglected and undervalued.

Listen to some of the verbatim comments that William H. Mercer Ltd. collected. "Frankly, the Department has not kept its word since I joined 15 years ago. Callousness is rife, although admittedly some individuals are less hypocritical than others. DFAIT [the Department of Foreign Affairs and International Trade] exists on the English public school model: when in middle management, one is cognizant of the inequities of the system, but plays the game, and claws up, to conveniently forget once in a position of privilege. Just like the old public school 'hazing,': you hated it when you got it, but gladly give it back once you have the chance!"[33]

And another one: "The survey does not even touch on one issue which is central to the morale problem – the frequent rudeness shown by staff, including senior staff, to colleagues and officers/staff of lower rank. Is it too much to ask for a thank you for a job well done: Is it all right for senior staff to grunt at or yell at staff? Why does the DFAIT culture permit open criticism of juniors by seniors? It is rudeness, not salary, which will push me out of DFAIT."[34] And another: "Place spousal employment centre stage. In other words don't just talk about it, actually put some money behind it, create spousal positions at each post, educate 'dinosaur' program managers/ Heads of Mission on how essential (not just 'important') spousal employment is."[35] Someone else struck the same note: "Recognize that foreign service officers live in two-income families. One cannot expect spouses to give up careers and pension because an employee is being posted."[36]

I have been very selective. There are eighty-nine pages of these comments, and many strike the same themes. Low pay, lack of a transparent promotion system, few opportunities for spouses, little sense of recognition or respect; they all recur. The portrait painted is of a bad place to work. And perhaps the most damaging statistic is this. Asked to comment on the statement "My department will take action on the findings of this survey," the answers broke down in the following way. Strongly agree: 1 per cent; agree: 12 per cent, for a total of 13 per cent. Disagree: 50 per cent; strongly disagree 36 per cent, for a total of 86 per cent. It is hard to imagine a clearer statement of collective disenchantment and bitterness.

What can be done to correct the situation? The simplest way, of course, would be to send money. Certainly, that was the recurrent theme in the verbatim responses to the Mercer Survey; answer after answer was simply that. These are people who see their private sector colleagues earning much, much more for what is often similar work. Some of the worst problems were resolved in the last round of salary negotiations. But many of the systemic problems persist.

CONCLUSION

When Paul Martin was sworn in as prime minister on 12 December 2003, Bill Graham was one of the only ministers to retain his portfolio. Suddenly, he became a senior minister in a cabinet full of newcomers. While he still had a prime minister who was deeply interested in foreign affairs, he was able to embark on the foreign policy review that Chrétien had limited to a public consultation. Graham's satisfaction was short-lived; in the Cabinet shuffle that followed the 28 June election, he was shifted to National Defence.

The Speech from the Throne on 2 February 2004 made it clear that, while there would be a change of emphasis and an explicit effort to improve Canada-US relations, many of Chrétien's initiatives would remain: the increase in aid contributions, and the desire to address the HIV/AIDS crisis in Africa. The ambiguity of Chrétien's policy towards the US ballistic missile defence, which laid the groundwork for Canadian participation while insisting on opposition to the weaponization of space, continued.

While Martin had implied that Canada might have taken a different position on the war in Iraq had he been prime minister, as the US experience turned sour he felt obliged to say that he supported the decision not to have Canada participate in the war.

But if the substance was similar, Martin seemed to bring a different, more conciliatory tone to his international relations. When he met George W. Bush at Monterrey and visited him later in the White House, the chemistry between the two leaders was positive. Martin met the Dalai Lama in Ottawa, which Chrétien had refused to do. Martin promised to harness the idealism of young Canadians by creating a Canada Corps, an initiative which seemed improvised at first, but expressed Martin's desire to engage Canadians in the world.

Jean Chrétien had proved, in foreign affairs as in so many other things, to be shrewd, sometimes unpredictable, and consistently underestimated. When he became prime minister, he seemed uncertain and unsure of himself on the foreign stage, but he became increasingly comfortable. The decisions he made in his last sixteen months in office – committing Canada to double its foreign aid, ratifying the Kyoto Accord, making Africa a central part of the G-8 Agenda in Kananaskis, refusing to have Canada participate in the Iraq War – were sometimes surprising and seemed almost willful. However, unlike many of his Cabinet appointments, those decisions survived the transition to the new Martin government.

Paul Martin came to office saying that he wanted to emphasize Canada's international role. He is the son of a former secretary of state for external affairs, and a former high commissioner to London. As a young man, he wanted to work in the developing world, and did work for the one of the institutions that laid the ground work for the European Union. As finance minister, he was active in the World Bank and the International Monetary Fund, and helped create the G-20.

Through much of his campaign for the leadership of the Liberal Party, he hinted – and his supporters said – that he would be doing things differently from the way Chrétien did. Certainly, he was comfortable in an international setting, sometimes more at ease with the complexities of international organizations than with the gritty realities of domestic politics. Martin took some initial steps to indicate that Canada was prepared to help the US deal with some of its international problems, announcing that Canada will spend $300 million in Iraq and $180 million in Haiti over the next two years. At the same time, in his first speech after the 28 June election, he warned the US that, if the border is not opened soon to Canadian beef, a continental cattle industry will unravel and Canada will create its own production facilities and compete with US beef in Asian markets.

Despite the change in tone, most of Chrétien's innovations prevailed. Bill Graham was moved to Defence and Pierre Pettigrew succeeded him as Foreign Affairs Minister, but there was little indication that this was a sign of a shift in policy. Rather, as was the case in 1993, Martin was faced with the challenge of a powerful contingent of 54 Bloc Québécois MPs, and the need to display a strong roster of Quebec ministers in powerful positions. In his first few months in office, continuity was more noticeable than rupture. But if Martin is serious in his desire to re-establish Canada's place in the world, he will have to address some of the systemic problems in Canadian diplomacy, defence and development policy.

NOTES

1 Conversations with various Canada-watchers on election night in Washington.
2 James Blanchard, *Behind the Embassy Door: Canada, Clinton and Quebec* (Toronto: McClelland and Stewart), 1998, 81.
3 Blanchard, 94; Gordon Ritchie, *Wrestling With the Elephant: The Inside Story of the Canada-US Trade Wars* (Toronto: Macfarlane Walter & Ross, 1997), 193.
4 Blanchard, 99
5 Ritchie, 193.
6 Stephen Clarkson, *Uncle Sam and Us: Globalization, Neoconservatism and the Canadian State* (Toronto: University of Toronto Press, 2002), 390.
7 See Eldon Black, *Direct Intervention: Canada-France Relations 1967–1974* (Ottawa: Carleton University Press, 1996), and J.F. Bosher, *The Gaullist Attack on Canada, 1967–1997* (Montreal and Kingston: McGill-Queen's University Press, 1999).
8 Luc Bernier, *De Paris à Washington: la politique internationale du Québec* (Sainte-Foy: Presses de l'Université du Québec, 1996), 69.
9 "La France devrait être sans aucun doute au premier rang de ceux qui diraitent au Québec que nous marchons avec luis. Si [le référendum] est positif, je pense qu'un certain nombre de pays notamment francophones, dont la France, devraient tout naturellement reconnaître la réalité d'une décision populaire, une décision qui est l'expression d'une souveraineté populaire." Cité par Pierre Duchesne, *Le Régent, Jacques Parizeau Tome III* (Montreal: Québec-Amérique, 2004), 345.
10 Bastien, 345.
11 Ibid., 346.
12 Louis-Bernard Robitaille, "Petit succès personnel pour Jean Chrétien à Paris," *La Presse*, 14 mai, 2002.
13 *Globe and Mail*, 10 April 1997.

14 Graham Fraser, "In Praise of Ambiguity," *Policy Options* (January-February 2000), 21–26.
15 Jean Chrétien, Address to Duke University, 3 December 2000.
16 Joseph S. Nye, Jr., "The Misleading Metaphor of Decline," *The Atlantic*, 265, 3 (March 1990), 86–95.
17 "Why Military Power is No Longer Enough," *Observer Worldview*, 31 March 2002; "The Decline of American Soft Power," *Foreign Affairs*, 83, 3 (May/June 2004).
18 Lloyd Axworthy, *Navigating a New World: Canada's Global Future* (Toronto: Knopf Canada, 2002), 57.
19 Allan Thompson, "Canada's New Face," *Toronto Star*, 20 January 2001.
20 *Time*, 31 December 2001–7 January 2002.
21 Paul Wells, "'We Don't Pull Our Weight': Manley," *National Post*, 5 October 2001.
22 For a rigorous dissection and criticism of the legislation as excessive, see Ronald J. Daniels, Patrick Macklem and Kent Roach, eds., *The Security of Freedom: Essays on Canada's Anti-Terrorism Bill* (Toronto: University of Toronto Press, 2001).
23 Remarks, "North American Integration: Migration, Trade and Security," a conference organized by the Institute for Research on Public Policy, 1 April 2004.
24 CBC News, 6 September 2002; "PM Wants Proof before Backing Attack on Iraq," http://www.cbc.ca/stories/2002/09/05/iraq_pm020905.
25 Jeff Sallot, "Refugees' Images Haunted Chrétien; PM's weekend spent on phone," *The Globe and Mail*, 14 November 1996.
26 Katherine Wilton, "Canadian Soldiers Hope to Redeem Reputation in Zaire," *Irish Times*, 18 November 1996.
27 James Bartleman, *On Six Continents: A Life in Canada's Foreign Service, 1966–2002* (Toronto: McClelland and Stewart, 2004), 233.
28 "A Question of Relevance: Canada's Foreign Policy and Foreign Service in the 1990s," in Christopher J. Maule and Fen Osler Hampson and, eds, *Global Jeopardy: Canada Among Nations 1993–94* (Ottawa: Carleton University Press, 1993), 38.
29 Clarkson, 393.
30 Axworthy, 43.
31 Joe Clark, "The First International Country," *International Journal*, LII, 4 (Autumn 1997), 545.
32 William H. Mercer Ltd., *Foreign Service Retention Survey Report on Findings* (Department of Foreign Affairs and International Trade, 26 July 2001).
33 Ibid., Appendix 2: Verbatim Comments, 6.
34 Ibid.
35 Ibid., 8.
36 Ibid., 51.

PROSPECTS

12 The Communications Revolution and Canadian Foreign Policy

CHRISTOPHER WADDELL

It is easy to find consensus that the ability to communicate instantly is changing the world dramatically, but there is less agreement in the foreign policy community in Canada on how to respond to those changes. Some institutions such as NGOs both in Canada and around the world have jumped on the bandwagon, adapting their activities to exploit the advantages the Internet offers. But the Department of Foreign Affairs has been slow to change. A series of events in 2003 involving a Canadian deported from the United States and tortured in a Syrian jail demonstrated both the department's shortcomings in using the new communications technologies and the potential benefits Canada could derive from an aggressive approach that takes advantage of the Internet to promote Canadian interests worldwide.

In the case of Syrian-born Canadian Maher Arar, the simplest of plans using the power of instant communications forced the Canadian government to retreat and do what it had never intended doing. A chronology of facts, checked and re-checked for accuracy and then widely distributed in the summer of 2003, ultimately pushed Prime Minister Paul Martin and his senior officials into a corner. They finally concluded they could only escape by calling a public inquiry into how Mr Arar ended up being held and tortured in a Syrian jail for a year.

Mr Arar's supporters decided in June 2003 that, if they wanted to apply pressure on the Canadian government to be more aggressive in demanding that Syria release him and return him to Canada, they needed a chronology of what had happened to him. He had been pulled aside at New York's John F. Kennedy airport the previous September 26 upon landing from Zurich on his way to Montreal. Held in custody with no opportunity to speak to anyone until allowed a two-minute phone call on October 2, Mr Arar was shipped to Jordan and then Syria, via Washington, on October 9. That began almost a year of solitary confinement, beatings and torture in prison cells, designed to force him to admit that he had links with al Qaeda and international terrorism. In October 2003 Mr Arar was suddenly released and returned to Canada.

He began a series of selected media appearances telling his remarkable story and demanding to know why the Canadian government had allowed a Canadian citizen to be treated in this fashion. Answers were not available from the Department of Foreign Affairs, a fact Mr Arar regularly noted in interviews. He was forthcoming about all his experiences and kept asking why the government of Canada was not equally open in describing its activities in his case. The goal was to force the Liberal government of first Jean Chrétien and then Paul Martin to explain Canada's role in Mr Arar's arrest and deportation to Syria by the United States and to ensure this would never happen again to other Canadian citizens.

The federal government responded by trying to explain away Mr Arar's ordeal and his statements about ill-treatment. It didn't work. Canadians listened and accepted his explanation of events, and concluded that the Department of Foreign Affairs had not done enough to help Mr Arar while he was in prison. Foreign Affairs Minister Bill Graham even had to defend Canada's decision not to recall its ambassador to Syria over the case. At another point, Mr Graham admitted that his officials had provided him with incorrect information. Documents released in early January 2004 demonstrated that Canadian officials gave Prime Minister Jean Chrétien and other cabinet ministers incorrect or incomplete information about the government's actions in the case between the time Mr Arar was arrested in New York in late September 2003 and his deportation two weeks later.[1] In addition, the Canadian government has never clearly explained what information the Royal Canadian Mounted Police and other Canadian police, security and intelligence agencies provided to United States authorities leading to Mr Arar's arrest. Canadian authorities also engaged in a systematic campaign of leaking information perceived to be damaging to Mr Arar. The Royal Canadian Mounted Police even raided a journalist's home and her *Ottawa Citizen* office in a clumsy attempt, apparently, to determine the source of a leaked document about the Arar case. Finally, on January 28, 2004, after consistent and growing public pressure, Prime Minister Martin called a public inquiry.

The straightforward, factual Arar chronology released to the media and the public had triumphed over all attempts to discredit it and him. The document laid out the dates and facts of the case with no hyperbole, no editorializing and no pleading of his case. It was just the facts, double and triple checked before the chronology was released. Any errors or mistakes would have undermined the credibility of Mr Arar and his supporters and completely undercut his demands for a public inquiry. Canadians were generally skeptical about Mr Arar and the claims by his wife, Monia Mazigh, that he was innocent. The case was so complicated that many Canadians couldn't follow its many twists and turns. There was also a sense that he would not have been stopped if there were not something suspicious about his activities. All that created potential for confusion and doubts about his case. The chronology challenged those doubts directly. It was distributed widely to the media and made available on Amnesty International Canada's web site to anyone who wanted it.[2] Other news organizations created their own chronologies based on the Arar document.

The effectiveness of the chronology is a lesson in the power of widely distributed and easily available facts and straightforward information. Journalists used it to counter evasive responses from government officials about what happened and when it happened, and to undercut government leaks designed to damage Mr Arar's credibility. The reporters would repeat the dates and events from the chronology to counter assertions from authorities trying to "leak" information that Mr Arar was involved in questionable activities at specific times. At the same time, Amnesty International Canada used its urgent action network to call on supporters across the country to write to the federal government in support of Mr Arar.

The easy availability of a detailed, factual chronology built credibility for Mr Arar's case. It was one example of how the rapid and widespread distribution of information by e-mail and on the Internet confronted and ultimately undermined attempts to challenge Mr Arar's story about what happened to him. This occurred at the same time as the Canadian government faced pressure about the treatment of other Canadians held in foreign countries. The relatives of Canadian William Sampson claimed he was being tortured while being held in a Saudi jail on questionable charges related to a bombing, and they accused Canadian officials of not working hard enough to secure his release. Canadian photojournalist Zarah Kazemi was murdered in an Iranian prison, with human rights groups demanding that the Canadian government apply pressure on Iran to force it to prosecute those responsible.

Collectively, the Canadian government's response to these events revealed major questions about the accuracy of the information the government used in reaching decisions on the cases. Non-governmental organizations and other activist groups using e-mail and the Internet provided Canadians with accurate and specific details about the conditions faced by Canadian prisoners in each of these cases, while only vague statements that did not confirm the use of torture came from the Canadian government and its Department of Foreign Affairs. Whether government officials didn't know or wouldn't say what was happening in each of these cases, it didn't matter. The Canadian government appeared to have no information about these cases. Others were willing to fill that void and quickly gained credibility as authoritative spokespeople on the issues at the expense of the Department of Foreign Affairs.

It was a perfect example of the failings of traditional diplomatic caution in commenting on issues when faced with twenty-first century high-speed communications. NGOs now routinely gather and distribute information quickly and globally. This allows them to compete with governments in Canada for the attention of the media and public on the substance and facts of international as well as domestic issues and individual cases. As participants noted at a 2003 conference on how the Internet is changing diplomacy, organized by the Washington-based Aspen Institute, it is now much more difficult and in some circumstances impossible, for governments to control and manipulate information for their own benefit.[3]

In the cases of these three Canadian citizens, the Department of Foreign Affairs paid a serious price in diminished public credibility for not understanding how much its own diplomatic world had changed. There is nothing new or startling about e-mail and the Internet changing diplomacy and changing the world as well. What is surprising is how slowly diplomats in Canada and other countries have responded to those changes and the challenges that flow from them. The Aspen Institute conference echoed what others have noted. Information technologies are a driving force that is changing world affairs by allowing a wide variety of other groups into debates, sometimes using factual information but also creating opportunities for malicious attacks with computer viruses or disinformation campaigns.

The ability to gather and spread news and information almost instantaneously gives a platform to everyone from NGOs to protestors to groups of exiles to put forward their views on both international and domestic issues and build constituencies supporting those views.[4] They use the Internet to organize, respond to government statements and mobilize public opinion. It is inexpensive and easy for all these groups to participate and to bypass such information gatekeepers of the past as diplomats, the media and governments and multinational corporations. The Aspen study argued that "powers that were once the monopoly of nation-states – participation in international politics, control of transnational communications, credibility as sources of accurate information – are now being exercised by a much wider array of players."[5] It concludes the result is the replacement of *realpolitik* with what it calls *netpolitik* and describes it as using the Internet's power as a communications tool to apply moral legitimacy to influence and shape cultural identity, public perceptions and the values of a society.[6]

The Arar and related cases demonstrated how a new diplomatic world is emerging in which both competing forces and those working in concert on issues will increasingly employ the Internet to advance their causes. Everyone from NGOs promoting human rights to organizations advocating radical overthrow of governments and societies will be on the Internet, all competing for public attention and legitimacy. In that world, there is an opportunity for Canada and Canadian diplomacy to build on the country's diplomatic history, international reputation and multicultural and multiethnic society to carve out a new international role for Canada suitable for the twenty-first century by using the communications technologies that will dominate the globe. That requires leadership and new openness on foreign policy within all levels in the Department of Foreign Affairs. A new approach must focus on promoting Canada's interest in such issues as human rights, democratic development and peace building, by replacing old methods with bold and imaginative use of Internet communications to bring Canada's moral legitimacy on these issues directly to a worldwide audience. It is a strategy advocated by a former deputy minister, Gordon Smith, in 1999.[7] In the five years since his proposal, the world of diplomacy has changed dramatically while the department has not.

There is a lot of catching up to do because the Canadian government and other governments have fallen far behind in exploiting the advantages of the Internet. NGOs have used it for almost two decades, at first mostly to recruit members and build support for their causes. As Craig Warkentin has noted in his examination of NGOs and the Internet, that initial involvement had six objectives for NGOs: improving internal communications, shaping public perceptions, providing greater member services, disseminating information, encouraging political participation and promoting innovative ideas.[8]

Greenpeace was one of the first to understand the power of the Internet. It has used it since the mid-1980s as a focal point for members and prospective members and to speak directly to the public, circumventing the media. That effort has become more sophisticated as technology has improved with web cameras, and the ability to stream audio and video and deliver a point of view instantly from almost anywhere on the planet to the homes and workplaces of millions of people around the world. It can provide information and analysis, but for groups like Greenpeace, the Internet is most important as an advocacy device to build coalitions in support of its policies.

NGOs also take advantage of the fact that the Internet has increasingly become an interactive tool. NGOs can communicate with their members, solicit opinions and forward their views to governments or other players involved in policy debates or confrontations over specific issues. Those NGO policies can also be quickly modified or changed in response to events, based on polling members or other direct communications that collect members' instant reaction to changing developments on an issue. This was a key reason for the ultimate success of the campaigners who killed the proposal to create a Multilateral Agreement on Investment (MAI). What took weeks or months can now be done in hours, and the results tabulated and used to promote the NGO's interests and policy positions or to organize letter-writing campaigns or demonstrations. Governments have been slower to take advantage of the Internet's ability to link people and groups instantly and obtain feedback. Their attempts have been sporadic, lacking the consistent approach of NGOs and usually not resulting in quick changes in policy direction.

NGOs also use the Internet very successfully to send timely material supporting their points of view to more traditional channels: newspapers, radio and even television. An example is OneWorld, an online network that promotes sustainable development and human rights largely through its massive web site, www.oneworld.net, with links to more than 700 other NGOs. OneWorld circulates audio and video interviews, stories, and images worldwide using the Internet. The material can be downloaded and distributed or broadcast by local and independent radio stations, newspapers, and magazines. In this case, the speed of the Internet facilitates the widespread distribution of NGO points of view through more traditional media, reaching those who have no Internet connection.

The Internet has become the central tool for organizing widespread international mobilization and demonstrations against perceived injustices and policy proposals from governments and international economic institutions. Over the last decade there have been many examples. One of the first was the sudden emergence of the Zapatista movement in Chiapas, Mexico in response to the North American Free Trade Agreement (NAFTA) in 1994. Even with no direct link to the Internet from Mexico's southern jungles, information passed from Chiapas to those outside Mexico was then immediately distributed over the Internet. It created an international audience waiting for each new development in Chiapas even without the media present on the ground. The ability to spread information immediately was the basis for the international movement that gave wide attention to the Zapatista cause, forcing the Mexican government to negotiate rather than use military force against the rebel group.[9]

Another example of the effective use of modern communications is the grassroots opposition against the Multilateral Agreement on Investment in the late 1990s. Instant communications, and the ability to share information and analysis immediately and to distribute portions of drafts of the agreement's text among different groups of opponents around the world, built a powerful and vocal coalition against an agreement negotiated out of the media spotlight by trade experts. At the outset, most governments considered the MAI to be too arcane for the public to notice. By the end of the campaign, the NGOs had succeeded in killing the agreement. The anti-globalization movement and related international protests that began in Seattle in 1999 at the World Trade Organization meetings were also a product of the Internet and instant communications.

Building international coalitions and circumventing the media and other institutions for worldwide protests is one way of using web-based communications successfully, but just as important has been the use of the Internet and e-mail by NGOs in building coalitions within Canada to press the Canadian government to change its position on international issues.

One of the best examples of the power of global communications was the 1990s campaign to push Canada to support East Timor, led in Canada by the East Timor Alert Network (ETAN). "We were effective with policy makers and we were effective at raising public awareness but the issue wouldn't have passed the Tim Hortons test," concludes Kerry Pither, the key ETAN organizer who also played a major role in building support for Mahar Arar. "If we walked in to Tim Hortons and said, 'What do people think about East Timor?' it would be unlikely anyone would know what we were talking about."

But ETAN persuaded the Canadian government that Canadians cared and that was all it needed to do. The visibility that the East Timor issue ultimately acquired among the media and political class in Canada almost certainly played a role in Canada's decision to send troops to East Timor as part of a UN force that supervised a referendum on independence, even though sending Canadian peacekeepers risked alienating Indonesia and undermining Canada's economic interests there. Only after East Timor's independence did ETAN discover how successful it had been. ETAN used the Access to Information Act to request all government documents relating to Canada's position on East Timor. The federal government ultimately released boxes of material that demonstrated ETAN's success. "The documents revealed that we were much more effective than we knew at the time. Memos warned about what ETAN would do if information about military sales to Indonesia became public," noted Ms Pither. "The minutes of a meeting between [President] Suharto [of Indonesia] and then Foreign Affairs Minister Lloyd Axworthy revealed we were the first item on the agenda – Suharto actually opened the meeting by threatening to cancel his 1997 trip to Canada unless the Canadian government could rein in ETAN."

That response from the Indonesian government was a direct result of the effectiveness of the global information network linking supporters of East Timor around the world. At the centre was the East Timor Action Network in the United States. It had the financial support of philanthropic foundations, and used that money to hire full-time staff to build and administer a web presence and e-mail lists that linked East Timor supporters around the world. The e-mail and web links created an international community of East Timor activists, with each pressing his or her government to take a stand in favour of independence for the country. The activists never met in person, but shared information daily and worked tirelessly and collectively towards a common goal. Their success came from the skilful use of their instant electronic information exchange. It allowed the whole network to:

- *Obtain the latest news.* For much of the decade before independence, East Timor was a closed society under strict Indonesian military control. Almost no news of what was happening inside the country emerged to the rest of the world. The network distributed news on a daily basis to supporters around the world. That included both the infrequent media reports that appeared from or about East Timor and information smuggled out of the country. Everyone received the same information at the same time. Supporters of the cause in each country exchanged ideas and reactions on a daily basis with everyone else in the network by highlighting how campaigns inside each country used the information they received.
- *Apply pressure to government.* Ideas were shared instantly so that all supporters had information and passed it on to their domestic media, often before their own governments knew what was happening. ETAN distributed news to its network of supporters within Canada, and encouraged them to write and fax the Canadian government and the foreign affairs minister, expressing concern and calling on Canada to speak out whenever a new development

occurred in East Timor. That campaign contained potential risks to the group's credibility if incorrect information distributed to supporters and the media could be quickly discredited by government. So ETAN was careful to ensure accuracy in everything it said. That was crucial in establishing and maintaining credibility.

- *Maintain morale.* Sharing information and ideas daily with an international network boosted the morale of those promoting the East Timor cause. They were part of a collective experience, not just individuals in Canada or elsewhere fighting a lonely battle for a far-off land. They knew that their actions would be supported by similar actions in other countries. The network also offered limited support to independence activists within East Timor because they knew they had the backing of an international movement. For much of the 1990s, though, there was very little information entering the country. Indonesia had effectively sealed it off from the rest of the world, making communications sporadic with the international network of supporters.
- *Strategy and tactics.* The network's members traded the details of specific tactics that did and did not work in individual countries as the organization tried to apply pressure on governments to support independence for East Timor. For instance, strategies on how to organize a large protest against a Suharto visit to Germany were shared with ETAN. It used the same approaches to organize successful demonstrations against Suharto's visit to Canada for the APEC conference in 1997.
- *Build trust.* The personal connections made over the network made it easy for activists around the world to work together when they arrived in East Timor to assist in preparations for the referendum. They already knew each other from their years of almost daily e-mail communications. That built instant trust among them and with the East Timorese working for independence. As a result, they believe that they were collectively more effective on the ground than a group of unknown outsiders simply arriving on the scene to offer help.

Although ETAN disbanded in Canada by the time of East Timor's independence in 2002, the U.S. group maintains the international network, and serves as unofficial watchdog over the actions of the World Bank and other development organizations on the ground in East Timor.

Building and successfully operating a co-ordinated international campaign to force change upon governments isn't the only way that NGOs are using new communications technologies to challenge and on occasion undermine traditional diplomacy. Internet technologies are also being used as early warning tools to aid in conflict prevention through monitoring activities within a country that might help predict everything from the impending failures of states to the potential for genocide.

In the Maher Arar case, the simple facts contained in the chronology completely undercut evasive responses from an ill-prepared government unable or unwilling to release whatever factual information it had about the case. It also showed how NGOs use the Internet, e-mail and instant communications to embarrass governments and diplomats. At issue were the claims of Mr Arar's supporters that he was being tortured while in prison and the conflicting statements from the Canadian government that it had no evidence about torture, despite several visits to Mr Arar from Canadian consular officials in Syria during the year he was in detention.

In mid-summer 2003, a report from a London-based organization that publicizes information on human rights violations, the Syrian Human Rights Committee, mentioned the Arar case and stated he was being tortured in prison. The committee based its report on information from dissidents within the country. Mr Arar's supporters read about the reference to him in the report and found the document on the Internet. They then discovered that the United States State Department considered the Syrian Human Rights Committee to be a reputable voice on torture in Syria. An e-mail request to the editor of the Committee's publication quickly produced a more detailed letter that described Mr Arar's torture in Syria. Mr Arar's wife, Ms Mazigh, released the letter at a widely covered news conference in Ottawa in early August to support the campaign fro Mr Arar's release. "So we were able to go public and say he's been tortured," said Ms Pither. "We have confirmation he has been tortured from the Syrian Human Rights Committee. The description of the torture is consistent with what the U.S. State Department says happens [in Syria] and by the way the source that says he's been tortured is used by the U.S. State Department." This all ran counter to the statements of the Department of Foreign Affairs that it did not have evidence of torture in the Arar case.

Mr Arar's supporters did not use the Internet effectively over the winter of 2003–2004, even though some of them were veterans of the successful ETAN campaign. They did not assemble a web-based campaign to press the Canadian government to explain what happened to him and what role Canadian officials had played in his arrest and transfer to Syria. Amnesty International Canada issued an urgent action alert asking its members to write the federal government to press for an inquiry. Beyond that, support for an inquiry built slowly but spontaneously among Canadians. It was not enough, though, to change the opposition of first the Chrétien and then the Martin government to such an inquiry.

By mid-January 2004, Mr Arar's supporters concluded that their last hope was to launch a web-based pressure campaign to demand an inquiry. They created a web site that included Mr Arar's proposed draft terms of reference for an inquiry. It requested that all supporters write to their local member of parliament and the prime minister, calling for a public inquiry under the terms proposed by Mr Arar's supporters. While NGOs rely on e-mail for their own internal communications and communications with members, they continue to believe that e-mails can be too easily ignored and so are not as effective as a tool to force change on governments. Pressure campaigns are often supported by web sites that allow visitors to send a fax to government simply by clicking a button on the web page; NGOs believe this strategy has more impact with the recipients.

The Arar web site was completed at 2 am on January 28, to go live on line later that morning after a news conference by his supporters to announce the site and a renewed push for an inquiry. Then, at 8 am, federal government officials told Mr Arar's supporters that an inquiry would be announced that morning. The site had to be rebuilt. The government's decision was not directly related to the threat of a web campaign from Mr Arar's supporters, but rather reflected the rising public criticism of government intransigence that had been growing for weeks and took on new life after the RCMP raid on the home and office of the *Ottawa Citizen* reporter.

While the Department of Foreign Affairs seemed unable to match the skill of NGOs in using the Internet, others in the federal government were very conscious of the potential use of the Internet to mobilize public support for Mr Arar's demands. The night before the planned news conference and unveiling of their web site, a radio reporter called Arar supporters about 11 pm to ask about the web site. He had just been faxed all its pages by an official in the federal government.

In fact, the site was live that evening for only a few minutes to check the operation of the domain name. It was then pulled down. In that few minutes, the federal government copied its contents. Perhaps it was just a chance discovery but it is more likely that Canada's electronic eavesdroppers, the Communications Security Establishment, were routinely sweeping the Internet for Arar-related material and discovered the site. They then passed on its contents to others in the federal government.

Unlike the diplomatic officials, the reaction of Canadian security and intelligence agencies demonstrates that they are well aware of the potential of the Internet to organize protests against government and in support of those making demands for changes to government policies. Their discovery of the Arar web site probably shows the degree to which they are constantly searching the Internet for information, looking beyond the traditional intelligence sources to the huge volumes of material on the wide-open Internet.

As the Arar and East Timor cases demonstrate, the Department of Foreign Affairs was outmaneuvered in its limited use of the Internet, but it has not been completely inactive in modernizing its communications technologies. Canada was one of the first countries to introduce electronic communications for Foreign Affairs officials through secure interactive desktop networks, well before many other foreign ministries, including the U.S. State Department.

Almost all communications between Ottawa and its posts and diplomats around the world rely on the same e-mail system used by millions of Canadians. These e-mails are neither marked nor considered confidential. The department maintains a network to encrypt and transmit information between embassies, consulates and Ottawa, but it is only very rarely used. Employees see it as too cumbersome and complicated. E-mail is faster and easier. Only messages on issues such as bargaining positions in trade negotiations and some consular matters (to protect the privacy of those seeking government assistance) remain confidential. Employees still are shown classified and confidential documents that are usually read and immediately returned but these most often involve intercepted communications, information provided by another government or material from confidential debriefings. Virtually everything else is sent as simple, unencrypted e-mail.

The communications revolution has reverberated through the department. While formal memoranda are still written on issues where it is important to maintain a permanent record of a decision, much of the rest of what happens is recorded only by e-mail. It is then up to individuals to devise their own approaches to message storage, deletion and archival retrieval. The situation is just as chaotic across government departments dealing with international issues. There is no guarantee of compatibility and ability to share information between computer programs used by Foreign Affairs, the Canadian International Development Agency and the Department of National Defence.

Other countries have made similar changes in diplomatic communications. Nabil Fahmy, Egyptian ambassador to the United States, told the Aspen Institute conference that four-fifths of his communications are now sent unencrypted over the Internet. He only sends confidentially his opinion on issues and on opinions he solicits.[10] The switch to non-secure e-mail has been a mixed blessing for Canada's Department of Foreign Affairs. Anyone in the department or at any post can now communicate quickly and confidentially to anyone else, with the positive benefit of breaking down the diplomatic hierarchy. Anecdotally, it appears most e-mail is answered more promptly than traditional mail, as the natural response to seeing a new message on the screen is to reply right away. It has also changed how information is shared. The groups of people knowledgeable about individual issues may also be larger, reflecting the ease of adding names to e-mail lists. Those groups may also be more irregular because there is no guarantee of consistent distribution lists for e-mail messages.

Despite these shortcomings, a system is in place for the easy and instant transmission of information between Ottawa and missions abroad, and only a miniscule amount of that communication is classified. As Evan Potter has noted, by 1999–2000 Foreign Affairs was spending 7.4 per cent of its budget on informatics, but virtually all of that was for internal communications.[11] Ignored in all this were Canada's communications with the rest of the world, just as that was taking on increasing international prominence and communications were becoming cheaper and easier.

The communications system can be the groundwork for a wider, more dynamic and creative approach by many people in the Department of Foreign Affairs to diplomacy and representing Canada and Canada's interests both to Canadians and to people around the world. Critical to that transformation is the Department's presence on the Internet. The original Foreign Affairs web site was designed from a commercially available template and looked curiously like the site for the now defunct Canadian Airlines. It appears that both were built from the same web site design kit. The old Foreign Affairs site has been replaced by one containing a wide variety of information that can be found without extensive searching skills. Within the overall site, there are more specific sites such as the Canada International gateway[12] and the Canada and the World section, breaking down the world into regional sites each of which offers information about the region, trade, diplomacy and Canadian activities.

Yet there are virtually no standards on how the Department's web sites are used or what material they must contain. Most Canadian embassies and high commissions and some consulates maintain their own separate web sites. Employees at each location decide what goes on the site, how often the site is updated, and how the site is used. It amounts to every post for itself. The department began only last year to enforce a degree of uniformity on its web sites by ensuring that information was in both official languages and that each site used common government of Canada identification.

There are small missions with large web sites and large missions with small web sites. Excellent sites, in locations where a staff member is keen on the Internet, contain a great deal of information that is updated regularly. That's the sign of an active site that attracts repeat visitors to view regularly refreshed content. If the web site administrator at the post is transferred to another country and replaced by someone who has limited or no knowledge, interest or experience in web work, the site quickly becomes a cyber equivalent of a ghost town, filled with old and outdated information. Web readers quickly notice that and stop visiting the site.

There is a similar lack of consistency and common standards applied to regional sites in the Canada and the World section of the department's overall site. While there is an Internet governance committee within the department (and a committee that determines what appears on the main Foreign Affairs page that pops up right after the introductory English/French selection page), the regional assistant deputy ministers have great autonomy over their sites. Those from the pre-electronic era are generally less enthusiastic about the potential of the Internet. Their sites reflect that. Nor does the department have detailed records of who visits its sites and why. While it can determine how many hits each site receives and break that down between those originating in Canada and outside the country, not much more is known about site usage.

As with internal departmental communications, the Foreign Affairs presence on the web can be a building block for something much more significant. It exists in an Internet world in which almost anything can be found by plugging words into a search engine. At the same time, anyone can put anything on the Internet and code it correctly for search engines to find. There is no accurate method to assess or categorize that information or its source. There is no way to determine who is reliable and who isn't, to figure out which interests or organizations finance web sites that contain information and promote points of view, to weed out propaganda and lies, to sort truth from fiction and opinion from fact.

Media outlets have filled some of that void with their presence on the Internet. Individual news organizations use their names to extend whatever credibility they have in their main medium, whether it is print, television or radio, to their web operations. The same is true for NGOs and corporations. The name or brand of the web site is critical for readers in assessing the truth and accuracy of the material on that site.

As the Aspen Institute suggests, the Internet provides researchers with an almost infinite amount of information on almost any subject or issue, but none of the tools required to assess the validity or accuracy of that information. The Institute's conference report suggests what is required are new editorial intermediaries that can "select important information, interpret it and warrant what is trustworthy and what is not."[13]

Canada has the reputation, experience and international credibility to play that role. It can become an internationally recognized source for the world of credible information about the world. The Department of Foreign Affairs has the communications systems and some of the people in place to do that. But more is required.

Potter notes that unlike many nations, Canada has no well-marketed international focal point either on the Internet, in television or as he sees as most important, short-wave radio broadcasting. He is critical of Canada's failure to present a modern image to the world that reflects the country and its views on international issues. He argues persuasively that "there is an urgent need to create a vibrant public democracy, using all the communications and technological tools at Ottawa's disposal, both to defend Canada's sovereignty and to promote its values and economic development. A renewed international information strategy, one that emphasized international broadcasting, can play a pivotal role in projecting an informed sophisticated image of Canadian views and concerns in a knowledge-based environment."[14]

Such an approach will allow Canada only to catch up with what other nations are doing. With the current pace of change in communications, that will not be sufficient. It is important to leap ahead of where others now are. To move to the forefront, the public democracy advocated by Potter must be built around the Internet, and radio and television broadcasting incorporated within a broader web presence for Canada. Start by reorganizing the web sites and make available as much as possible of the already unclassified Foreign Affairs e-mail traffic as possible, the perspectives of Canadian diplomats on the world around them. Add to that information provided by NGOs to make the Foreign Affairs web site an authority that people around the world could use to separate what is fact from fiction, and what works from what does not, on such issues as the promotion of human rights, freedom of expression, open societies, democracy and democratic reforms, elections, environmental protection and sustainable development. Canadians pride themselves on their country's successes in these fields and want Canada to promote and export these values around the world. The Internet is an excellent way to make progress towards those objectives.

While some argue that Canada's international role and diplomatic influence is in long-term steady decline, that is not true in terms of the stature of Canada and Canadians in the worlds of international business, arts and culture and diplomacy and development. Whether it is Margaret Atwood, Margaret MacMillan, Rohinton Mistry, Diana Krall, Mike Meyers, Peter Jennings, Nickelback, Avril Lavigne, Sarah McLachlan, Celine Dion, Bombardier, Research in Motion, Nortel, Encana, Louise Frechette, Louise Arbour, Romeo Dallaire, John de Chastelaine, Peter Cory or Stephen Lewis, Canadians are more influential internationally across a broader range of activities than ever before. Peter Harder, deputy minister of foreign affairs, argues that "when people say Canada has lost influence in the world, they are often thinking along very traditional lines of state-to-state relations, and have missed the dramatic changes in the world and in Canada that Canadians have capitalized on so effectively. By that measure, Canada – the people as well as the government – has a lot more influence and impact than our critics give us credit for."[15]

In addition to that growing international stature and recognition, Canada's ethnic diversity opens doors to countries around the world through the links Canadians have with relatives and families in almost every nation. Increasingly these communities of recent immigrants exchange money, information, hopes and dreams over the Internet, staying in touch with friends and political movements at home through e-mail and providing them with financial and moral support in much the same way that NGOs use the Internet. A major internationally recognized Foreign Affairs presence on the Internet can bring those Canadians into discussions and debate about the country's foreign policy. It might allow them to express their views on how Canada should relate to their home country by using the Internet's interactive capability. It can also build recognition and appreciation for the positions Canada takes on international issues by using the credibility of Canada and its values as perceived by immigrants and refugees. The benefits they see in their new lives in Canada can translate into how their relatives in their home country perceive Canada's positions in international affairs creating an additional audience for a Canadian view on the Internet.

The timing is also right. The Internet is predominantly a communications tool of the developed world but mobile and satellite telephones, wireless communications and satellite links are changing that quickly, bringing the Internet and instant communications to developing countries. That will accelerate tremendously as other nations follow China and India in the expansion of Internet access.

There are changes even in the developed world that make the time right for a large Canadian Internet presence as a tool of foreign policy. The Internet, as a source of information and a means of collecting and distributing it, is replacing other forms of media and communications much faster than most people realize and at speeds that allow millions to rapidly transfer audio and video material, not just printed words. For instance, a December 2003 Ipsos-Insight survey of thirteen global markets found that half of Internet users now use high-speed DSL, cable or optical fibre connections. South Korea, Japan, Germany, Canada and urban China are leading the world, each with about three-quarters of users connected via broadband. The United States, at 47 per cent, is catching up quickly.[16] The Pew Research Center's Internet and American Life research project found in March 2000 that 52 million Americans logged on to the Internet each day. By August 2003 that had grown to 65 million.[17] Last year's dramatic drop of 12 per cent in television viewing in the United States among 18–34 year old males, as reported by Nielsen Media Research, suggests this age group is giving up on television to spend more time on the Internet. It is even more pronounced for those males 18–24, where television viewing dropped by 20 per cent.[18]

There is nothing to suggest the situation is any different in Canada. While young males may use the Internet primarily to play computer games and to talk to their friends through instant messaging services, for many other people the web is quickly supplementing and even supplanting print, radio and television as a major source of information on public and social policy, economic and international relations. This is precisely the material an aggressive Canadian presence on the web, mixing NGO, government and private sources of information could provide to Canadians and people around the globe.

The Pew Research Center regularly surveys political attitudes and how Americans get their political information. A survey conducted in mid-March 2004 showed how quickly the Internet has become essential for those most interested in politics. It discovered "one in five Americans say they have gone online to get news about the elections; 15 per cent say they go online at least once a week to get such news. That represents an increase since January when 14 per cent said they had at some point gone online for election news and 10 per cent reported going online at least weekly for that purpose. The percentage of Americans who had gone online for news or information about the 2004 election is already comparable to the percentage doing so at the end of the 2000 campaign (18 per cent)."[19] The same study concluded that American are using the Internet for much more than the cyber equivalent of radio talk shows. In addition to campaign news, the survey found "16 per cent of the public (24 per cent of Internet users) say they use the web to research candidates' positions on the issues. Roughly half as many (8 per cent of the public, 12 per cent of Internet users) go online to get information about local campaign organizations or activities, or to visit the web sites set up by groups promoting candidates or positions. Seven percent say they have visited candidates campaign web sites, and just 3 per cent of the public reports participating in online discussions, blogs or chat groups about the elections."[20]

It is clear that the international audience for the information Canada could provide on the Internet is large and growing. Canada also possesses advantages that other nations do not have in adopting such an aggressive Internet strategy. However, there are also some impediments that must be overcome. Updating and maintaining a major web presence is both time consuming and costly. It would require a much larger budget for the department's web activities, but has the offsetting potential to reach millions of people around the world. That would increase Canada's stature and influence significantly and could justify reallocating money spent in other areas to ensure an adequately financed web presence. Both equipment and people would be required. Determining what information to post on the site would require editors and staff, plus overall direction and decisions from the department's senior management about the content, focus and emphasis on the site. Those changes would be necessary in Ottawa and around the world. The department would require employees who could collect, synthesize and send information back to Ottawa for publication on the web site and maintain complementary sites at the various posts. In some cases, the information might be very similar or identical to the material now being passed back from some posts to senior management. In other cases, the demands would be totally different, requiring employees with different skills than those currently in the jobs.

The opportunities are significant and very different from traditional diplomacy. As the Aspen Institute suggests, "unlike asymmetrical interdependence in trade, where power goes to those who can afford to hold back or break trade ties, information power flows to those who can edit and credibly validate information to sort out what is both correct and incorrect." Thus, credibility is the crucial resource and asymmetrical credibility is a key source of power. "Establishing credibility means developing a reputation for providing correct information, even when it may reflect badly on the information provider's own country."[21] Developing that credibility ultimately comes down to the knowledge, experience, analytical abilities and communications skills of the people Canada places around the world in its embassies, high commissions and consulates.

Using the Department of Foreign Affairs as an intermediary to filter information and become a reliable Internet source for the world on issues where Canada has traditionally taken a strong stance would be a change in the department's role. But now is an ideal time to implement major change. The world of international relations and the way Canada conducts its foreign affairs are changing dramatically, creating the opportunity for Foreign Affairs to establish a new role for itself and Canadians in the world. The department is no longer as much of a direct intermediary between foreign governments and departments of the Canadian government or provincial governments on many issues. Federal government departments, such as Environment Canada and Fisheries and Oceans, have their own international branches and work directly with foreign governments, often bypassing Foreign Affairs completely.

This is a time for Department of Foreign Affairs to develop partnerships with Canadians and Canada's NGOs community to use the Internet in the ways NGOs have already mastered: to gather and distribute information worldwide, building bridges and promoting the interests of Canada and Canadians around the globe. This would require abandoning the traditional roles and reticence of diplomats. It could mean the release of information and assessments that may even offend or alienate some of our allies. But it is an opportunity Canada would be shortsighted to ignore and let pass by.

NOTES

1 Jeff Sallot, "Chrétien Was Kept in the Dark about Arar," *Globe and Mail*, 9 January 2004, A1.

2 Amnesty International Canada, "Mahar Arar: A Chronology of Events: 26 September 2002 to 5 October 2003," available at http://www.amnesty.ca/canada/Arar_Chronology.php.

3 David Bollier, *The Rise of Netpolitik: How the Internet is Changing International Politics and Diplomacy* (Washington: Aspen Institute, 2003), 12.

4 Ibid., 38–9.

5 Ibid., 1.

6 Ibid., 2.

7 Gordon Smith, "Reinventing Diplomacy: A Virtual Necessity," United Institute of Peace, 25 February 1999.

8 Craig Warkentin, *Reshaping World Politics: NGOs, the Internet and Global Civil Society* (Lanham, Maryland: Rowman & Littlefield Publishers, 2001), 35.

9 Greg Elmer, *Critical Perspectives on the Internet* (Lanham, Maryland: Rowman & Littlefield Publishers, 2002), 106.

10 Bollier, 6.

11 Evan Potter, "Information Technology and Canada's Public Diplomacy," in Evan Potter, ed, *Cyber-Diplomacy: Managing Foreign Policy in the Twenty-First Century* (Montreal: McGill-Queen's University Press, 2002), 182.
12 Department of Foreign Affairs (FAC), Canadian International Policy website, available at http://www.dfait-maeci. gc.ca/cip-pic/menu-en.asp.
13 Bollier, 7.
14 Potter, 196.
15 Peter Harder, Luncheon Address to the Retired Heads of Mission Association, Ottawa, 17 March 2004.
16 Peter Wilson, "Canada at Forefront of Switch to High-Speed Internet Access," *Vancouver Sun*, 19 February 2004, D4.
17 "The Growing Web," *The New York Times*, 29 December 2003.
18 John Schwartz, "Leisure Pursuits of Today's Young Man," *The New York Times*, 29 March 2004.
19 Pew Research Center, "Far More Voters Believe Election Outcome Matters," 25 March 2004, available at http://www.people-press.org/reports/display.php3?ReportID=207 and http://people-press.org/reports/display.php3?PageID=800.
20 Pew Research Center, "Cable and Internet Loom Large in Fragmented Political News Universe," 11 January 2004, available at http://www.people-press.org/reports/display.php3?ReportID-200 and http://people-press.org/reports/display.php3?PageID=800.
21 Bollier, 20.

13 The Turbulent World of Water: Threats and Implications for Canada's Foreign Policy

MARGARET CATLEY-CARLSON

"The World is in Water Crisis" says the BBC. The UN Secretary General asks, in a year end broadcast, if the next wars will be water wars. "Water is the twenty-first century gold," avers a Middle Eastern research group. Behind the drama of these headlines is the daily reality of two and one half *billion* people suffering the indignities of being without sanitation facilities, and fully half that number suffering the effects to their health and livelihood of not having access to clean water. The result? Six thousand people, mostly children, die every day. Rains fail, water tables drop, crops wither, roots die, lands erode, and soil blows away. Rivers dry up before they reach the sea and fertile lands are ruined by salt. Lack of food or fear of its lack stunts the lives and bodies of millions of rural poor.

What is going on? Doesn't it still rain? Aren't there still rivers and lakes? What *is* the problem? And do these problems really touch Canadian interests? Among all the potential activities Canadians might take on, are there useful actions Canadians should undertake with regard to water? Is anyone asking for this involvement?

Here is the world of water in brief. We all know the world is mostly made of water. But within this watery world, only 2.5 per cent of the world's water is fresh water, with less than 1 per cent available for use. We draw down fully 56 per cent of the 1 per cent of water that is actually *accessible* to us. Since the 1960s, the population has doubled, with 3 billion additional people. Water use, however, has sextupled. What will the situation be in 2050 when we add the next 2–3 billion? Sextupling isn't possible. We are already over the halfway mark.[1]

Some things have already changed. We all require water for the agricultural and industrial goods that we use, perhaps for the energy we consume, and for personal use. With the huge population increase in the world has come a reduction in the absolute amount available *per person* for these purposes. Because of the enormous temporal and spatial variability in water, this hits some areas much harder than others. As well, humankind has invented about 100,000 chemicals to help us with food, industry, and daily life; we use the streams and rivers around us to dispose of these and other agricultural and human waste products. For instance, ninety per cent of the South's waste water goes untreated into the streams and oceans, with consequences for those downstream and for the reefs and coastal regions. As a consequence there is less water available for each of us, and what water there is is sometimes polluted to the point that it cannot be used, often to the point where it causes illness.

We can talk about water globally but the real impacts and all solutions are local. There are about 450 million people in twenty-nine countries facing water shortage; by 2025 about 2.7 billion, or one-third of the expected world population, will live in regions facing severe water scarcity.[2] About one quarter of the fresh water fish species are endangered. Major rivers no longer reach the sea for weeks on end, every year. The Aral Sea is drying up. Fully 50 per cent of the global wetlands disappeared in the twentieth century.[3] Mangrove swamps are being pulled out. Aquifer levels are falling, not everywhere but in far too many places.

The individual consumption levels of water are what counts. If we look at one of the most unstable areas of the world, we see a truly disquieting water picture. In the Middle East and North Africa region, the population doubled from 1970 to 2001. In 1960 there were 3,500 cubic meters of water per capita available for all purposes – food, industry, personal use; by 2025 that will be down to 600 cubic meters per person, a *six*-fold decrease. Although this part of the world is now 60 per cent urban, irrigated agriculture uses a hefty 85 per cent of the water in the region. The scarcity will increase for agriculturalists and urban users alike. The Arabian Peninsula, Jordan, Palestine, Israel, and Libya consume more water than the annual renewable supply, with Egypt, Sudan, Morocco, Tunisia, and Syria close behind. Jordanians consume about 163 cubic meters per person per year, Yemen 133. How can prosperity be achieved in these circumstances?

If we take an even closer look at water in Israel/Palestine, the drama intensifies. Everyone needs about 100 cubic meters/year for washing, water, and preparing food; Palestinians have about 85 cubic meters per year, and 25 per cent of the population does not have running water.

Israel has an average of 447 cubic meters per person, and the Settlements often have lawns. As much as 25 per cent of Israeli water comes from the Mountain Aquifer, which is largely, but not totally, within the West Bank.

The impact of water supplies on people's lives and livelihoods depends on who they are and where they are. Poor people suffer most when water is unavailable and suffer disproportionately from health problems due to dangerous water quality or low water and quantity.

It would be difficult to exaggerate the impact that the lack of clean water has on the lives of the poor. At any one time close to half the population of the developing world is suffering from diarrhea, ascarids, guinea worms, hookworm, and schistosomiasis, all of which are water-borne diseases. (A well-designed water system reduces the incidence of schistosomiasis by close to 80 per cent.)[4] There are 4 *billion* cases of diarrhea yearly which cause 2.2 million deaths. Fully 6 million individuals are blind from trachoma, a disease that could be largely prevented if there were enough water for people to wash their faces and if the habit of doing so could be taught and learned. The naturally occurring arsenic in Asian groundwater has diminished the quality of life for hundreds of thousands of the millions whose life expectancy has increased because they no longer face cholera.[5] Cholera means not only loss of life but also loss of livelihood: Chile's losses in fruit and vegetable export earnings after their 1990s cholera scare took years to recover from and cost infinitely more than improved water systems would have.

Poor water impoverishes the poor in other ways. About 73 million working days are lost in India to problems associated with poor water quality and its health impact, with $600 million lost in treatment costs and in the cost of lost production. A staggering 40 *billion* working hours in Africa are lost to carrying water. This is considered women's work and if women cannot do it their daughters come out of school to fetch water.[6]

To add complexity, water availability varies greatly according to time and place. For instance, some parts of India receive 90 per cent of their water in five days of rain, perhaps spread over two intervals a year. If they cannot store this water, they lose it and have no more for months to come. To add even more complexity, 263 of the world's river basins are shared by two or more nations and about 40 per cent of the global population lives in these shared basins.

How is Canada affected by changing water trends? Canadians are of course involved in their own national and local water management and have strong views on continental water issues. Why might it make sense for there be a deliberate foreign policy decision to encourage greater Canadian involvement in water resource management issues around the globe?

The following factors might draw Canada toward greater involvement: our concern to reduce tensions in areas of particular difficulty; our wish to improve livelihoods threatened by water shortage, inter alia reducing out-migration toward our borders; a general concern to preserve clean rivers in order to protect environmental resources; and, most of all, the desire to support poverty reduction, which underlies Canada's development assistance programme.

ABSURDITIES, REAL THREATS, NOT-YET THREATS, AND PROMISES

Absurdities

By common consent, water problems are problems of water management. There are a great number of absurdities in the way we use water worldwide. These also show where there is potential for change.

- Household consumption: In North America we store water by damming rivers, pipe it, filter it, add chemicals to it, preserve its purity – and then flush more than a third of it down the toilet (about 8 per cent worldwide).
- Mexico is chronically short of water but the average per capita daily consumption in Mexico City is double that of Berlin.
- One-third of Mexico's water is lost to leaking pipes and faulty systems; the city is sinking, and a lake is being drained to feed this inefficient system.
- Only 70 per cent of consumers in Mexico City get bills and only half of that number pays them. There are thus no funds to pay for repairs to pipes and systems.
- Australia, Ethiopia, and the Western United States all have about the same rainfall and climate, but while the US and Australia have around 5,000 m^3 per head of water storage capacity, Ethiopia has only 50 m^3, and Africa and the Middle East as a whole have only 1,000 m^3.[7] Each US citizen has fully one hundred times as much stored for him or her as each Ethiopian. Given this, how can Ethiopia grow more food, provide conditions under which industry might be established, and meet peoples' needs for water?[8]
- China has about 50 per cent of its agriculture under irrigation; as much as 70 per cent of that water lost to wasteful methods.
- In China it takes 25 to 50 tons of water to produce a ton of steel; Germany, Japan, and the US use 5 tons of water to make 1 ton of steel.

- The Aswan high dam was built where summer temperatures reach 44°C. Had it been built further upstream, the evaporation losses would have been cut substantially.
- Saudi Arabia uses "fossil" water from deep, underground aquifers (i.e., water laid down eons ago, which is not replenishable) for agriculture.
- India and China between them probably pump about twice the Nile River's worth of water per year from underground sources for irrigated agriculture – *more than rainfall will replenish*. Often the electricity and the water are both free.
- The poor pay more for water and use less, often to the detriment of their own health.

Real Threats

Food Security Water scarcity is a threat to the security of food supplies. Probably the most important series of numbers in understanding water is 17/40/80. Although only 17 per cent of agriculture is irrigated, this irrigated land accounts for more than 40 per cent of all agricultural production and accounts for about 80 per cent of all the water humans use. We have fed an additional 3 billion people since the mid-point of the last century through *intensifying* agricultural production, primarily through Green Revolution techniques and substantially but not uniquely through irrigation. Had this not been done, the burgeoning world would have fed itself by *extensive* means, i.e., clearing more forests, more tropical lands, and denuding more hillsides.

Decrease in Irrigation Investments Investments in irrigation have declined continuously since 1980 and have in any case virtually not touched Africa. A combination of factors are responsible for this state of affairs:

- agricultural water storage involves dams, now rarely financed by concessional funding sources;
- past projects are perceived to have performed poorly (there are hardly ever water charges or budget appropriations to keep the systems in good working order);
- irrigation projects are more costly than education or social projects;
- irrigation investments were crowded out by lending for structural adjustment in 1980s and later by increasing focus on the environment;
- irrigation investments became less attractive with declining international food prices[9] – declines that help the urban poor but not the

rural poor. Both rural and urban have to make money to buy anything better. Some 70 per cent of the poor are still rural.

Floods and Disasters Hotter air holds more water than cold air. As temperatures rise, more water accumulates. Rain becomes torrential in more places, more often. We are not imagining that there are more hurricanes in the world – there are. Climate variability is having an enormous impact on water management and will have an impact even greater in the future. Flood damage claims per year since 1950 have risen from US$39.6 to US$607 billion,[10] with the curve still climbing sharply. Loss of lives in flooding has dramatically decreased in the industrialized world as early warning measures and long-term disaster prevention measures take hold, helped by skyrocketing insurance premiums. Loss of lives, however, has increased dramatically in the developing world as burgeoning populations build in flood plains and less well-organized societies try to cope with a stream of adverse weather events, which are increasing in frequency and violence in tropical regions.

One of the results of climate change is a steep rise in the intensity of forest fires, as Canadians have learned. As well, for the first time a conference is being held on water scarcity in Canada.[11]

Population Increase Population increase is the biggest threat to water security. Although population growth rates have decreased dramatically, the human race is expected to increase by another 2 to 2.5 billion before population levels stabilize. With higher levels of development come higher demands on water for energy, food, and personal use. Water use increased by a factor of six when the world's population doubled, with 3 billion people added to the planet since the mid-point of the last century.

Emerging Threats

Water Wars Two Middle Eastern cities once armed themselves and went to war directly over water.[12] But that was 4,500 years ago and while in the subsequent millennia participants have often been edgy, violence has erupted only at the local level. Shots have been fired in Egypt, Ethiopia, Sudan, and Jordan. Landmines have been put down in Uzbekistan and a dam blown up in Oregon. But generally and amazingly, nations have found more to cooperate about over water than to fight about. The reality is a fairly rich tradition of transboundary cooperation, with India paying Pakistan for the costs of building and operating dams that Pakistan continued to build and operate right through several periods of Indo-Pakistan hostilities. The Mekong River treaty held, with some difficulties, through the Vietnam War. The Jordan

River Treaty is also more generally observed than it is violated.

A study of the last fifty years shows that two-thirds of all events involving water issues between two or more states have in fact been cooperative, with acute violence being rare. Where there is violence, the water issue is usually a subset of other difficult issues. US intelligence reports suggest that shortages have often stimulated cooperative arrangements for sharing scarce water resources.[13] However, as countries come up against tighter and tighter limits, conflict may increase. Wolff's Axiom says that "the likelihood of conflict rises as the rate of change within the basin exceeds the institutional capacity to change."[14] Thus, for example, the strong links of history, technical capacity, and managerial competence of the Canada/US International Joint Commission will help our two countries find solutions to new challenges, such as deformed fish, zebra mussels, and declining Great Lakes Water levels. In the Aral Sea, given the weak links between the countries in the region, it is much less likely that solutions will emerge easily.

Water-related violence exists throughout today's world, but the most intense conflicts are intrastate, intercommunity, and even intervillage. Pastoralists and planters do come to blows. And when we wonder about water and violence, we should also think of the women at the well who sometimes come to blows to maintain their position in the daily line. "I have become a warrior for water," says one woman with pride and resignation.[15] But it is unlikely that we will be as aware of their bitter daily conflict as we will be of those conflicts where armies line up and command camera attention.

With Canada often in a leading position, the international community has tried to forestall tensions over shared waters. The Nile River Treaty tries to create a win-win situation through finding agreement on and financing for an impressive range of development projects for all of the countries in the region. The price tag is very steep, but wars would undoubtedly cost more on any scale of measurement.

The new transboundary issues are complex and are unlikely to be about water availability alone. A rich mix of issues will plague the 260 shared river basin countries: water dumping in times of flood risk, toxic dumps near water sources, inadequate industrial protection, salinity and agricultural wastes in streams, and the building of dams and infrastructure without consultation. Climate variability will add to the complexity of this mix.

Promises

More water The time-honoured solution to water problems has been to increase supply; i.e., build dams, extend pipelines, and pump more out of the aquifer. China is busy moving part of the Yangtze River to the North, and India is talking very seriously about joining its rivers in a national grid. The Red–Dead Sea Connector talks go on throughout the Middle East atrocities.

Supply-side management has serious consequences for rivers, aquifers, and displaced populations. Many unnecessary dams have been built, with benefits to be sure but also a great deal of ancillary damage for the simple reason that it is a lot more politically rewarding (and, in many countries, a major source of corruption income) for governments to supply more water than to attempt to reduce the demand of their populations.

As of two years ago, there were 47,655 large dams in the world and about 800,000 small dams.[16] Most are constructed in the medium-to-rich countries. Anti-dam protesters in the industrialized world, through their pressure on industrialized state governments and international financial intuitions, have ensured that IFIs no longer fund dams. As a result, even needed water-storage capacity has not increased in the poorest countries.[17] Middle class countries such as Turkey, Iran, China, and many others have gone on building dams using other resources. The poorest cannot finance these with their own resources, and therefore do not have the storage they need. Countries with variable rainfall cannot become prosperous without being able to store water. There is almost no storage capacity in the poorest countries, almost all of which have highly variable rainfall patterns. Unless this changes, these countries will stay poor.

Desalinization has become a more and more interesting option for some, given that sea water comprises 97 per cent of the earth's water. Some 12,500 desalinization plants now dot the planet, with two-thirds of these in the Middle East and fully one quarter in Saudi Arabia. Plants are being built in Florida, California, and the Caribbean. There is a new generation of low-cost, small-scale, individual water lifting and application devices. Only 1 per cent of water use is accounted for by desalinated water, but the percentage is growing.[18]

Membranes, biotechnology, and nanotechnology all offer promises for water remediation. Why not re-circulate all of the gray water in an apartment building? Indeed, if the membrane is good enough, why not re-circulate all of the water? Why not build whole neighbourhoods on this principle? Why have huge water mains and sewer mains if the processing can be done locally by membrane?

If engineered microbes can eat oil in oil spills, and might be designed to transform arsenic to less harmful compounds, why not engineer them through nanotechnology to take on the heavy metals in our waste water (and then use bulrushes to purify the organic wastes, a delightful mixture of high tech and low tech!)? These are just some of the possible solutions that are available to reduce demand and make more effective use of the water supply we now have.

Better Science for Water for Food. For the first time in world history, water demand for nonagricultural uses is growing more rapidly in absolute terms than water demand for agriculture.[19] The task is to "reinvent irrigation for the twenty-first century."

There is, for example, a wide technology gap between irrigation practices required for wheat, barley, corn, cotton, sugar beet, potatoes, and tomatoes and the actual water application in most areas. Improved water-use efficiency also means high potential water savings. The "free ride" we have had while we have depleted groundwater resources is coming to its inevitable end.

New technology can and will help in this process. There are many new and exciting techniques we can use to help us make water supplies go further. They include:

- Watershed modeling;
- Integrating simulation techniques with GIS projections;
- Maps and graphs of natural resource impact;
- Daily temperature data and soil and land management data collected from meteorological data; and
- Satellite imagery.

The evidence that these techniques can work is provided in compelling figures. I have the honour and pleasure of being the chair of the Board of the International Center for Agriculture in Dryland Areas (ICARDA). The Center has special expertise in the areas most likely to be most affected by climate change. Some of ICARDA's findings suggest that:

- A 50 per cent decrease in irrigation water used in wheat irrigation in the ICARDA area results in only 10 to 20 per cent loss in cereal production.
- ICARDA has found that if lentils and chickpeas are planted earlier to catch the Mediterranean rain, yields are doubled.
- New drought-tolerant cultivars offer huge potential for improved yield in dry conditions.
- It is estimated that if 70 per cent of the 30 million hectares of land left fallow every year in West Asia and North Africa could be sown to forage legumes, enough feed for 80 million sheep would be

produced, and the nitrogen fixed could be increased by 1.4 million tons.[20]

Saltwater and Wastewater Agriculture. We can also find "new" water for food if we redirect research priorities and put in place effective regulatory frameworks. These include regulating framework for water harvesting, brackish water use, and treated effluent where the key issue is how much treatment? This has to be one of the most exciting potential areas for "finding" water; for example, each 100 cu meter increase in water consumption in a city results in 70 cu meter of waste water production; the hazard for re-use is that industrial and biological wastes are often mixed, with toxins and heavy metals in the mixture.

Rainwater Harvesting. Old techniques are being rediscovered and reapplied to yield more water for topical use. Eavestroughs collect water from schools and public buildings to provide water for community use. Families are collecting rainwater all over India, but also in Germany. Tanks are being rebuilt and watersheds refurbished in the process; rivulets are flowing in formerly denuded landscapes.[21] Communities are putting water back into the subsoil and aquifer by the conscious channeling of rainwater. Global satellites may help us to do this on a global basis.

Demand Management. Anywhere there is metering, demand drops. California's Pacific Institute "Waste Not, Want Not" estimates that up to one-third of California's current urban water use of more than 2.3 million acre-feet could be saved using existing technology. And at least 85 per cent of this (over 2 million acre-feet) could be saved at costs below what it would cost to tap into new sources of supply without the social, environmental, and economic impacts that any major water project brings.[22] Composting toilets reduce the demand for water, as do innovative pit latrines for communities of modest means.[23] Separating feces and urine allows latrines to be treated as resources.

Reallocation. Some of the real answers will have to come through allocation decisions. Pragmatic but sometimes difficult steps can lead to dramatic consequences. For instance:

- In Jordan, a 5 per cent transfer from agricultural use would increase domestic supplies by 15 per cent.
- In Morocco, where 92 per cent of water is used for agriculture, a 5 per cent diversion would effectively double the supply to the domestic sector.

- In California, the San Diego and Imperial Valley accord charges municipalities for water, allowing investment in improved irrigation facilities. The water used in Imperial Valley agricultural use would provide water for domestic use for 12 million people.
- In Mexico, the Costa de Hermosilla proposals to improve agricultural use patterns could avoid the need for desalination plants.

If, by common consent, there is enough water – although *just* enough in many areas – can't we improve management? This is not as simple as it sounds. Moving to a conscious, transparent, publicly announced allocation of available water is a process fraught with risk and almost guaranteed to generate more enemies than friends for the party doing the allocating. The move toward charging for water services offers opposition parties an instant election issue. Managing across boundaries and agreeing to share the benefits of water, often between neighbours with centuries-old traditions of mistrust, is not easy. Current arrangements favour the powerful. Who will speak for the weak or the environment? In many countries irrigated-land agriculturalists have much more power than either the rural or urban poor. There are also taboos against waste water re-use. Yet, unless these tough issues are addressed, the world's growing water "shortage" problem will only get worse. Much worse.

WHAT CAN THE WORLD DO?

Water cannot be created; it can only be managed. Better forms of management mean that public authorities must establish appropriate policy and regulatory frameworks. We must also reform and develop new institutional frameworks. For example, transparency is needed where water use is subsidized. There must be some move to full cost pricing and greater interest in market mechanisms to allocate this scarce resource. The private sector also has a role to play in addressing some of the non-performance issues, such as leaks, needed investment, leaky distribution system, lack of investment in water systems, and the problems of billing consumers.

The Millennium Summit Development Goals' pledge is by 2015 to reduce by half *the proportion* of people who do not have access to safe water. The Johannesburg Earth Summit includes a similar target for sanitation. These goals sound wonderful but are incredibly ambitious, if not impossible, to implement. In the 5,000 days remaining till 2015, approximately 290,000 people each day will have to gain access to clean water and over 500,000 to sanitation for these goals to be met. Although many countries are on track to meet these goals,[24] in the poorest countries, it is not going to happen under anything like current circumstances. Nonetheless, one positive outcome of the Johannesburg Earth Summit was a Plan of Implementation, including a specific directive calling for all countries to develop Integrated Water Resource Management (IWRM) and water efficiency plans by 2005. IWRM is an approach "which promotes the coordinated development and management of water, land and related resources in order to maximize the resultant economic and social welfare in an equitable manner without comprising sustainability of vital ecosystems."[25] Specifically, Paragraph 26 of the Plan of Implementation, issued in September 2002, called on all countries rich and poor, water scarce and water plentiful, to develop integrated water resources management and water efficiency plans by 2005.

WHAT CAN CANADA DO?

Canada is a nation well endowed with water. Only one in two hundred people on the planet is Canadian, and we have somewhere between 7 and 12 per cent of the world's available fresh water, depending on the criteria. Regardless of the amount, it is a goodly sum. This does not mean we are without problems, or that we should be complacent. The Milk River can run dry and droughts can encourage forest fires, as we have seen in British Columbia, Ontario, and Quebec. Prince Edward Island has perennial dry spots, there are mercury-polluted zones in lakes in the North, and the Great Lakes still have zebra mussels and fish abnormalities. On the water and sanitation front, a crisis like that of Walkerton, Ontario, in the late 1990s could happen again. We have more empathy with the world on water issues than we might have had a short while ago.

Development Assistance. Canada has a long tradition of assistance in the water area: from dams to hydro to boreholes to community projects to municipal water works we have been there. We played a signal role in drawing the international community toward the Nile River Basin Treaty. CIDA is helping a few countries with their 2005 IWRM plans. Canada, represented by either Environment Canada or CIDA, attends international water meetings, playing a moderate, sensible, and forthcoming role on most issues.

Comparatively, Canada is seen as quite a good aid donor for water, in the relative sense, since few developing countries request aid in this area. About 4 per cent of Canadian aid goes to water and sanitation, a figure not greatly out of line with most donor countries, although Germany and Japan are significantly higher. Of this assistance for water, 22 per cent goes to the thirty highest priority countries: Honduras and Peru, for example, get more.[26]

There are good things happening within Canada in water management and therefore interesting practices to share. Consider the following three examples:

- Quebec has a new water law, based on water basins;
- The Ontario Stewardship Program has interesting governance concepts, which have had good results; and
- Drinking water practices in Canada have brought new attention to how regulations should work.

We can provide this expertise either by selling our professional services or via development assistance. Although Canadian expenditures in these areas have been declining, we are very good at the science, the technology, and the administrative implications of water resource management. From the science of aquifer management and measuring, to our capacities in disaster preparedness for water events, we can be useful. Our cities and utilities have good practices to share as well managed entities.

If asked, we could provide information and experience on conciliation mechanisms, particularly those related to shared river basin management and the proud tradition of the International Joint Commission, which plays host to dozens of policy-seeking visitors every year.

At the same time, it is important to recognize that Canadians do have some difficulties with water policy issues because of a preoccupation with bulk water exports to the US. But not all water issues concern bulk water exports, and Canada can play an active role in this area without prejudice to our position on this issue. Bulk water export is almost uniquely an issue in the Canada-US relationship. The subject rarely if ever comes up in water meetings, and bulk water is far from being a useful all-purpose way of looking at water issues. I have met Canadian officials who hesitate to speak up on any issue of water management, "lest it be read as selling out to the United States." But there are reasons to question whether there will be an increase in American demand. US per person use continues to decline.[27] In some places, the United States is using desalination plants for water and sanitation. There is also the reality of NAFTA provisions, untested perhaps for their validity for water, but this cannot be our total global lens.

The main problem is that there is a politically correct side of water issues and then another side. Dams, private investment in water, payment for water – all of these are difficult issues. Why would the Canadian government espouse the difficult side of these issues, which are vitally important in the developing world but have no direct impact on Canada? For example, if Canada is serious about fighting poverty, we have to recognize that *all* of those countries with variable rainfall patterns that have become prosperous have done so by storing water so that farmers, industries, and cities will have it in rainy and dry seasons alike. Canada should take a long look at the policies and administrative provisions we have allowed to evolve in IFIs regarding stored water. Is it really reasonable to deny the poorest water storage via procedures that make it virtually impossible for bankers and lenders to take on these projects?

Are we ready to take on the "payment for water issue"? Providing potable water to the poor communities in the world is still a challenge for humanity. In most of the poor parts of the big cities, the poor are served by vendors and often pay ten times the price paid by those who are connected to a network. The extension of areas served by networks would reduce prices tremendously for the poor, but increase somewhat the price for the already served; subsidies, though essential, will never be big enough to cover the needed costs. Neither the rich in the developing world, especially farmers or industrialists, nor the many very active NGOs in the industrialized world accept water pricing: it is dismissed as "commodification." So systems continue to degrade and under-perform. Whether the systems are private or public, they need funds to perform, to allow maintenance, and to continue service delivery.

In some countries, the utilities simply cannot raise the capital, or manage the technology, to get from where they are now to where they want to be. Some want to conclude service contracts with private service managers; this does not "privatize" water assets or the reservoirs, pipes, or system. Yet Canadian churches have raised money to prevent this type of contract from happening in Ghana.

Agriculture is the biggest water-using activity and is responsible for 70 to 80 per cent of a country's water consumption. It warrants careful attention. Billions are spent in subsidies to farmers throughout the world, but they are allocated without any consideration to water problems, thus artificially creating a water crisis, which will manifest itself as a food security crisis.

The water problem is as much a financial problem as a water problem. There is no solution to the water problem without a complete overhaul of the way agriculture is subsidized, water is priced, local authorities are vested with the responsibility to provide water to their inhabitants, good managers are engaged, and sustainable financial resources are allocated.

CONCLUSION

All of this changes every day. Every day, the population grows and the amount of water available per person decreases. Every week, somewhere in the world, there are manifestations of climate variability that will have a marked impact on water resources. Every month, pollution increases. Meetings are held to assess how best to intervene. And every morning, the women walk a little further to find water to keep their families alive.

NOTES

1 Igor A. Shiklomanov, in *The UN World Water Development Report: Water For People, Water For Life, World Water Assessment Programme* (UNESCO Publishing, 2003).
2 IWMI International Water Management Institute, Colombo, Sri Lanka.
3 Kirsten Schuyt and Luke Brander, *Living Waters: Conserving the Source of Life: The Economic Values of the World's Wetlands* (Amsterdam: World Wide Fund for Nature, 2004).
4 UN Millennium Project on Water, *Interim report*. See http://www.unmilleniumproject.org/documents/tf7interim.pdf.
5 UN Millennium Project.
6 Millenium Water Task Force.
7 World Bank estimates.
8 World Bank estimates.
9 IWMI.
10 United Nations, International Committee on Climate Prediction (ICCP).
11 "Confronting Water Scarcity," University of Lethbridge, 13–16 July 2004.
12 Aaron Wolf, in *WATER 21*, February 2003 (Department of Geosciences, Oregon State University).
13 US National Intelligence Council Global Trends, 2015
14 Wolf.
15 *Voices from the Poor*, video shown to UN Committee on Sustainable Development, April 2004.
16 World Commission on Dams WCD 2001.
17 World Bank Water Week 2004; waterweek 2004@worldbank.org.
18 http://www.globalwaterintel.com/Management%20Reports/desalination.htm.
19 Mark Rosegrant et al, *Global Water Outlook to 2025: Averting an Impending Crisis* (International Food Policy Research Institute (IFPRI) and the International Water Management Institute, 2002).
20 ICARDA, Aleppo Syria.
21 The Global Rainwater Harvesting Collective, The Barefoot College, SWRC, Tilonia, Madangunj, Rajasthan, India: grwhc@sancharnet.in.
22 Pacific Institute, http://www.pacinst.org.
23 Sulabh Institute, Delhi.

24 Human Development Report, UNDP, 2003.
25 Global Water Partnership, TAC paper #4, Integrated Water Resource Management.
26 CARE, OXFAM, WATERAID and others, "A scorecard assessment of developing country and donor progress," prepared for UN Committee on Sustainable Development, April 2004, www.wateraid.org.
27 http.pacinst.org.

14 Energizing Canadian Foreign Policy Through Science and Technology Innovation

PETER A. SINGER, HAELI GOERTZEN, ANDREW D. TAYLOR, ELIZABETH DOWDESWELL, and ABDALLAH S. DAAR

This paper offers a vision of Canada as a world leader in using technological expertise to help solve health and environmental problems in poorer nations. Canada has great strengths in its research institutions, universities and science and technology (S&T) firms. We see a tremendous opportunity to leverage our nation's innovation resources into a significant foreign policy plank. We propose a strategic move to employ these assets, now embodied in a variety of S&T and development research institutions, to accomplish the vision. The result would see the use of Canadian innovations in ways that provide a service to developing countries, and would create opportunities, particularly for small and medium-sized Canadian companies.

The first section of this paper outlines the challenge, and Canada's opportunity and role in addressing health and environmental challenges of developing countries. The next section provides a vision and a list of resulting benefits for a change in Canada's foreign policy focusing on science, technology and innovation. The following section presents six policy goals required to achieve the vision. The final section of this paper outlines an actionable option to address the vision and policy goals, as well as the recent commitment from Prime Minister Paul Martin of devoting no less than 5 per cent of our R&D investment to developing countries. *Canada Science International (CSI)*, as a concept, and ideally as an arms-length foundation, will leverage existing and future Canadian innovation investments and organizations to maximize impacts on global health and environmental challenges.

If successful, this new direction for Canadian foreign policy on development can serve as an innovative policy model for other industrialized nations, leading to social and economic benefits on a global scale. We have an opportunity to make a mark. Just as the Canadarm, the mechanical device mounted on the space shuttle built in the 1970s, demonstrated Canada's skill at reaching out into space, so this project could show our ability to reach out to those who need help to achieve a better life on our shared planet.[1]

THE CHALLENGE AND CANADA'S OPPORTUNITY AND ROLE

The Challenge

While life expectancies in industrialized countries are about eighty years and rising, in a number of developing countries, especially due to HIV/AIDS in sub-Saharan Africa, life expectancies are forty years and falling. This gap is perhaps the greatest ethical challenge of our time. Underlying the differences in health are inequities in knowledge. Most people are familiar with the "digital divide." However, the S&T gap also extends to biotechnology and nanotechnology[2] sectors (the "genomics divide" and "nano-divide"). Despite discussions about the roles which research and technology development (and technology transfer) should play in helping developing countries achieve greater economic and social stability, the S&T divides between developed and developing countries continue to grow. For example, the Global Forum for Health Research has documented that 90 per cent of all health research is targeted at problems affecting only 10 per cent of the world's population.[3] This so-called "10/90 gap" threatens to create even greater inequities between wealthier and developing countries, posing a critical challenge to the application of new knowledge and innovations for global human welfare.[4]

Science and technology have long been recognized as significant factors in the economic health of nations, as well as an important tool for improving the human condition and addressing the needs of developing countries and the disadvantaged. Canada has a moral obligation to share the fruits of its large, domestic investments in research to help poor nations. At the same time, the economies in many of these poor nations (including new and emerging markets such as Brazil, India and China) are growing at a far faster rate than those of richer countries (mature markets like Canada, the US and much of the European Union) and will become increasingly significant players in the global economy, in absolute terms, over the next decade. If Canada does not undertake a concerted effort to a) understand the opportunities inherent in these markets; b) develop new business models to meet their challenges; and c) begin to foster deep and abiding relationships built on mutual understanding and respect with key stakeholders in these nations, then the country faces the very real prospect of becoming an increasingly marginal player in the key emerging markets of the twenty-first century.

The Opportunity

In every great challenge lies an equally significant opportunity. The federal government has invested over $13 billion[5] since 1997 in innovation initiatives, such as the creation of new research institutions and programs like the Canadian Foundation for Innovation, the Canada Research Chairs, Genome Canada and the Canadian Institutes for Health Research, which complement the work of the National Research Council and International Development Research Centre (IDRC).[6] Of this substantial investment, however, the current annual R&D expenditure for international developmental S&T is significantly less than 1 per cent of total annual R&D expenditures. This S&T represents the front end "input" into the process of value creation (research and development), value capture (commercialization), and value expansion (markets), the success of which will allow Canada as a country both to address the pressing development challenges of the day, and to increase its presence in new and emerging world markets. As such, Canada will need to greatly increase its focus on S&T, oriented towards the challenges of developing countries, if it wishes to take advantage of the opportunities that are present in those markets.

There is a real opportunity to use Canadian investments in S&T innovation to address development challenges, and to do so in a way that will promote innovation and economic expansion both for public and private sector institutions in Canada and in developing countries. This opportunity involves both aid to the poorest countries and trade with the middle-income countries. New Canadian technologies can be targeted to address development challenges in ways that will create opportunities in the emerging export markets of the future. Through the development of a national strategy for increasing and coordinating research into the challenges of new and emerging markets, coupled with timely strategic investments and capacity building activities, Canada can become both a world centre for R&D on how to use technology to deal with global health and environmental issues and a significant player in the most important export markets of the coming century. Success in these endeavours will attract significant foreign direct investment in Canadian companies and institutions in the form of international science and technology partnerships.

Canada's Role

We recommend the creation of a Canadian science and innovation system that works to alleviate development problems, particularly in the fields of health and the environment. Of course, technology itself is necessary, but there also needs to be a major element of partnership with developing countries to determine their needs, and design technology appropriate to their particular circumstances with due attention to policies and delivery systems, so that technology brings real benefits to people. This vision can add a new direction to the Canadian research and innovation agenda, an element of inspiration to researchers, and could contribute to a new and unique Canadian foreign policy.

VISION AND BENEFITS

Vision

By 2010, Canada will be a world leader in developing and applying technological innovations to help solve health and environmental problems in low and middle-income countries in partnership with them.

The vision calls for Canada to employ its domestic science and technology assets, both research infrastructure and human capital, to help solve health and environmental problems in developing countries. We can do this by creating new approaches that link domestic innovation and foreign policy. These will provide a quantum leap in how we can internationalize our S&T expertise.

We can make this happen by fostering strategic alliances and partnership involving research, policy and industry. This approach will link experts in Canada and developing nations, along with colleagues from other nations, to find innovative science and technology-based solutions for the needs of developing countries. Because both researchers and business people are involved, there will be practical and economically viable applications of knowledge, as well as employment opportunities. This approach represents a tangible way in which Canada can advance its long-standing commitment to help other nations achieve more sustainable forms of development.

This policy approach will help to reduce inequities around the world, foster international understanding, enhance Canadian science and technology innovation capacity, and position Canada as a global leader in research for development.

Benefits

Reaping the benefits[7] of the vision calls for the bold action that characterized Canada's "spirited internationalism" of the past. Creating a new foreign policy plank by leveraging Canada's innovation assets recognizes the complementarity of commercial and moral arguments for addressing global development needs. It draws on the strengths of government, S&T institutions and the private sector in a synergistic process to meet development challenges effectively.

POLICY GOALS

We also set out a series of policy goals to achieve the vision. The public sector must catalyze the advancement of S&T for development, while harnessing the strengths of the private sector for effective application of the vision.

Policy Goal 1

The first policy goal is to raise Canada's annual R&D expenditures for international developmental S&T to the prime minister's target of 5 per cent. In 2002, Canada invested $21.70 billion in R&D to foster S&T innovation.[8] Current R&D expenditures in S&T targeting health and environment problems in developing countries is currently estimated to be approximately $142.8 million and is, therefore, *significantly less than 1 per cent* of total R&D expenditures.

Prime Minister Martin has indicated that he favours a 5 per cent target. In his 3 February 2004 reply to the Speech from the Throne, Mr. Martin said that: "Our long-term goal as a country should be to devote no less than 5 per cent of our R&D investment to a knowledge-based approach to develop assistance for less fortunate countries."

In order to reach the goal of 5 per cent of total R&D expenditures earmarked for international developmental S&T, both public sector and private sector will need to increase funding for such research. This can be achieved through an allocation of public funds for international developmental S&T research, accompanied by policies that provide incentives for the private sector to prioritize a portion of their R&D for international developmental S&T research.

Policy Goal 2

Enriching Canadian international policy by strengthening the innovation dimension is the second policy goal. According to a submission by the North-South Institute and the Canadian Association for the Study of International Development to the April 2003 Canadian Foreign Policy Review, "the object of foreign policy must be to promote a peaceful and just world; without addressing the enormous, and growing gaps between developed and developing countries such an objective cannot be met ... The well-being of Canadians as well as their hopes for a peaceful and just world necessitates a continual focus on international development."[9] These statements respond to concerns raised by former Prime Minister Lester Pearson about the dangers of a world where, "a few rich countries with a small minority of the world's population alone have access to the brave and frightening new world of technology and science, while the majority live in deprivation and want."

These foreign policy views resonate at a time when Canada is being challenged to reclaim its ability to punch above its weight overseas.[10] At the same time, Canada faces the added challenge of maintaining significant ties with the United States while distinguishing ourselves as a visionary global player. It is recognized that the opportunity exists for Canada to build a twenty-first century economy, and ensure itself a proud and dignified place in the global arena.[11] The vision encapsulates an innovative solution to meet these goals and contribute to Canada's sense of global achievement by sharing the benefits of S&T.

There is growing sentiment among international leaders that science is a necessary component of development.[12] The UN Development Program made its position clear with the 2001 Human Development Report,[13] stating the importance of science and technology in reducing mortality rates and improved life expectancy in the period 1960–1990. The World Health Organization's report on Genomics and Global Health[14] suggests that genomics-based solutions have the potential to meet the needs of developing countries. The Grand Challenges in Global Health initiative proposed by the Bill and Melinda Gates Foundation (BMGF) is grounded on the assumption that, with greater encouragement and funding, contemporary science and technology could lead to increased progress against diseases that disproportionately affect the developing world.[15] Therefore, the knowledge of science to understand developing country problems and the technology to tackle them[16] is central to this initiative and will act as a vehicle in the progression of countries from aid to trade. From Canada's perspective, this can be done best by leveraging current S&T assets.

Existing Canadian efforts and initiatives follow a relatively rigid and slow developmental pathway. Markets are segmented into Canada's current industrialized trading partners (e.g., United States and the European Union), emerging markets and growing economies which include Department of Foreign Affairs priority countries such as China, and least-developed nations like Bangladesh and other countries that are currently recipients of CIDA aid, but which may become markets in the long term.

Our vision also breaks down some widely held dichotomies. It represents neither *foreign* nor *domestic* policy alone. It is both. It represents neither a *moral* nor a *commercial* purpose alone. It is both. It represents neither *aid* nor *trade* alone. It is both. These concepts are often viewed as distinct, but this initiative recasts them as mutually supportive.

The slow and laborious progression from aid to trade can be accelerated through the global partnerships envisioned by the proposed initiative, which will re-vitalize the thrust of development by leveraging Canadian S&T innovation.

Canada can foster partnerships involving our scientific experts and business people with colleagues in developing nations. These partnerships can address critical health and environmental issues which poor nations are ill equipped to tackle alone. The results will include not only humanitarian aid, but also the development of new business opportunities for people in both countries. Through the vision, developing nations gain access to technology, and Canada establishes new trading partners in emerging markets. The novel approach of this initiative helps to accelerate the progression of "Aid-to-Trade" through policy approaches that will reclaim Canada's role in the world of development.

We hope this paper can influence the current international policy review in promoting science and technology as a major focal point for Canada's international policy.

Policy Goal 3

The third policy goal aims at leveraging Canadian S&T innovation investments and institutions for development. To strategically leverage Canadian S&T innovation for development, it will be essential to combine the strengths of Canada's existing institutions to capitalize on their expertise. For example, IDRC offers more than thirty years of expertise in understanding developing countries' priorities through its collaborative work with developing country researchers and policymakers. This could be greatly complemented by the

National Research Council's (NRC) capabilities in commercializing new science and technology. The research granting councils (CIHR, NSERC, SSHRC), as well as Genome Canada, and the Canada Research Chairs and CFI programs, offer access to Canada's most highly qualified researchers, and possible co-funding opportunities on projects. The NCE program offers expertise in the development of national research networks.

In order to capitalize on Canada's expertise among existing institutions there needs to be a stronger link between our domestic R&D strengths and our international development and trade capabilities. To translate this vision into operation, a new institutional arrangement should be established. In essence, the whole needs to be greater than the sum of its parts. In the fourth section below, we will offer an institutional concept to address this policy goal.

Policy Goal 4

The fourth policy goal encourages the development of strategic partnerships between Canadian and developing country firms and research organizations. New international partnerships in science and technology are likely to be extremely effective in realizing the vision we present. A good example is found in the collaborative effort to address Bangladeshi arsenic poisoning through bioremediation techniques.

Bangladesh faces the largest mass poisoning of a population in history due to naturally occurring groundwater arsenic contamination. An integral contributor to this problem could be bacterial activity in Bangladesh sub-surface aquifers. A number of bacterial species exist that can either metabolize arsenic and release it into the groundwater, or can perform the reverse process, taking arsenic out of water and immobilizing it in soil. Scientists in the US and Australia have discovered and characterized bacterial species that can perform this interesting chemistry that can lead to potentially valuable bioremediation tools for Bangladesh.

Genome Canada, NRC, and the University of Toronto Joint Centre for Bioethics are leading a coalition that will take a new approach to this problem, based on Canada's science and technology assets. Working in partnership with Canadian, Bangladeshi, and US and Australian scientists, the coalition will sequence the genome of both kinds of arsenic-eating bacterial species at the same Canadian sequencing laboratory in Vancouver that sequenced the SARS virus. Although it is difficult to move from genome sequence to intervention, the difference in sequence between these two bacteria with diametrically opposed functions will lead to novel insights for tackling the problem of groundwater arsenic poisoning in Bangladesh.

We also see a need to strengthen capacity building both in Canada and in developing countries through training of researchers, technical experts and policymakers. A good example of how to do this in a developing country is seen in the Genomics and Health Policy Courses, supported by IDRC and Genome Canada, which have so far been conducted in Africa, India and the Eastern Mediterranean region. They gave participants and opinion leaders a forum for multi-sectoral discussion on the current status and implications of genomics and biotechnology for health in the region, and provided information useful for public policy development. S&T capacity building will also take place as scientific experts from developing countries now living in Canada partner back to their countries of origin.

Partnerships play a vital role in fostering sustainable development by enhancing innovation system capacity in developing countries. While developing countries recognize the importance of S&T and are developing their own innovation systems, there is evidence that a bottleneck arises when moving from R&D into implementation. The capacity of the private sector in many developing countries to commercialize new innovations is quite limited. Thus, partnerships between private firms in Canada and those in the developing world can build a much needed commercialization capacity within the developing world for job and wealth creation. This policy goal will be expanded upon below in the form of an R&D Fund.

Policy Goal 5

Building a twenty-first century Canadian economy by supporting globally competitive SMEs in new and emerging markets is the fifth policy goal. Canada has made great investments in S&T in recent years. It is time to leverage these investments and initiatives most effectively by creating a new foreign policy model that links humanitarian goals with business know-how to deliver goods and services to people. If we do it right, it will not only build on our humanitarian legacy, but will serve as an example to other nations.

Developing countries are evolving their own domestic S&T innovation systems in biotechnology, nanotechnology and other technologies.[17] Often, S&T capacity building efforts are focused on local needs, as seen in the case of Cuba. In response to a domestic epidemic of meningitis B, Cuba has developed the world's only meningitis B vaccine which, despite the trade embargo, is undergoing clinical trials conducted by Glaxo-SmithKline in the United Kingdom, with an ultimate goal of marketing the vaccine in the United States.[18] This example shows that linking national S&T capacity to local needs is a significant way of meeting development challenges in health and environment. The Indian biotechnology company, Shantha Biotechnics, has indigenously developed and produced Hepatitis B vaccine[19] at the low price of US$0.29 per dose for the Indian market and for other developing countries. This vaccine recently received WHO certification, allowing UNICEF to procure 8.5 million doses of Shantha's Hepatitis B vaccine for distribution in the developing world.

Partnerships with Canadian high-tech companies can build capacity to address gaps within developing country innovation systems, particularly with respect to the private sector. Partnerships with companies like Shantha, or others in emerging economies like India, Brazil, China and Africa can provide Canadians with access to new markets, and opportunities, while at the same time boosting global innovation and improving global health.

The Prometic-Tunisia partnership on drugs provides a good example. In October 2003, Prometic Life Sciences, a Montreal-based biotechnology company with close links to the NRC Biotechnology Research Institute, established a biopharmaceutical company in Tunisia that will manufacture and commercialize affordable drugs against hepatitis and cancer for 500 million people in Africa, the Middle East, and part of Europe. The company is a Toronto Stock Exchange listed Canadian company with a market cap of $165 million CDN, expecting revenues of $30 million CDN over the next three years from this Tunisian venture. The potential market opportunity resulting from this venture is over $2 billion Canadian.

In building the twenty-first century economy, the goals of research and training need to include the commercialization of research results in Canada and abroad for dissemination in developing countries. This is the key challenge in distributing S&T solutions for development.

The process of commercializing Canadian S&T innovations will lead to innovative partnerships with the private sector and timely commercialization and dissemination of technologies, as highlighted by the UN Commission on Private Sector and Development report: *Unleashing Entrepreneurship: Making Business Work for the Poor.*[20] This report underscores the importance of partnerships with the private sector in working to achieve the United Nations' Millennium Development Goals. UN Secretary-General Kofi Annan announced the initiative by saying that, "a large part of the work for development, after all, is about preparing the ground for sufficient private sector activity to provide jobs and income needed to build a more equitable and prosperous society."[21]

Recent reports on the biotechnology sector suggest that small and medium sized companies have an increasing role to play in S&T innovation,[22] although in Canada a lack of venture capital relative to the United States poses a challenge to these firms.[23] Internationally, the creation of a venture capital fund could maximize the ability of smaller firms to partner and market new products to address development needs. This policy goal will be elaborated upon below in the form of an *International Commercialization Fund.*

Policy Goal 6

The sixth policy goal will develop a program for engaging young Canadians in S&T for development. It is essential to gain public support for new science and technologies. Effective and constructive public engagement is becoming a strategic keystone for accelerating the transformation of science-based sectors throughout the world. The vision we propose for Canada will only be successful if it engages the imagination of the public, especially youth, on Canada's contribution to the world.

There is a generation of young Canadians pursuing S&T oriented careers committed to a vision of a better world.[24] Imagine combining the fascination of Canada's youth with technology (think video games) and their commitment to serving the poor (think Canada World Youth). What a powerful combination!

A significant technology platform to engage this group and the public at large is being pursued by the Joint Centre for Bioethics through CFI grant support. The Information and Communication Technology Platform for Public Engagement to Optimize Canadian Innovation is one possible tool to invigorate public interest and involvement in S&T innovation for development.

Another way of mobilizing the public around S&T issues would involve specifically engaging Canadian youth through educational modules, similar to the "ENGAGE – Stem Cells" modules created and disseminated to 5,000 Canadian high schools by the Joint Centre for Bioethics, with support from Genome Canada and the Stem Cell Network.[25] Through a *Youth Engagement Strategy (YES)*, outlined below, we will translate this policy goal to action.

CANADA SCIENCE INTERNATIONAL

As noted above, Prime Minister Paul Martin has recently set a long term target for Canada to devote no less than 5 per cent of our R & D investments to a knowledge-based approach for development (policy goal 1). The international policy review provides an ideal forum to focus attention on this goal by elevating science and technology innovation to a key plank of Canada's foreign policy (policy goal 2).

This section provides a blueprint on how to implement the prime minister's target in the context of the international policy review by leveraging Canadian science and technology innovation investments and institutions for development (policy goal 3). The institutional blueprint is called *Canada Science International.* At the moment, CSI is a concept but it could easily be launched as an arms-length foundation to work in partnership with other groups to help achieve the prime minister's bold new direction for Canadian international policy. CSI itself will address the other three policy goals.

Vision, Mission, and Goals of Canada Science International

Vision of Canada Science International By 2010, Canada will be a world leader in developing and applying technological innovations to help solve health and environmental problems in low and middle-income countries in partnership with them. CSI would be recognized as a focused response to the knowledge that stark and growing inequities exist between the world's richest and poorest nations and that wealth creation and standard of living are tied to science and technology innovation. If successful, this vision will be internationally and domestically acknowledged and adopted as a singular foreign policy model that defines and energizes Canada's role in the world.

One of the key roles for CSI will be to provide a coherent strategy for the internationalization of Canadian research and development through an intermediary position. Through an institutional arrangement, this strategy will build on and complement the work of existing federal departments and agencies and, by aligning their strengths, create a new synergy for development.

The vision of CSI recognizes, supports and will enable the important ongoing contributions of other Canadian agencies and organizations in the application of Canadian research and development to the challenges of developing countries.

The vision of CSI, and the development of its organizational structure, will be informed by the following mission: 1) maximize the impact on health and environment problems in developing countries; 2) leverage existing Canadian innovation investments and organizations, and strengthen other efforts to internationalize S&T; 3) strengthen research and business partnerships with developing countries; and 4) strengthen S&T capacity and infrastructure, including social innovation, in developing countries.

Canada Science International fills a unique niche, but it would want a close partnership with existing organizations. There are existing excellent models of internationalization of Canadian health research, such as the IDRC-CIHR partnership (with CIDA and Health Canada) known as the Global Health Research Initiative. By employing existing Canadian innovation investments and organizations, we want to emphasize that these other efforts should be strengthened as well. The goal is to avoid replication and to build on existing strengths. Therefore, the organizational structure of CSI would be the lightest structure needed to achieve its objectives.

In addition to its vision and mission, CSI will focus on the delivery of three specific goals: 1) create strategic partnerships between Canadian and developing country firms and research organizations; 2) build a twenty-first century Canadian economy by supporting globally competitive SMEs in new and emerging markets; and 3) develop programs for engaging young Canadians in S&T for development, with a possible link to the Canada Corps. If boldly implemented, these strategic goals can capture the imagination of Canadians, strengthen Canada's identity and make Canadians proud of their role in the world.

CSI R&D Fund In accordance with the prime minister's commitment of devoting no less than 5 per cent of our R&D investment to development, CSI proposes to implement an R&D fund to address the current health and environment problems of the developing world.

The *CSI R&D Fund* would focus its investment on science and technology research applied to large-scale projects that address the health and environment needs of developing countries. The goals and objectives of this competition closely relate to the $200–million global health research initiative, *Grand Challenges in Global Health*,[26] announced by the Bill and Melinda Gates Foundation in 2003.

The Global Health initiative was proposed on the assumption that, with greater encouragement and funding, contemporary science and technology could remove some of the obstacles to more rapid progress against diseases that disproportionately affect the developing world.

A grand challenge was described as "a call for a specific scientific or technological innovation that would remove a critical barrier to solving an important health problem in the developing world with a high likelihood of global impact and feasibility." A grand challenge is meant to direct investigators to a specific scientific or technical breakthrough that would be expected to overcome one or more bottlenecks in an imagined path toward a solution to one or preferably several significant health problems. The efforts to identify Grand Challenges in Global Health relied on financial and administrative resources of two collaborating foundations, the BMGF and the Foundation for the

National Institutes of Health (NIH); a selection panel (scientific board) of twenty scientists and public health experts from thirteen countries, including several from the developing world; and on the scientific community to supply ideas for challenges.

Following the announcement of the Grand Challenges, the Foundation for NIH issued a Request for Proposals to address each of the challenges with grants of up to a total of $20 million over five years or less. How many grants will be made toward each challenge and how many of the fourteen challenges will have funded grants will depend on the quality of the proposals and the available resources.

Applications will be invited from anywhere in the world, from one or multiple institutions or countries in the developed or developing world, and from non-profit and for profit institutions. The Foundation for NIH will oversee the application and award processes, will encourage the participation of developing-country researchers and will be available to advise about organizing inter-institutional or international consortia where appropriate. The scientific board expects to seek candidate challenges through solicitations of ideas, the convening of workshops with invited speakers on defined topics, and continued discussion among members of the board. In the very design of its gift, the BMGF has challenged the world's scientists to produce a program that has the potential to improve the lives of many people. The following list outlines the goals of the Grand Challenges identified through the above initiative: 1) to improve childhood vaccines; 2) to create new vaccines; 3) to control insects that transmit agents of disease; 4) to improve nutrition to promote health; 5) to improve drug treatment of infectious diseases; 6) to cure latent and chronic infections; and 7) to measure disease and health status accurately and economically in poor countries.

Through a peer-review system similar to the *Grand Challenges in Global Health* initiative, proposals will be judged on their ability to maximize the impact on addressing health and environmental problems in developing countries. Our call for scientific and technological innovation for development will also build on a recently published report by the University of Toronto Joint Centre for Bioethics, *The Top 10 Biotechnologies for Improving Health in Developing Countries*,[27] which highlights biotechnology applications that have the potential to improve the health of people in developing countries. This includes: molecular diagnostics; recombinant vaccines; vaccine and drug delivery; bioremediation; sequencing pathogen genomes; female-controlled protection against sexually-transmitted diseases (STDs); bioinformatics; nutritionally enriched genetically modified crops; recombinant drugs; and combinatorial chemistry.

To maximize the impact of S&T for international development, CSI will need to develop strategic partnerships between Canadian and developing country firms, universities and research organizations, as well as encouraging systemic knowledge flows and learning in these countries. In that way CSI goes further than the *Grand Challenges in Global Health* by explicitly promoting systemic capacity building and learning in developing countries, and focusing not only on technological but also social innovation.

International Commercialization Fund The recent Canadian Federal Budget[28] has a strong emphasis on commercializing domestic S&T innovation. In building the twenty-first century economy, we believe a strong emphasis on international S&T innovation should also be included within Canada's commercialization strategy.

As highlighted by the UN Commission on Private Sector and Development report, *Unleashing Entrepreneurship: Making Business Work for the Poor*,[29] the process of commercialization for development involves the dissemination and facilitation of knowledge flows between public and private sectors of both developed and developing markets. Through targeted international policy reforms, the commercialization and internationalization of SMEs is critical to eradicating the poverty, health and environment problems of the developing world.

The objective of the Commission (co-chaired by Prime Minister Martin) was to identify the legal, financial, and structural obstacles blocking the expansion of the indigenous private sector in developing countries, with a special focus on the poorest regions and communities. This report provides answers that draw on the expertise of internationally-recognized leaders in business, development economics, and government from both the industrialized and developing worlds.

The following is a brief outline of the chapters in the report: Chapter 1 deals with why the private sector is so important in alleviating poverty. Chapter 2 outlines three major structural challenges confronting the private sector in all developing countries, to varying degrees: 1) micro-enterprises and many SMEs operate informally; 2) many SMEs have barriers to growth; and 3) lack of competitive pressure shields larger firms from market forces and the need to innovate and become more productive. Chapter 3 focuses on specific actions that are needed, relating to fostering the rule of law and creating a level playing field for entrepreneurship, as well as improving access to financing and the availability of skills and knowledge. Chapter 4 provides an analysis of how better to engage the private sector in addressing the development challenge. Through private actions and public-private partnerships, the power of linkages and networks will foster enormous potential for sustainable development, improving corporate governance and advancing corporate social responsibility standards. Chapter 5 outlines recommended actions within the Public Sphere, the Public-Private Sphere, and the Private Sphere.

This UN report addresses some of the systemic failures currently affecting developing countries, especially the potential for the private sector to promote growth in domestic markets. Through the facilitation of cooperative partnerships between central actors of the public and private sphere, the private sector of developing countries will be able to promote sustainable learning and development.

By adapting the role of science and technology towards innovation, the *International Commercialization Fund* would focus on helping Canadian SMEs internationalize into new and emerging markets targeting the health and environment demands of developing countries. As a social venture capital fund, there would be a strong focus on generating economic and social returns within Canada and in developing countries through innovative partnerships. In order to implement this fund, initial federal investments are needed for important proof-of-principle opportunities. This process is important in establishing the knowledge and investments needed to support the development of joint venture relationships between Canadian and developing country SMEs.

Youth Engagement Strategy (YES) An essential component of the CSI vision, mission and ultimate legacy is premised on engaging the imagination and untapped potential of Canadian youth. In cooperation with Canadian youth organizations, CSI will develop and implement a *Youth Engagement Strategy (YES)* in S&T for development. This strategy will harness the energy of young Canadians to address health and environment challenges of the developing world. By leveraging existing youth movements in S&T, a unified platform through CSI will provide the opportunity to create international partnerships and knowledge exchanges on a domestic and international level.

The following goals will guide the focus of this strategy:

1 To increase the *awareness* of current health and environmental problems in low to middle income countries, and the importance of S&T in addressing these issues.
2 To *engage* youth in an action orientated way through new and existing strategies/organizations.
3 To *utilize* the multicultural diversity (diaspora communities) of Canadian youth for knowledge enhancement.
4 To *leverage* the skills, interests and untapped energy of our youth in

partnership with existing youth movements toward action orientated goals.

5 To *celebrate* the success of existing youth strategies with an international development purpose and the future success of youth programs through CSI.

A significant focus of CSI will be the development of youth capacity to think in new ways through the launch of innovative programs centering on science and technology for development. This vision of *YES* is grounded on the notion that the youth movement should "learn by doing and experiencing." Canadian youth need opportunities to present their concepts and the resources to put their ideas into action in partnership with Canadian and developing country firms and organizations around the world.

Internationalization of Canada Science International Canada can become the world leader in developing and applying technology to help solve health and environmental problems affecting low to middle income countries. *Canada Science International* can become a model for other industrialized countries. We can foresee a similar global pledge from other nations with a strong commitment to sustainable development, such as Sweden, Finland, Denmark and the Netherlands. Through relationships with international institutions, such as the United Nations, G-8, G-20 and bilateral groupings, Canada can take a leading position in the twenty-first century global economy through science and technology innovation.

NOTES

1 The first three sections of this paper are based on a white paper developed by the Joint Centre for Bioethics in consultation with Genome Canada, IDRC and NRC. We are grateful to Marc LePage, Paul Dufour, Tim Dottridge, Peter Hackett, and Richard Isnor for helpful comments.

2 Nanotechnology is the creation of functional materials, devices and systems through control of matter on the nanometer length scale (1–100 nanometers), and exploitation of novel phenomena and properties (physical, chemical, biological, mechanical, electrical...) at that length scale. NASA definition: http://www.ipt.arc.nasa.gov/nanotechnology.html.

3 S. Davies, "The 10/90 Report on Health Research 2000," Global Forum for Health Research, Geneva, 2000.

4 UNDP, *Human Development Report 2001; Making New Technologies Work for Human Development* (New York, United Nations: 2001).

5 "Speech from the Throne to Open the Third Session of the Thirty-

Seventh Parliament of Canada," 2 February 2004, http://www.pm.gc.ca/eng/news.asp?id=201.

6 D. Watters, "The Canadian Institute of Developmental Science and Technology," 2003.

7 Ibid.

8 Statistics Canada, Federal Government Expenditures and Personnel in the Natural and Social Sciences, 1993–1994 to 2002–2003, http://www.statcan.ca/english/IPS/Data/88f0006XIE2003009.htm.

9 North-South Institute and the Canadian Association for the Study of International Development, "Joint Submission to the Canadian Foreign Policy Review," April 2003.

10 Andrew Cohen, *While Canada Slept: How We Lost Our Place in the World* (Toronto, McClelland & Stewart: 2003).

11 P. Martin, "Making History: The Politics of Achievement," 15 November 2003.

12 J. Sachs, *New Scientist*, 175, 2352 (2002).

13 UNDP, Human Development Report, 2001.

14 World Health Organization, *Genomics and World Health* (WHO: Geneva, Switzerland, 2002).

15 H. Varmus, R. Klausner, T. Acharya, A.S. Daar, and P.A. Singer, "Grand Challenges in Global Health," *Science*, 2003, 302: 398–9.

16 A.S. Daar, Elizabeth Dowdeswell and P.A. Singer, "Genome Diplomacy: Canada's Crucial Role," *Policy Options*, September 2003.

17 H. Thorsteinsdottír, A.S. Daar, Tirso W. Sáenz and P.A. Singer, "Building a Health Biotechnology Innovation System in Cuba: Growth Through Linkages," forthcoming. E. Court, "Scientific and Social Contributions of Developing Countries to Nanotechnology."

18 H. Thorsteinsdottír et al., "Building a Health Biotechnology Innovation System in Cuba: Growth Through Linkages," forthcoming.

19 The Hindu Business Line, "Shantha Bio Launches New Drug for Cancer," 19 April 2002, http://www.thehindubusinessline.com/bline/2002/04/19/stories/2002041901090400.htm.

20 Commission on the Private Sector & Development, *Unleashing Entrepreneurship Report* (New York: United Nations, 2004).

21 News Release, "Secretary-General Calls on Newly Launched Commission on Private Sector and Development to Foster Millennium Development Goals," 25 July 2003, http://www.un.org/News/Press/docs/2003/sgsm8793.htm.

22 Karl Leif Bates, "Big Pharmacy Relies on Small Biotech Firms to Succeed" (Life Sciences Institute, University of Michigan, 18 February 2002).

23 Canadian Program on Genomics and Global Health, KPMG Proposal

Document, "Developing Health Genomics: An Investment Fund to Bridge the Gap," February 2002.

24 For more information, see http://www.impactanation.com.

25 For more information, see the Joint Centre for Bioethics website, at http://www.utoronto.ca/jcb/main.html.

26 "Grand Challenges in Global Health."

27 University of Toronto Joint Centre for Bioethics, "Top 10 Biotechnologies for Improving Health in Developing Countries" (Toronto: University of Toronto Joint Centre for Bioethics, 2002).

28 Canada Budget 2004: http://www.fin.gc.ca/budtoce/2004/budliste.htm.

29 Commission on the Private Sector & Development, "Unleashing Entrepreneurship: Making Business Work for the Poor" (New York: United Nations, 2004).

15 The UN in the Twenty-First Century

PAUL HEINBECKER

Predictions of the demise of the United Nations are, Mark Twain–like, greatly exaggerated. Ambitions for a new world order mediated by American power are running aground in the inhospitable realities of Iraq. As one of the most multicultural and cosmopolitan of states, a good global citizen in word and often in deed, with interests in every corner of the globe, Canada benefits from its close relationship with the United States and from an effective multilateral system of governance. Managing relations with the United States is a perennial preoccupation for Ottawa, but Canada, whose principles largely constitute its power, equally needs a UN that is effective as both stage and actor. The health of the UN is not robust, however, and the membership is fractious at a time when the institution is being tested as rarely before. Clearly, reforms of the world organization are overdue and innovations in international governance are necessary. It is manifestly in Canada's interest as well as in its ability to assist the UN to meet the challenges of the 21st century.

It was not long ago that fate had seemed to smile again on the United Nations. In December 2001, Secretary-General Kofi Annan accepted the UN's eighth Nobel Prize for its "work for a better organized and more peaceful world."[1] The shame of the UN's failure in Rwanda was receding in the collective consciousness, if not conscience. The guns were silent in Bosnia, and the UN was back in charge in Kosovo after sitting out the war. Following rocky starts, the UN's military interventions in East Timor and in Sierra Leone and between Ethiopia and Eritrea were succeeding and saving lives. In the fall of 2000, seventy-five heads of government – record attendance at the time for a diplomatic conference – had come to New York for a Millennium summit and established very ambitious international economic and social development targets, the Millennium Development Goals.[2] The subsequent "Monterrey Consensus," achieved at the 2002 conference on financing for development, seemed to express a new financial compact between rich and poor.[3] The secretary-general had personally put HIV/AIDS back at the top of the international agenda, persuading (some say coercing) drug companies and governments to cooperate and, himself, raising hundreds of millions of dollars for the cause.

Scant months later, the Security Council split over Iraq and some of the UN's harshest critics happily began writing its obituary. International public support for the UN was sagging, in the US because the world organization did not support the war in Iraq, and in the Muslim world especially, but elsewhere as well, because it did not prevent the war. The UN, at least the Secretariat, was reeling from its tragic personnel losses in Iraq and burdened by the alleged scandal in the UN Security Council's Iraqi Oil for Food programme. Further, the sheer weight of coping with the world's most intractable problems was proving draining for a long-serving secretary-general and his increasingly fatigued staff.

It is evidence of the UN's resilience that it has persevered in the face of such difficulties and, even, begun to rally. Member countries have rediscovered the old maxim that multilateral cooperation is a necessary means to some important ends. The UN is not irrelevant, as President Bush implied in his UN General Debate statement in September 2002, but indispensable to the good management of international relations. As a consequence of the Iraq experience, it has become evident that the general concurrence of the world expressed through the UN remains necessary in order to confer legitimacy on acts of war and that that legitimacy is a prerequisite to broad-based, effective cooperation in the management of war's aftermath. Resolution 1546 of 8 June 2004, among other resolutions, helps to re-situate the UN at the heart of international relations.

In an integrating world, where international decision-making authority is allocated by means of informal "subsidiarity,"[4] it is more evident than ever that overarching economic and social problems, such as climate change and communicable diseases, can best and often only be resolved globally. Most governments have come to the realization that the UN *per se* is central to such global cooperation. All of this is not to say that the UN is sufficient unto itself. Nor that the universality of membership of the UN, which is integral to the organization's unique legitimacy, lends itself to efficiency. Nor that the UN is ready for the new challenges of a new era. Nor, more fundamentally, that a constitution written in and for another age, i.e., the Charter, which has come over time to contradict itself, can go on forever unamended. Reform is clearly and urgently needed.

DISSATISFACTION WITH THE UNITED NATIONS

Although by no means the only member dissatisfied with the UN, the discontent of the United States has been the most prominent and most consequential. In contemplating the way ahead, it is worth remembering that antipathy to the UN has not been a basic operating principle of past US administrations. President Franklin D. Roosevelt, early in his career a member of his country's League of Nations delegation, was the driving force internationally for the creation of a world body, against the judgment of some of America's major wartime allies. President Harry Truman was equally convinced of the need for such a world body, and made its establishment literally his first priority.[5] President John F. Kennedy called in 1963 for the United Nations to become "a genuine world security system ... capable of solving disputes on the basis of law."[6] President Richard Nixon said the US would go the extra mile to make the UN succeed. More recently, speaking at the inauguration of the Reagan Library, President Bill Clinton recalled that Ronald Reagan had said that the UN stood as a symbol of the hopes of all mankind for a more peaceful and productive world. For most of the UN's existence, then, United States administrations have seen an effective UN as in American interests and constructive participation in the UN as a civic duty. It is not evident that either proposition remains true today.

The US, whose domestic exercise of power is governed by a system of checks and balances, progressively came to realize that, with the demise of the Soviet Union, American power no longer faced check or balance abroad. In addition, American will and capacity for international leadership continued undiminished at a time when others, particularly other industrialized countries, were content to see Washington lead if it wanted to, in part because of the US's sheer capacity to do so, in part because they saw no international threat to themselves or obligation to others requiring heavy investments in military capability. They preferred to spend their money and effort on domestic programme needs. As a consequence of the leadership role others readily conceded to the US, and because of the considerable costs and risks of its self-appointed mission to propagate democracy, many in Washington on both sides of the political aisle came increasingly to see the US as bearing a disproportionate burden and meriting exceptional dispensations from international law and norms.

The notion of America-as-exceptional harks back to the Puritan landing at Plymouth Rock[7] and has ebbed and flowed in the American psyche ever since. De Tocqueville observed it in nineteenth century America[8] and Margaret MacMillan discerned it in her recent study of the Paris peace talks of 1919.[9] US "exceptionalism" gained modern currency in the 1980s when President Reagan borrowed from the Bible[10] and from John Winthrop[11] for his favoured portrayal of the United States as the "shining city on a hill," the exemplar of democracy.

As Harold Koh of Yale, a former assistant secretary of state for democracy, human rights and labor has written, American "exceptionalism" unquestionably has its positive as well as its negative characteristics.[12] The US has exercised exceptional leadership, for example, in the development of postwar institutions, in the promotion of human rights and the development of international law and in the preservation of stability, particularly in North-East Asia. But from Iran in the fifties, to Vietnam in the sixties, to Chile in the seventies, to Iraq in the eighties, the US has chalked up some considerable errors. In its more self-serving expressions of exceptionalism, the United States has also questioned the applicability to itself of the UN Charter and of international law writ large, alienating many others in the process. It has also progressively eroded the equality principle that most UN members consider integral to the democratic character of the UN Charter, much as the legal equality of American states is integral to the US Constitution, even if in both cases actual power correlations are otherwise. The US abuse of the UN Security Council and the Charter, in giving effect to its opposition to the International Criminal Court, was seen by many as exceptionalism taken to counterproductive lengths, an unvarnished and unapologetic assertion of one law for the goose and another for the gander.

It was not always thus. At the end of the Second World War, when the US bestrode the world even more colossally than it does today, President Truman told the assembled UN delegates in San Francisco that "[w]e all have to recognize that no matter how great our strength, we must deny ourselves the license to do always as we please."[13] Now, many in the US seem to expect to lead, not by example, but by exception.

September 11 2001 did not "change everything," but it did change some things, especially in the United States. A country that had pursued a policy of invulnerability by means of a high cost, high tech defence found itself unexpectedly vulnerable to a low cost, low tech attack, with horrific consequences. In response, the US administration propounded a national security strategy positing not just pre-emption, which is foreseen in international law, but prevention, which is not. The war in Iraq was actually preventive – to bring down a tyrant with potentially malignant intentions and capabilities – but was presented as pre-emptive, to stop a tyrant who already had weapons of mass destruction.[14] A preventive attack should, in theory, be based on unassailable evidence that an adversary has not just the capability but the intent to do great harm. It, also, presumes very high quality, if not irrefutable, intelligence on the part of the attacker, which was catastrophically absent in the Iraq case. The new national security strategy of the United States articulated an intent to dominate which, if carried to its logical conclusions, could eventually generate major, preventive wars, directly violating international law and US treaty obligations under the Charter.

Undermining the UN would in some American minds be neither an incidental nor an unwelcome consequence of American policy. Richard Perle, until the spring of 2003 chairman of the US Defense Policy Board, probably spoke for many members of the current US Administration when he professed to see two benefits from the war in Iraq: first, the disappearance of Saddam Hussein and, second, the end of the United Nations. "Thank God for the death of the UN," he wrote in *The Guardian*, in March 2003.[15]

It is not only the far right in the United States that has been expressing its dissatisfaction. More moderate Americans, such as Ivo Daalder, who served in the Clinton White House, have called for an Alliance of Democratic States that would either enhance the effectiveness of the world organization or replace it.[16] The common values of an Alliance of Democracies, it is argued, would confer a legitimacy on its decisions that would attract the respect of Americans, which the UN, a supposed rogues' gallery of despots, human rights abusers and mini-states, had definitively lost. This thesis confers too much rectitude on democracies, which are capable of self-serving action and chicanery and which have, contrary to popular belief, frequently been far from peace-loving. In any case, the UN membership is already two-thirds free or partly free.[17] Resistance to US policy on Iraq was led in the Security Council by democratic governments. Further, it is precisely the non-democracies that must be persuaded if progress is to be made, for example, when human rights are at stake.

There was little in the reaction of the international community to the tragic events of September 11 to warrant putting sixty years of the development of international law, most of which previous US Administrations had promoted (and all of which was significant to

Canadian interests), into jeopardy. After the Al Qaeda attacks on New York and Washington, the UN General Assembly and the Security Council acted sympathetically to the United States and with despatch. On 12 September 2001, the General Assembly, which is not a decision-making body, issued a unanimous declaration of solidarity with the American people. Within days of September 11, the UN Security Council, whose decisions are legally binding in international law, proscribed cooperation with terrorists, ordering member states to deny them both safe haven and the use of national banking systems to finance their operations. The Council also established an oversight committee to monitor member states' compliance and to promote capacity-building in the poorer states. Many governments, the Canadian government included, sent troops to Afghanistan to fight the Taliban and Al Qaeda alongside the Americans. Many, also, committed themselves to spending substantial sums to lift Afghanistan out of its failed-state status, so that it would not again become a rear operating base for terrorists. Afghanistan became the largest recipient of Canadian funding, both in the Official Development Assistance and military categories.

By portraying the war against terrorism in indiscriminate and monolithic terms, Washington gave itself mission impossible. Terrorism is a heinous tactic but a tactic nonetheless, not a tangible enemy such as the Al Qaeda network that can be defeated. It also gave itself a hunting license to attack Iraq, despite the most tenuous of links between Al Qaeda and the Iraqi regime and the absence of hard evidence of the existence there of weapons of mass destruction. The US also rode roughshod over the objections of the great majority of UN members, isolating itself in world public opinion. By conflating Iraq with the Palestinian-Israeli issue, US foreign policy became, in the eyes of many, the problem. It has not helped matters that throughout the latter part of 2002 and the first quarter of 2003 some senior administration figures in Washington directed a steady stream of invective against the UN, an institution that, however flawed, most other members considered central to their national interests. In the process, the UN weapons inspectors were treated with surprising contempt, given that US and other intelligence services had depended on them to investigate third-party allegations. Those in Washington who still favoured multilateralism appeared to want it *à la carte,* to be a selective instrument for validating US action when Washington so wanted and to be ignored when it proved uncooperative.

Many influential Americans persuaded themselves that the potential nexus of terrorism and weapons of mass destruction meant that US security was best, in fact only, assured by the US acting free of the constraints of international law, multilateral institutions and quarrelsome allies. Books appeared describing self-serving theories of the inevitability of American dominion, justifying both its exceptionalist and unilateralist manifestations. Feckless allies were considered to owe the hegemon a decent loyalty, at least when it decided an action was in its vital interest, as in Iraq.[18] There was no patience with disagreement, which was regarded as manifesting moralistic qualms or strategic quibbles. At no time did it seem to register in official Washington that a large number of UN member states disagreed that war in Iraq was necessary and urgent and that their disagreement mattered, not least to the US's prospects of success there. Washington had tuned dissonance out.

Washington's dissatisfaction with the UN was mirrored in public opinion polls taken after the Iraq war that showed that the UN had lost support in two very different quarters: among the war's proponents, because the UN failed to sanction the war, and among the war's opponents, because it failed to prevent it. Although 55 per cent of Americans continued to view the UN positively, this was substantially down from pre-war figures. Outside of the US, a majority of those polled in Muslim countries had a much more negative opinion of the UN. For example, more than seven in ten Jordanians and nearly as many Moroccans expressed an unfavourable opinion.[19] Turkey was the single exception to this trend; a bare plurality viewed the UN positively.

Washington, with the bottom falling out of its standing in the Arab world,[20] its Iraq enterprise in jeopardy and the November 2004 elections at risk, came to see the utility of greater UN engagement. And, in fact, the UN played an indispensable role in the creation of an interim Iraqi government. Washington appeared to recognize that it needed the cooperation of UN and its members. What was less clear was the extent to which a weakened UN could help retrieve such a flawed enterprise.

THE UN HAS ITS OWN PROBLEMS

In attacking Iraq against the will of the international community, and in mishandling the occupation, the US did itself, and the UN, incalculable harm. Nevertheless, it would simply be wrong to lay all the UN's misfortunes at Washington's door. Rote apologies for the UN are no less damaging than mindless attacks on it. The UN Charter was written in and for a different age and treats national sovereignty as an absolute and constant good. As a consequence, over time a contradiction has arisen between the most basic purpose of the UN, "to save succeeding generations from the scourge of war," and one of its cardinal tenets, state sovereignty.[21] Because most of today's wars, the Iraq war being a significant exception, arise within the borders of existing states, the inhabitants often cannot be protected without intervention from outside. There is no consensus on how to respond to this new reality. Equally, there is no agreement on how to reform the ageing, unrepresentative Security Council, still the most important political/security body on earth.

Fundamentally, the UN's strength, universal membership, has also become its weakness. Its membership has swollen to 191 countries, making the achievement of consensus on any issue a Sisyphean task. As the UN has expanded and the world economy has been globalized, disparity between the richest and poorest has deepened, making the North-South economic divide ever more pronounced. Poverty eradication and development became the near exclusive compass points of the South, which often dismissed security as an issue of interest primarily to the North and of little consequence to the South. The poorer countries, feeling vulnerable to the more powerful states, especially to the sole superpower, banded ever more resolutely together in the hoary Non-Aligned Movement (NAM) and G-77. Combined with the strong preference for consensus in the General Assembly, this herd instinct made lowest-common-denominator outcomes the norm and provided a ready tool for political mischief, which was happily exploited by spoilers in the service of long dead ideologies and activists and reactionaries with dubious political objectives. Further, faced with the impossibility of moving the Security Council on Middle Eastern issues, largely because of the US veto, the Arabs under Palestinian leadership made the General Assembly their default forum. They have ready allies in much of the South, which has only relatively recently emerged from occupation and/or colonialism and which identifies with the Palestinians' powerlessness and plight.

Meanwhile, regional groups, which are indispensable to the efficient administration and management of the business of UN bodies, have themselves sometimes produced destructive electoral outcomes, notably in the stunningly counterproductive election of Libya to the chair of the Commission on Human Rights. Under these various pressures, the General Assembly has come to be seen in some countries, notably in the US, but also in Canada, as more theatre than parliament, with performances that are usually ignored outside the UN's immediate precincts, except where they censure Israel.

The world has also changed. There is very little international agreement on what the most important issues are, much less on how to resolve them. Most fundamentally, there is little common perception of the threat, including terrorism. There is correspondingly little agreement on how to respond. Some of the most dangerous confrontations attract only episodic Security Council engagement: the China-Taiwan issue, the Korean peninsula division and the South-Asian nuclear standoff. While the number of interstate conflicts has declined in recent years, the proportion of intrastate conflicts has increased and it is here that the contradictions inherent in the UN Charter itself have become a central issue. Further, economically and socially, the world is polarized between rich countries and poor. There is no real consensus about the contributing factors of the all pervasive issue of poverty and how to remedy it. At once seen as a cause and a cure, globalization has generated great wealth and considerable disparity within and between countries and revealed how inadequate existing institutions are for coping with the problems of the twenty-first century.

THE UN REMAINS INDISPENSABLE

None of this is to say that the UN has failed definitively and that it is time to walk away from it. Warts and all, it remains indispensable. Most fundamentally, the UN Charter is at the heart of the development of international law. Few outside the ambit of American exceptionalists doubt that the rule of law is preferable to the law of the jungle; a world governing itself by freely accepted laws is likely to be safer and more stable than one run by the self-appointed and self-interested powerful. In forty years time, would Canadians be content to grant similar, exceptional dispensations from international law to China as they might concede to the US now? Would Americans?

Global problems can only be solved through over-arching cooperation. From security to trade to finance to the environment to human rights, in sum, the complex of treaties, conventions, norms, institutions and formal and informal networks that the world has created, and continues to create, is integral to international order and prosperity. Multilateral cooperation, not multilateralism as an ideal or end in itself, is essential. For example, while the UN is often an object of uninformed criticism on terrorism, the UN General Assembly has passed a dozen basic counter-terrorism treaties. As these treaties have been progressively absorbed into domestic legislation around the world, norms and standards of international behaviour have been established and performance and compliance enhanced. What is true for terrorism is equally true for human rights, where the UN has passed six core treaties, including on women's rights; for arms control and disarmament, where the UN is at the heart of the nuclear non-proliferation regime, including its weapons inspection capability; for health, where the World Health Organization is central to the effort to control and eradicate communicable and other diseases such as HIV/AIDS, malaria, and SARS; for the environment where the UN has generated seventy-six treaties, including the ozone treaty so important to the health of Canadians; for international trade and investment, where GATT and WTO-written rules have fostered an explosion of international commerce, and so on. Beyond rules, norms and laws, there is an alphabet soup of UN acronyms IAEA, ICAO, IPU, ITU, WMO, WIPO, among many others, that stand for organizations helping the world to manage one aspect or another of international interchange.[22]

The UN is also indispensable to international humanitarian operations. For example, UNICEF has inoculated 575,000,000 children against childhood diseases, the World Food Programme fed over 100,000,000 people last year alone, the UNHCR has protected 22,000,000 refugees and internally displaced people, and the UN Mine Action Service has reported the destruction of over 30,000,000 landmines, which has saved countless limbs and lives. This work has been belittled by some as mere international social work. It may be social work but it delivers very real human and international security benefits.

TOWARDS REFORM OF THE UNITED NATIONS

The UN suffers from excessive caution and diplomatic sclerosis at a time when it is facing decidedly new demands. The fundamental political and legal challenge facing the UN is to determine when and under what conditions the international community is justified in intervening in the internal affairs of member states. The grounds on which there is a disposition to contemplate reform in descending order of practicability, include humanitarian crises, the illegal development or acquisition of weapons of mass destruction, the provision of safe haven for terrorists and the overthrow of democratic governments. Officials from countries that gained their independence in the living memories of their citizens see sovereignty as a crucial bulwark against once and future domination and are understandably reluctant to risk creating new pretexts for interference by others. Their worries are entirely comprehensible but not, nevertheless, a sufficient basis on which to protect the interests of their citizens in a changing world. As Secretary General Annan said in his Nobel Prize acceptance speech: "[t]he sovereignty of States must no longer be used as a shield for gross violations of human rights."[23] Elsewhere he argued, "[t]his developing international norm in favour of intervention to protect civilians from wholesale slaughter will no doubt continue to pose profound challenges to the international community. In some quarters it will arouse distrust, scepticism, even hostility. But I believe on balance we should welcome it."[24]

The tragic losses of September 11 raised a related challenge. Does the nexus of WMD and terrorism provide another justification for outside intervention in a state's internal affairs? Secretary-General Annan also put this issue starkly, in his seminal address to almost one hundred heads of government gathered in New York for the 2003 General Debate: "[s]ome say ... since an armed attack with weapons of mass destruction could be launched at any time ... states have the right and obligation to use force pre-emptively." The secretary-general clearly was referring to the US Administration. "This logic represents a fundamental challenge to the principles on which, however imperfect, world peace and stability have rested for the last fifty-eight years ..." He told the leaders assembled that "we have come to a fork in the road and that we must decide whether radical changes are needed."[25]

The secretary-general has done his part to respond to changing needs, using his bully pulpit to urge reform and establishing a blue ribbon panel to propose specific remedies to the UN's problems, both as regards what the UN does and how the UN does it, in that order. It is incumbent on UN member states to acknowledge the new dangers we all face collectively and to find the will and creativity to adapt the world organization to changed times. All UN members but particularly the developing countries are going to have to come to a new understanding of the limits of state sovereignty and the advantages of sharing and pooling it, if the UN is to be effective. The onus to adapt does not fall, nonetheless, exclusively on the poorer, younger countries. The United States and some others are also strongly attached to the idea of sovereignty. The US will need to resist the temptations of exceptionalism and unilateralism and resolve to cooperate on global issues, which can only be resolved multilaterally.

Nor is security the only major problem facing the UN. The yawning gap between rich and poor belies many western countries' charitable self-images, bedevils multilateral cooperation and undermines international security. The international community is not on track to achieve the economic and social goals leaders set themselves at the Millennium Summit. Rich and poor country governments, business and civil society organizations, all get a failing grade in the effort to meet the voluntarily chosen targets.

CANADA AND THE UNITED NATIONS

Canada can help the UN to reform itself. As much by virtue of our values, of who we are as a society, as by what we do in the world, although that needs our urgent attention too, we do have the standing to contribute. Other countries rightly see Canada as one of the very few countries where minorities' rights are protected and diversity is valued. Our years of peacekeeping and putting the protection of people at the heart of our foreign policy have gained us considerable respect. Our position on the Iraq war has earned us substantial political credit with the less powerful among the UN's members and with many, probably most, of the more powerful, as well. Canada is well positioned to carry out an effective foreign policy.

An effective foreign policy requires a beefed-up, combat-capable, peace-building-trained military, especially ground forces capable of intervening in conflict, a contemporary rather than a prospective financial commitment to poorer countries, and a diplomatic service with the resources to meet our own and others' expectations of us. Finally, our will needs to match our wallet, which has never in Canadian history been better able to afford an effective foreign policy.

On the two overarching challenges the UN faces, the absence of a common threat perception and the stubborn disparity between rich and poor, Canada, with its long tradition of bridge-building among different international constituencies, can play an important role, as the secretary-general reminded Canadians in the Canadian Parliament in March 2004. Perhaps the most important such role is to help the world and the US reconcile their very considerable differences. This means taking the initiative to impart to others the particular insights into what motivates the United States that we gain from geographic proximity and political and cultural propinquity. In an effort to alleviate American isolation and insecurity, and to be credible to others, we will have to "speak truth to power" in Washington. This means not shrinking from dealing frankly, albeit courteously, with US administrations when we think they are wrong, as many Canadians believe they were on issues as diverse as Iraq, the International Criminal Court, Kyoto, and the development of still another generation of nuclear weapons and missile systems. It, equally, means not shrinking from supporting and defending American positions when we think the US is right, as for example, on North Korea, on Taiwan and on the propagation of democracy by example, generally. It also means, finally, not subordinating foreign policy imperatives to bilateral anxieties.

Redressing the insecurities of both the US and the developing world is impeded by rigid interpretations of sovereignty on both sides. In the developing world, there is a historically understandable, albeit irrational, fear of too much outside intervention but an all too true and present reality of too little, as Rwanda tragically demonstrated, and the conflicts in the Congo and Sudan continue to confirm. In Washington, an atavistic interpretation of sovereignty often fuels exceptionalist policies and frequently encumbers the negotiation and even precludes the ratification of treaties.

We need to use our political capital to persuade developing world countries, the Africans above all, that by limiting and pooling their national sovereignty they can serve their own interests. It is Africans who have most desperately needed intervention in recent years. The African Union charter is a pudding that will be proved in the eating. We can work to alleviate the concerns of Latin Americans, who hear in the US invasion of Iraq echoes of the Monroe Doctrine and of a century of intervention. We can urge Asians to recalibrate their surprisingly strong attachment to the seventeenth-century European idea of Westphalian sovereignty. We need to work to understand, and to persuade others to address, Washington's sense of unique vulnerability.

Canada can also help the secretary-general to rebalance the international agenda, and to empower the United Nations to organize a global response to the global challenges of disease control, hunger, lack of schooling and environmental destruction.[26] The past thirty years have seen some dramatic improvements in the developing world. Life expectancy has increased by eight years. Illiteracy has been cut nearly in half, to 25 per cent. People surviving on less than $1 a day has been almost halved in the 1990s. Still, some fifty-four countries are poorer now than they were in 1990. In twenty-one, a larger proportion of people are going hungry. In fourteen, more children are dying before age five. In twelve, primary school enrolments are shrinking. In thirty-four, life expectancy has fallen. Such reversals in survival were previously rare.[27]

The Millennium Development Goals address these daunting challenges. They present an effective framework for delivering on the commitment to alleviating poverty. Many of the solutions to hunger, disease and lack of education are well known. UN-bashers notwithstanding, the specialized UN programs and agencies have extensive expertise and hands-on experience in dealing with these challenges. Here, Canada could help by marshalling talent from across our widely respected public service and civil society organizations to support the UN's efforts to build capacity in the poorer countries, in order to enhance the quality of their own governance. As we help others build their own effective institutions, we also help the UN regain its effectiveness, an interest that we and the Americans share.

Reform of the United Nations system is necessary but not sufficient to meet the challenges of the twenty-first century. The weaknesses of other international bodies need remedying and the lacunae between them need filling. The Bretton Woods organizations, for example, have representation and voting rights anomalies. The World Bank has grown to dominate others in the field and its role vis-à-vis the regional development banks and especially vis-à-vis the UNDP needs recalibrating. Nor, in a floating exchange rate world, is the IMF's mandate clear, including vis-à-vis the more powerful countries which currently can and do ignore its prescriptions. NATO, a trans-regional alliance, is also struggling with the reality that neither the values of its members nor the threats they face are as common as they once were.

The G-8, while effective in mobilizing the major industrialized countries on key issues, such as HIV/AIDS and the New Economic Partnership for Africa's Development (NEPAD), is nonetheless handicapped in achieving broader objectives by virtue of its limited membership. Prime Minister Paul Martin's proposal for the creation of a larger, north-south group that would be more representative of power and population realities now and foreseen is one possible answer to this problem. Such broader-based participation would facilitate broader-based "buy-in" by developing countries. Because heads of government have both the horizontal perspective and political authority that their individual ministers by definition do not have, a G-20 at leaders' level could make breakthroughs on intractable problems. Prospects for progress on HIV/AIDS and other communicable diseases, on trade and agricultural subsidies, on terrorism and WMD, on international financial reform, on the Millennium Development Goals and, not least, on the reform of the UN itself would be enhanced if the world's leading countries could sensitize each other and reach general understandings among themselves. Such a group would complement rather than compete with the UN, which would retain its unique legitimacy by virtue of its universal membership, its statutory responsibility for peace and security and the centrality of its Charter to international law. A G-20 could also facilitate the work of the UN, including the Security Council, by helping reduce North-South economic polarity and US-"other" security gaps that often bedevil UN deliberations.

International organizations are notoriously difficult to reform, the UN perhaps most difficult of all. Still, no one can be confident that absent a determined effort at innovation the world organization on which we count for nearly every facet of international relations and global governance will muddle through. The system of laws, norms and treaties that the UN represents, backed up by formal and informal networks of officials and experts on economic and social cooperation, human rights, the judiciary, the police and security, is crucial to Canada's well-being and independence. It is manifestly in Canada's interest to promote UN reform so that the organization functions effectively as a universal forum for the deliberation on and collective management of the world's global problems. Overcoming the fear of change is neither easy nor certain but the attempt to do so is timely and necessary. The suffering of the Second World War generated the international will to create the United Nations. It is not too much to hope that the shock of the second Iraq war will generate the collective resolve to reform it.

NOTES

This paper reflects the views of the author alone.

1 The Norwegian Nobel Committee, "The Nobel Peace Prize 2001," (press release), Oslo, 12 October 2001.

2 The Millennium Development Goals were established at the UN Millennium Summit in September 2000, when member states reaffirmed their commitment to assess development progress and achieve specific development goals within specified time frames. 147 heads of state adopted the UN Millennium Declaration, and it was passed unanimously by all the 189 members of the UN General Assembly. See http://www.un.org/geninfo/ir/millen-main.htm.

3 The Monterrey Consensus was adopted on 22 March 2002 in Monterrey, Mexico. Heads of state and government gathered to address the challenges of financing for development. The consensus, effectively, held that increased financial flows and sounder governance were both prerequisites to achieving the Millennium Development Goals. See http://www.un.org/esa/ffd/aconf198–11.pdf.

4 A European Union term for distributing decision-making to the level of government international, regional, national, local best positioned by circumstance to succeed.

5 "Flags of Convenience," *The Economist*, 368, 8341 (13 Sept. 2003), 76–7, review of Stephen Schlesinger, *Act of Creation: The Founding of the United Nations* (Boulder, Colo.: Westview Press, 2003).

6 Theodore C. Sorensen, "Arrogance and Ignorance," American University commencement address, Washington, DC, 11 May 2003.

7 William Ames, "Emergence of Puritan Technology," in Alden Vaughan,

ed, *The Puritan Tradition in America 1620–1730* (Columbia: University of South Carolina Press, 1972), 14.

8 Alexis de Tocqueville, *Democracy in America* (New York: Vintage Books, 1945), 14.

9 Margaret MacMillan, *Peacemakers: The Paris Conference of 1919 and Its Attempt to End War* (London: J. Murray, 2001), 22.

10 Matthew 5:13–16.

11 John Winthrop, the first governor of the Massachusetts Bay Colony, wrote from the deck of the ship that had borne him across the Atlantic: "We shall find that the God of Israel is among us ... when he shall make us a praise and glory, that men of succeeding generations shall say, 'The Lord make it like that of New England.' For we must consider that we shall be as a City upon a Hill, the eyes of all people are upon us."

12 Harold Hongju Koh, "On American Exceptionalism," *Stanford Law Review,* 55, 5 (May 2003), 1479–1527.

13 "Flags of Convenience."

14 Geoffrey Wheatcroft, "The Tragedy of Tony Blair," *The Atlantic*, 293,5 (June 2004), 56–72.

15 Richard Perle, "Thank God for the Death of the UN," *The Guardian*, 21 March 2003, 26. See: <http://www.guardian.co.uk/comment/story/0,,918764,00.html>.

16 Ivo Daalder and James Lindsay, "An Alliance of Democracies," op-ed in *Washington Post*, 23 May 2004, B.07.

17 Linda Stern, ed, *Freedom in the World 2002* (New York: Freedom House, 2002).

18 Timothy Appleby, "US still upset with Canada: Rice; Bush adviser says time needed to heal rift," *Globe and Mail*, 31 May 2003, A1.

19 The Pew Research Center for the People and the Press, "Views of a Changing World 2003: War with Iraq Further Divides Global Politics," 3 June 2003, 1.

20 Report of the US Advisory Group on Public Diplomacy for the Arab and Moslem World, "Changing Minds, Winning Peace," submitted to the Committee on Appropriations, US House of Representatives.

21 See especially *Responsibility to Protect*, the report of the International Commission on Intervention and State Sovereignty, Canadian International Development Research Centre, Ottawa.

22 IAEA International Atomic Energy Agency; ICAO International Civil Aviation Organization; IPU Inter-Parliamentary Union; ITU International Telecommunications Union; WMO World Meteorological Organization; WIPO World Intellectual Property Organization.

23 Kofi Annan, Nobel lecture, Oslo, 10 December 2001.

24 Kofi Annan, "Two concepts of sovereignty," *The Economist,* 352, 8137 (19 Sept. 1999), 49–50.

25 Kofi Annan, The Secretary-General's Address to the General Assembly, New York, 23 September 2003.
26 Jeffrey Sachs, "Weapons of Mass Salvation," *The Economist,* 365, 8296, (24 Oct. 2002), 101.
27 UNDP Human Development Report 2003, Millennium Development Goals Overview.

16 Summitry and Governance: The Case for a G-XX

GEORGE HAYNAL

The international system is stumbling in the face of new challenges. The facts are known to all. What is missing is a capacity to deal with them. Adjustment is necessary in the architecture, not just the plumbing, of international cooperation. Summitry is the innovative management formula of the last decades. It may be the only one that can help foster reorientation in the international system today. But the Summit structures we now have are inadequately representative.

A new, inclusive Summit, let us call it the G-XX,[1] could help address global challenges and reform international institutions. It would express the changing nature and balance of power in the world and assist our shared institutions to function better by providing them with the appropriate political direction. The practical challenges involved in establishing a new forum are formidable. A great deal of political capital and intense diplomacy will be required if a G-XX is to have a chance of success, and even then the initiative will be subject to unpredictable variables in an unsteady global system. The chances of success depend very much on the nature of the strategy for launching it.

Successive Canadian governments have used the leverage provided by summitry to further national interests in the international system. Canada is a uniquely open modern society, an externally oriented economy and a non-belligerent international actor. Its capacity to defend its interests in the world now depends heavily on exerting influence on, and through, a well functioning, rules-based international system. This country was in an extremely privileged position of relative power when the postwar institutions were established in the 1940s, and played a significant role in shaping them. It has maintained a global influence that is increasingly disproportionate to its relative power, by being a joiner, builder and user of the international system.

Any erosion in the international framework would leave Canada weaker and more vulnerable. It is in the national interest to have a meaningful role in shaping whatever Summit-level efforts are made to reshape the international system. Neither geography nor size guarantees Canada a role in doing that. We have always earned the right to participate in Summitry by dint of our dedication and capacity to contribute. Taking the initiative now to shape the discourse among world leaders could help us to secure a seat at the table when decisions about the future global system are made.

We are uniquely able to take on such a role. Canada is a dynamic member of virtually every international Summit group, including the G-8, APEC, the Commonwealth and the Francophonie. We were instrumental in founding the Finance Ministers G-20. Our experience allows us to help create a new mechanism at the heart of world power, and by doing so ensure that we remain in it.

THE INTERNATIONAL SYSTEM IS SHOWING ITS AGE

The multilateral system to which the world community looks as its principal tool for the management of shared challenges was established in a radically different age. It was created by the vision of leaders determined to avoid the kind of order that precipitated two world wars, the concern of waning imperial powers to retain influence and an American will to shape the international agenda.

The world also looked very different than it does today. There was no "developing world" then. Its foundations were being laid in the idealistic rhetoric that surrounded the bitter business of decolonisation. The post-1945 order was settling into what came to be the bipolarity of the Cold War. The global trading system was the preserve of a very small number of industrialized countries in the North Atlantic. It is less surprising that the system is showing its age than that it has been able to adapt as it has.

Though some have been more successful than others in responding to new realities, all the institutions that make up the system faltered in the last decade. The end of the Cold War and the triumph of liberal economics left the institutions unprepared for the new challenges of global insecurity and disorder, as well as for the potential of free markets to destabilize fragile economies. The institutions also suffer from being organized functionally. As the complexity and interconnectedness of the international agenda intensify, institutional stove piping is an ever more serious inhibition on the system's capacity to respond to the global challenges today that are posed by a stew of security, societal and economic issues. Dealing with them in isolation is much less likely to be productive than treating them as parts of one paradigm.

The institutions are all addressing their weaknesses, some more openly than others. They all need political support and energy to permit them to do so successfully.

THE UN SYSTEM IS UNDER SEVERE STRESS

The United Nations (UN) security system was, for most of its life, a podium for the Cold War, expressed as often as not in superpower standoff. It served weaker countries as a rhetorical vehicle for expressing their sovereign neutrality in the Cold War. When the Cold War ended, the United Nations were unable to find a unifying principle to put in its place. The 1990s were its decade of opportunity to establish a new basis for global security. The countries of the UN failed even to establish a workable method of stabilizing disintegrating polities, or of intervening when these turned genocidal within their own boundaries.

THE SECURITY COUNCIL IS INSECURE

Part of the reason for this failure is the unrepresentative nature of the Security Council membership. Its nominal composition has remained unchanged, even though two of its original permanent members (the Soviet Union and the Republic of China) have disappeared, two others (Britain and France) are merging their sovereignty within the European Union (EU), and new regional powers (including India, Brazil and South Africa), with a legitimate claim to a permanent seat, have emerged. The Council's crisis of legitimacy is driven in part by the demands of these rising powers for more representation.

It is also fanned by conflicts of principle between the United States and the other existing permanent members, who are all using the Council to try to impose their own visions for a new global order. Increasingly ideological divisions within the Council on the response to the proliferation of weapons of mass destruction and international terrorism makes shared effort to combat them elusive.

The Council is, in sum, part of the problem rather than of the solution to the failings of the international system. It cannot be looked to as the prime vehicle for addressing them, nor is it going to be able, unaided, to reconcile the conflicting visions of global security that now bedevil the world.

The failure to agree on a shared approach to global security has already hindered action in specific crises. It has sapped energy from achieving other, unrelated objectives, such as trade liberalization. It cannot last long without doing fatal damage to the whole system of global cooperation.

The Iraq war has highlighted only some of the UN's structural weaknesses. The UN secretary-general is trying to address them across the board. He has appealed for openness to radical change, and has established a High-Level Panel[2] to make proposals in this spirit. His initiative reflects despair that member states, whose diplomacy is at the root of the institution's problems, can agree on meaningful reforms. The Panel might well produce a report with cogent recommendations; good ideas on reform are not lacking. The problem will be that the exercise could let governments avoid grappling with the issues. The group's recommendations will have to be taken up somewhere, if they are to have an effect. That "somewhere" now is the Security Council and the General Assembly, the same fora on whose failure it will report. This could be a recipe for frustration and failure. A new forum with political will and authority will be needed to build consensus outside these bodies before they consider them. A G-XX, so mandated, could perform such a consensus-building role, and in the process, help the multilateral system address the new threats to global security.

Committing a group of leaders to take the Panel report as their agenda could be difficult. They would not want to make themselves hostages to the views of a group of independent experts. Nonetheless, if the secretary-general were to draw on the report from the Panel to submit his own recommendations, a meeting of a G-XX could be an appropriate informal venue to consider them, though there would be difficulties in justifying this way of proceeding to the countries that were not members of the group. If an informal consensus on directions was reached, Leaders could monitor progress in the international framework on achieving it. Monitoring would not equal management, but it would permit Leaders to instruct their own national delegates in a common spirit.

THE GENERAL ASSEMBLY IS TOO GENERAL

The UN General Assembly, which provides the world's primary forum for dealing with global issues, has expanded to over 190 members. The only truly universal body shared by the world community, the General Assembly has been obliged to trade effectiveness for representativity. The Cold War constraints are gone, but its capacity for constructive debate is still drowned in a sea of words. That being said, its committees have had more quiet success in raising global issues over the last decade than they are given credit for. Summits inspired by the General Assembly have produced global agreements to address poverty, health, environmental protection and education. Those agreements were incorporated in a shared commitment to action in the form of the Millennium Development Goals (MDGs). But these accomplishments have their limits. The General Assembly is too large and too remote from the loci of national power to sustain the pressure on developing countries and donors to meet the MDGs. Nor does it have the capacity more generally to bring coherence to the activity of the various components of the UN system.

THE SPECIALIZED AGENCIES ARE OVER-SPECIALIZED

The UN specialized agencies do come under the UN institutional umbrella, but are under-funded and receive little of the political attention that is focused on international security. They are, nonetheless, the ones performing what is often the most valuable work in the UN system, setting standards and fostering global co-operation in public health, telecommunications, transport, postal services, environmental protection, nuclear safety, agriculture, human rights and the treatment of refugees. They work with national governments and NGOs across the world. Their contribution to management within their own domains is often of a high order, but they are narrowly focused on technical areas and are provided direction from national governments by sectoral experts. They lack the coherent guidance and political support that would integrate their efforts.

National representatives at these institutions often resist the notion that the rules they negotiate need to be consistent with broader goals of the global community. This is not because they are innately narrow minded, but because their mandate and their expertise is circumscribed by policy and experience. Financial, development, trade, security, economic, agricultural and scientific experts are all under the same constraint, which they then impose on the institutions that they oversee on behalf of their national governments.

Though efforts are being made to bring coherence to the system by individual organizations, the only way to integrate the management of global issues and establish priorities among them is for national governments to decide that they should be managed on such a basis. The only level where the various threads of national decision-making come together is at the top. Global issues need coherent effort by international institutions. The G-XX could help push the system to provide it.

THE NEW GLOBAL ISSUES

Another dimension of the challenge of international governance is that new issues, driven by technology and change in demographics, have not found a place on the agenda of existing international institutions, and there has been little appetite to establish new arrangements to manage them. Among these issues, some of the most critical are: global terrorism and international criminality; fresh water management; governance of cyberspace; migration; and the application of genetics to agriculture and human health.

In some cases, like fresh water management, the issue is the domain of all institutions, and hence of none. In the case of global crime and terrorism, substantive co-operation is largely carried out among national intelligence, security and enforcement agencies. The political discourse that is required for broader efforts to combat the phenomenon and the root causes behind it has not yet advanced beyond the ideological. Governance in cyberspace has not yet become the focus of concerted international action, though the social, economic and security implications are already evident.

International migration is reshaping the world's social and economic structures, and has implications for international security. The discourse on migration, however, is at best haphazard and the co-operation in the area spread over many institutions in an uncoordinated fashion, though the World Bank is now focusing on a more integrated approach to migration.

Agreement on the rules for the genetic modification of consumables is elemental to securing the future of global agriculture and for safety of the human food supplies. Similarly, the implications for the application of genetics to medicine require some minimum consensus and rule-making for science to serve socially acceptable purposes. Yet there is no global institutional focus for a discourse that would create such a consensus. The issues are dealt with in stovepipes, if at all, and sometimes in ways that serve other ends.

The new global issues need consideration in a small but representative high-level group. No single country can address them successfully. They are highly complex and political. Before the international system can address them with any sense of confidence, key national governments will have to reach consensus on how it should do so.

The G-XX could, at a minimum, provide a forum where leaders could address these issues together, in a non-contentious setting. That in itself could foster better co-operation at lower levels. At the optimum, they could set priorities among these issues as guidance for the international system, and monitor their progress in addressing them.

THE DOHA PROCESS

The GATT served the international trading system well as long as the participants were largely like-minded industrialized countries trying to reduce tariff barriers among themselves. It began to falter, however, when the system expanded with the entry of significant industrializing economies, and as the acceptance of free trade reached its apogee with the foundation of the WTO. The Doha Round of negotiations that followed that landmark event has disappointed the expectations of the middle income and less developed countries. They had entered the Round because they had come to accept the need for liberalized trade, and regarded access to developed country markets as the key to their own development.

Their disappointment is the worse because the Doha Round was intended to focus on meeting their interests. It has failed in that so far, and has created North/South tensions that had been largely muted in the previous two decades. These tensions complicate efforts to establish harmony on other fronts, most particularly on a new international security order. Tensions on security, in turn, inhibit progress on trade.

The Round coincided with an upsurge in anti-free trade sentiment in industrialized economies. Economic liberalization proved to be socially and economically destabilizing in a number of emerging and developing economies. Regional trading arrangements in Europe and the Americas distracted the attention of industrialized governments from the multilateral process, and continue to do so. The industrializing economies, for their part, have not been willing to liberalize trade generally among themselves. They also sought out bilateral and regional arrangements when these were to their national advantage. The poorest countries have had little reason to push for a multilateral agreement, given their perception that the costs far outweighed the immediate advantages. They too have preferred to go the bilateral route whenever a large partner was willing to entertain it. Current tensions on international security further inhibit the transatlantic co-operation that will be necessary to make the Round a success.

The protectionists and mercantilists have won so far. The Round is stalled, although a framework agreement seems to have avoided its collapse. Much difficult work, however, remains if substance is to be given to the agreement itself. The United States and the EU have, in any event, pursued alternative regional and bilateral agreements. Their example is being followed elsewhere, most particularly in Asia, where China forms a new pole around which regional economies now gravitate.

A stasis in WTO negotiations threatens to leave the weakest, those who most need the opportunities created by stronger trade flows and the governance improvements they can bring, even weaker, both among countries and within them. If it persists, this failure will reverberate far beyond the trade domain. Isolating economies within regions or behind borders will eventually impoverish them, creating further destabilizing inequity within societies. Regional and superpower centred trading blocs will drive other forms of particularism and could rekindle security rivalries.

Should these trends prevail, they can only undermine efforts to address global challenges of public health, environmental sustainability, and international criminality and terrorism, among others. These are issues of the global commons, not trade policy; consideration of these long-term consequences of a failure to reach agreement on a new trade regime is beyond the remit of trade ministers. There is, however, no widely representative forum that can address the problem at a higher level and give an appropriate signal of determination to break the deadlock.

Under the right circumstances, a G-XX summit process could help to build a consensus to reinvigorate the Doha process. Leaders can weigh a broader range of considerations than can ministers of trade, and could thus help to find a more fruitful basis for the necessary compromises. In doing so, they would also help to establish a better political basis for a new global approach to security. Everyone has to have a more equitable stake in the system if they are going to be prepared to defend it. In this sense, the WTO and the Security Council agendas are closely linked, though that link has not yet been made by the protagonists. The G-XX process could help them to do so.

CONFLICTING PRESSURES ON THE INTERNATIONAL FINANCIAL INSTITUTIONS (IFIS)

The Bretton Woods institutions, though the target of insistent criticism, and self criticism, are perhaps the most responsive to changes in the world environment.[3] Nonetheless, both the World Bank and the International Monetary Fund (IMF) continue to face challenges of purpose and relevance. While the World Bank is moving to make the Millennium Development Goals the organizing principle around which to organize its work, it still faces criticism, especially from low income countries, that it is too slow to disburse resources to those countries that most need them to meet the MDGs. It is attacked on the grounds that some of its approaches are contradictory (for instance, in its policies relating to the management of fresh water resources). Others observe that it has not sufficiently integrated its own operations with those of other development institutions, particularly in the UN system.

The uneven success of its macroeconomic prescriptions and its performance in crises has failed to convince critical constituencies about the International Monetary Fund's capacity to guarantee stability in the world financial system. There are insistent criticisms about the lack of adequate representation in its decision-making bodies. The middle income countries, in particular, argue that the constituency structure has suppressed their voices, which is particularly problematic because they are the only ones over whose economies the IFIs has sway. They argue with some reason that the IMF prescriptions originate in a fiscal orthodoxy that the dominant economic powers practice only in the breach.

The Fund's perspective has been attacked as narrow and technical, but efforts to widen the scope of its remit have not yet produced a new approach. The Fund's capacity to integrate its own efforts and resources with those of the Bank and the UN system are also the subject of concern and criticism. The Fund's critics include financial market actors. Most recently, the Argentinean crisis has left some market participants doubtful about the need for the Fund at all.

The G-20 Finance Ministers have already addressed some of the structural issues in the IMF. The inclusion of all systemically significant economies in a politically sensitive discourse of equals has helped to build a greater sense of shared responsibility among members. Summit level support for this approach could add political weight to the effort of ministers, and sensitize leaders to some of the concerns that the G-20 was designed to raise.

A G-XX summit process could also provide a forum for validating the emphasis that the World Bank has placed on meeting the Millennium Development Goals and reinforcing the Bank's leadership role in the global effort to meet the MDGs, though there are difficulties with doing so in the immediate future.[4] It could monitor progress in meeting those goals among member states and in the manner in which global institutions are working to advance them. The nature of this monitoring would have to be carefully circumscribed. Rather than focusing on quantitative indicators of progress, the most effective focus might be on policy directions at the national level and in global institutions.

THE G-XX COULD HELP CORRECT THE GROWING MISMATCH BETWEEN POWER AND REPRESENTATION IN WHAT IS BECOMING A TRULY GLOBAL SYSTEM

Globalization and the end of the Cold War have brought a sea change in the international environment. The institutions that are intended to manage it were not designed for radical change, including in the way that they make decisions or that they accommodate the newly powerful.

The North Atlantic powers are over-represented, one way or the other, in all world institutions, whether it is in the Security Council or the IFI quota and constituency systems. Whether or not predictions that the economies of Brazil, Russia, India and China will be larger than the G-8 by 2050 are accurate, they underline an inexorable diffusion of economic power in the world. Demographic trends as well as military and technological advances point in a similar direction. New Great Powers are rising. The governance structures of our international institutions do not accommodate them. Nor do they permit other, weaker states to have an effective voice in the management of international organizations on which, being the weakest, they rely the most. Those with the most disproportionate power in these institutions resist "redistricting." The United States, for its part, argues that it has disproportionately little influence considering its real power, and is seeking to build a new international system that is at the same time more responsive to and less binding on it. These dynamics have led to a multilogue of the deaf in the international system, which makes coherence in the way institutions function increasingly elusive.

A new G-XX mechanism would not solve the problem of skewed representation in global institutions, but it could go some way to providing a meaningful forum with more realistic participation. A new forum that was designed specifically to include the emerging major powers would have strong symbolic value. If it were to be structured to work with a maximum degree of informality and to be a consensus body, it would also allow for a unique kind of personal interaction among leaders that now exists only at regional level and in restricted groups like the G-8. It could facilitate more collegial decision making in global fora, by providing coherent guidance to national officials and maintaining periodic oversight of progress on agreed priority issues. The G-XX would also be the best-positioned caucus in which informal agreements might eventually be reached on the most contentious representation issues, including the restructuring of the Security Council. Conversely, if no agreement were possible, the group could evolve into an informal surrogate for the Security Council.

STRUCTURING THE G-XX

There could be several ways to approach the formation of a G-XX. One would be to expand the G-8, but that is unlikely to work. The G-8 membership will evolve over time, but it cannot be expanded enough to be representative without changing its character altogether. Trying to make it into a consensus formation body would destroy its invaluable capacity for decision-making. Any new body should therefore operate in parallel, rather than seek to displace, the G-8. Formalizing G-8 outreach has been suggested as another alternative, but it is unlikely that inviting others to meet at the margin of G-8 meetings would be a viable long-term basis for shared discourse. Another approach would be to elevate the G-20 Finance Ministers forum to the Leaders' level. Though this course has the attraction of symmetry, it would overburden the G-20 process and pose more problems than it solves. This is not to say that the G-XX should distance itself from the G-20 experience. On the contrary, it should draw extensively on the pioneering model that finance ministers established, but do so without absorbing the original.

It is easy to identify a core G-XX membership. The G-8 would be one building block. The great regional powers of Asia, Africa and South America (China, India, South Africa, Brazil and perhaps Mexico) would be the other. Such a caucus would certainly represent the emerging balance of economic and military power in the world. But a whole different class of weak countries, ones that rely the most on the international system, would have to be added to this core of the powerful to make the group representative of what the world really looks like. Only their inclusion will oblige the group to focus on the management of the global commons as a shared responsibility.

The most practicable way to proceed might be to build on, but not be restricted by, the composition of the G-20. Adding a small number of members would make the group somewhat more representative, if not perfect, but still manageable in size. Representation from Africa would have to be raised. The Middle East would also merit greater representation. An additional country could be added from each of southeast Asia, the Americas, and the ex-Soviet bloc. Such an approach would bring the group to approximately twenty-six, making it more representative than the G-20 membership, but still manageable in size.

Whatever composition is decided upon, an invitation to Leaders to an initial meeting, rather than the establishment of a formal process, would provide the most flexibility at the least political cost. Attendance would be a function of the agenda and be at the discretion of the convening head of government. Though the implicit understanding would be that such a "one off" meeting could be the beginning of an informal process, the issue of inclusion/exclusion would be less divisive than if participants were invited to launch an immutable "group." The most critical participant in any such enterprise would be the United States. If the US president comes, everyone else will likely do so as well.

There is a good case to be made that a G-XX would be in America's interest. Whether the Administration could be persuaded to go this route, however, depends heavily on events in the UN, the situation in Iraq and, most important, on presidential election politics. Ironically, too, the G-XX cannot be made too attractive to the US. There will be little appetite by anyone to sign up to a group that would be either a pulpit or an anvil for the United States.

Potential participants will all have to be persuaded that the G-XX is in their interest. The other G-8 countries could be attracted by the prospect that the G-XX would be helpful in domestic political terms and could take pressure off the G-8 process for more engagement with non-members. China and the other regional powers would have to see the G-XX as a useful way to engage, and not as a second best to G-8 membership or bloc-to-bloc confrontation.

CONSENSUS IS INDISPENSABLE FOR MANAGING THE GLOBAL COMMONS

The G-XX's value lies in representing a diversity of interests. That commitment to diversity precludes decision-making as a realistic goal. Building mutual confidence across the rifts in world power is important in its own right and should be the first objective of the G-XX. The second should be consensus formation on directions and priorities in the management of the global commons.

Many issues require Leaders' attention, but there are several arguments for choosing international security co-operation as the initial focus for the G-XX. It is the subject that is most likely to attract US participation. The Group's support would also be helpful to the secretary-general in his efforts to reform the UN's peace and security role. International security would also be a broad enough subject to provide an umbrella under which linkages among global issues (e.g., Doha, migration, international health and the fight against terrorism) could be discussed. A "global security" agenda would therefore legitimately leave space for everyone's national and human security concerns.

LAUNCH LOGISTICS, AND CANADA'S ROLE

The objective of setting up a G-XX would be to establish an "ongoing conversation." The agenda, the objectives, the expectations and the rules of that meeting would have to be agreed beforehand. One vehicle for agreeing on that common base would be to hold an organizing meeting of the principals. Where and how would that be organized best? On balance, the most effective approach might be to associate the meeting with the UN General Assembly fall session, when Leaders are in attendance. This venue and timing would have both practical logistical advantages and potentially positive symbolic significance.

Who would call the preparatory meeting? Prime Minister Paul Martin was the first leader to champion the concept of a G-XX Summit. It would be reasonable to assume that he would want to be the one to launch it. Doing so would also be important in ensuring Canada's inclusion. Launching the meeting would involve considerable personal time by the prime minister and require structured follow up by the Canadian government.

There is a good deal of scepticism about summitry in G-8 countries, though this is not always the case elsewhere, regarding the lack of both transparency and concrete accomplishment. Effective communications will be essential. Realistic expectations, low-key stage setting, open agendas, costs kept to a minimum, a venue that is associated with other meetings and a candid chairman's report – all be helpful.

The direct costs associated with a G-XX could be enormous. They can best be kept under control if the meeting is held in the UN General Assembly context in New York. The indirect costs (pledging resources to agreed goals) could be kept within the realm of the feasible only if the G-XX is firmly framed as an effort at consensus building and direction setting, and that pledging (including pressure to pledge) is off the table.

CONCLUSION

It is definitely possible to construct a successful scenario for launching a new Summit, but it is also the case that a host of unpredictable events could scupper it at any stage. It is certain that the Canadian prime minister will have to invest a lot of time and capital in making it happen. The prospect of these obstacles, foreseen and unpredicted, could lead the cautious to advise against launching the Summit early in the new mandate, which presumably is when the prime minister will want to do so.

But the obstacles are only potential, and need to be tested. They do not disqualify the chances of success. The upside of success could be significant in systemic terms; the costs might be disproportionately small, which would be unusual in the Canadian experience of Summits. The effects of delay until later in the life of an uncertain government are unpredictable, except in one respect: the problems the initiative is meant to address will have had more time to simmer and corrode the international system. If it were done, it should be done quickly.

NOTES

This paper is a personal contribution of the author, and does not reflect the views of Bombardier.

1 I have used the term "G-XX" throughout, in referring to such a more comprehensive Summit process, both to distinguish it from the Finance Ministers process, and because the likely number of participants is a real and open question.

2 Chaired by former Thai Prime Minister Anand Panyaruchin. For the Panel's terms of reference, see http://www.un.org/news/dh/hl panel/terms-of-reference-re-hl-panel.pdf.

3 The criticism itself might account for the adaptation. Another is that the consequences of IFI failure are easier to appreciate because they are more immediate than those that attend the United Nations and of longer standing than those at the WTO. Another is that the institutions function on a basis that provides a better balance between representativity and effectiveness. The constituency system has allowed a far higher level of direct influence to smaller countries than the one country one vote UN system, and has allowed those with a larger stake in the world economy to be more effective in providing it with direction.

4 The MDGs are receiving a good deal of attention already in other contexts. The policy course for meeting the goals is still being established, and Summit level attention might have a negative effect on the dynamics of this early phase. It could, in particular, provoke the rhetoric of claims and counterclaims about financial pledges unmet or policy changes not implemented. If that were to happen, both the shared commitment to the MDGs and the G-XX process itself would be imperilled rather than advanced. The MDGs, however, are a critical part of the mix for managing global challenges, and would therefore be an important focus for the G-XX once it has been launched.

Contributors

ROBERT BOTHWELL is professor of history and director of the International Relations Program at the University of Toronto.

MARGARET CATLEY-CARLSON is chair of the Global Water Partnership, after a career in the Canadian public service which included a term as president of the Canadian International Development Agency.

DAVID CARMENT is associate professor at The Norman Paterson School of International Affairs, Carleton University, director of the university's Centre for Security and Defence Studies, and principal investigator of the Country Indicators for Foreign Policy Project.

ABDALLAH S. DAAR is professor of public health sciences and surgery at the University of Toronto.

JEAN DAUDELIN is assistant professor in The Norman Paterson School of International Affairs at Carleton University.

ELIZABETH DOWDESWELL is president and CEO of the Nuclear Waste Management Centre for Bioethics at the University of Toronto, and a former executive director of the United Nations Environment Programme.

GRAHAM FRASER is a national affairs writer and weekly columnist for the *Toronto Star*, and an adjunct professor at the School of Journalism and Communications at Carleton University.

HAELI GOERTZEN is a research assistant at the University of Toronto Joint Centre for Bioethics.

NANCY GORDON is senior vice-president at CARE Canada, and a former director of public programmes at the Canadian Institute for International Peace and Security.

FEN OSLER HAMPSON is a professor and director of The Norman Paterson School of International Affairs, Carleton University.

GEORGE HAYNAL is an adjunct professor at The Norman Paterson School of International Affairs and retired senior official of the Department of Foreign Affairs. He is now vice-president, public policy, at Bombardier.

PAUL HEINBECKER, recently retired as Canadian ambassador to the United Nations, is the inaugural director of the Laurier Centre for Global Relations, Governance and Policy, and senior research fellow at the Centre for International Governance Innovation in Waterloo, Ontario.

JEFFREY HEYNEN is senior research analyst at the Canada School of Public Service.

JOHN HIGGINBOTHAM is senior visiting fellow (international) at the Canada School of Public Service. His Department of Foreign Affairs service includes long experience in policy planning in Washington and China.

NORMAN HILLMER is professor of history and international affairs at Carleton University.

PHILIPPE LAGASSÉ is a doctoral student in the Department of Political Science at Carleton University, and a holder of the Canada Graduate Scholarship.

ROB MCRAE is director general of the Policy Planning Bureau in the Department of Foreign Affairs.

PETER A. SINGER holds the Sun Life Chair in Bioethics and is director of the Joint Centre for Bioethics at the University of Toronto, where he is also a professor of medicine.

ELINOR SLOAN is assistant professor in international security studies at the Department of Political Science at Carleton University, and a former defence analyst at the Department of National Defence.

GORDON SMITH, a former deputy minister of foreign affairs, is director of the Centre for Global Studies at the University of Victoria and chairs the board of the International Development Research Centre.

DENIS STAIRS is McCulloch professor of political science and a fellow in the Centre for Foreign Policy Studies at Dalhousie University.

ANDREW TAYLOR is a research assistant at the University of Toronto Joint Centre for Bioethics.

CHRISTOPHER WADDELL occupies the Carty Chair in Business and Financial Journalism at the School of Journalism and Communications, Carleton University.

Index